MAD FRANK AND SONS

DAVID FRASER, PATRICK FRASER AND BEEZY MARSH

PAN BOOKS

First published 2016 by Sidgwick & Jackson

First published in paperback 2017 by Pan Books
an imprint of Pan Macmillan
20 New Wharf Road, London N1 9RR
Associated companies throughout the world
www.panmacmillan.com

ISBN 978-1-5098-0795-6

1 3 5 7 9 8 6 4 2

A CIP catalogue record for this book is available from the British Library.

Typeset by Ellipsis Digital Limited, Glasgow
Printed and bound by CPI Group (UK) Ltd, Croydon, CR0 4YY

Visit www.panmacmillan.com to read more about all our books
and to buy them. You will also find features, author interviews and
news of any author events, and you can sign up for e-newsletters
so that you're always first to hear about our new releases.

MAD FRANK AND SONS

Patrick and David Fraser have both had long and varied criminal careers, interspersed with many stretches in prison.

Beezy Marsh is an award-winning journalist with a strong background in investigative reporting, who cut her teeth on the *Northern Echo*, before moving to the *Daily Mail*, where she regularly wrote the front page. She has always been fascinated by heroes and villains. Beezy is married with two children and now works freelance for the *Sunday Times*, *Daily Mail* and *Mail on Sunday*.

David – for my family
Patrick – for Jamie
Beezy – for my boys, Idris and Bryn

CONTENTS

FOREWORD

From the moment I could crawl, I'd thought of just about every way to thieve money. I'd nicked it from the till as a kid, burgled houses and shops, worked out ways of fiddling, robbed jeweller's and raided banks. You name it, I'd done it. If I hadn't done it, I probably wished I had.

Now, here I was, at the age of seventy-seven, an ex-con with forty-two years' bird under my belt. I'd done more time on bread and water than any man alive and spent most of my life behind bars. I was on the way to Reg Kray's funeral in London's East End in October 2000 when I realised that my fortunes had definitely taken a turn for the better. There were thousands of people lining the route. The last time I'd seen crowds that big they were the usual rent-a-mob jeering outside court. Now they were surrounding my car, chanting my name: 'Frank! Frank!'

So, this was all a bit of a turn-up.

Some kids who were not even born when I started my last serious bit of bird in the late 1960s were asking for autographs, stuffing twenty-pound notes through the car window at me. It was tempting to keep a few, I must admit, but I did right by them, signed them and handed them back.

There was quite a crush and I was worried someone would get hurt and I would get nicked for it – let's face it, with a reputation like mine, I am usually the first to get the blame. We were all travelling in black limousines through the Krays' old manor in Bethnal Green on the way to the church. Reg's coffin was in a traditional hearse, drawn by six black stallions with feathered head plumes; they looked really beautiful, they'd done him proud. The funeral procession even had cozzers on motorbikes as an escort. I'm sure the irony of that would not have been lost on Reg, who would have laughed his head off.

A funeral is always a solemn occasion, and rightly so, but there was something in the air that day, as Frank Sinatra's 'My Way' played out across the congregation and the crowds gathered outside in the churchyard, and it got me thinking. Reg's twin brother, Ron, had gone five years earlier, dying of a heart attack in March 1995, after spending years in Broadmoor – a place I also had a few spells in myself. He had a massive turnout for his funeral. But this was different. There was an excitement, a buzz. Poor Ron really went downhill after he and Reg were given thirty years each at the Old Bailey in 1969 for the murders of Jack 'The Hat' McVitie and George Cornell, but he wasn't always mad.

My name has often been linked to theirs and, in a funny way, it seems our paths were always destined to cross. We were supposed to be from rival gangs – they were the Krays and I was with the Richardsons – the brothers Charlie and Eddie, who were scrap metal dealers by trade. They were the

East End and we were south of the river. The truth is more complicated than that, and I intend for me and my family to set the record straight on quite a few things in this book. But, broadly speaking, it is probably fair to say we were rivals because we were not in business together, ever, and the twins would have loved a slice of the action that I had in the West End.

In fact, the downfall of our empires was tied to each other through violence that is now legendary in gangland terms. The murder of Dickie Hart in a shooting at Mr Smith's night-club in Catford in 1966 kicked it all off. I was acquitted of that and rightly so. Who pulled the trigger in the fight that killed him remains a mystery that the cops have never managed to unravel. I'm very glad about that.

With me and the Richardsons nicked over the Hart killing, the way was clear for Ron to blast several rounds into George Cornell in the Blind Beggar pub in Mile End, in broad daylight, the very next day. It was possibly because he had called Ron a 'fat poof', possibly because of the Hart killing, but certainly because I wasn't around to take care of the situation. So, one thing led to another.

Back then shootings weren't ten a penny like they are now. The public felt like London was the Wild West and these two violent gangs were behind it all, with the police after us, the dangerous criminals. The press headlines whipped it all up into a frenzy of an all-out turf war. Things were going to get a lot worse for the Krays and me after that – we were public enemy number one and it was twenty years of bad luck in my case, with no remission.

Reg died of cancer just eight weeks after his release –

which was a liberty, he should have been let out earlier; he was no risk to anyone anymore and he had already served more than thirty years. His passing marked the end of an era and that is what the funeral was all about for the public. I realised then that people looked on me not as some low-life, but as part of a criminal age that was no longer with us. I came from a world where women and children were kept out of it and men settled scores among themselves and didn't involve the cozzers. The Krays were people who were held in that sort of respect in people's minds.

Now Reg was about to be laid to rest alongside his brother Ron, with the world's media watching, and I was there – so people felt they could reach out and touch me and get a part of that history through the car window on the way to the funeral, I suppose. We were still the bad guys, but when it comes to it everyone loves a villain, don't they? And with the way crime has got more violent with more innocent people caught up in it, I think people remember the days of the Krays, the Richardsons and me in a different way. It was only those who had it coming who got hurt on my watch and I was a bit handy with a razor or an axe.

It was all a very long time ago now but still it fascinates people. Everyone loves the stories, the half-truths, the what-ifs? Well, to know what really happened, you had to be there. Sometimes the real truth is ugly, hard to stomach if you are not used to that way of life.

The thing is, me and my family, we were there; through the days of the big gang bosses of 1930s Soho, the blackout and the Blitz in London, the heyday of 1950s clubland and the rise of the razor gangs, to hitting the big time as a gang leader in the 1960s. My sister Eva was a top-class 'hoister' – a shoplifter – in the Forty Thieves gang, which traced its roots back to Victorian London. She regularly emptied many a West End shop of furs, designer dresses and jewellery with her light-fingered pals. My boys, Frank, David and Patrick, took it on to the next generation, becoming burglars, jewel thieves, bank raiders and armed robbers in the 1970s and 1980s, through to drug running in the 1990s. Me and my boys were all in the nick together at some point.

The Fraser family has carved its niche on the wrong side of the law at every stage of twentieth-century British criminal history, and that is something I am extremely proud of. Thinking about it, if you put all of our sentences together, we'd be pushing a hundred years at Her Majesty's pleasure. How many families out there can say that?

Through it all, I have gained a reputation as a hardman; 'Mad' Frank, an enforcer who pulls people's teeth out with pliers. There's been a lot of lies written about me, stuff that made us all laugh really, but it has never done me any harm to have a tough reputation. Those who know me know I've done a lot worse.

When people ask me if I have any regrets, I always say my only regret is getting caught, and I think the same goes for the rest of my family. I'm proud of everything they have ever done – whether it is on the wrong side of the law or the right one. I know which one I prefer.

Families have many secrets, things you only know if you have lived through it together. I'm happy, at the end of my days, to share ours. It's been a life of crime and I wouldn't have it any other way.

Now it's time for us to set the record straight.

Frankie Fraser, 2014

PROLOGUE

1933

'Go on, Frank!'

As two boys grappled on the greasy cobblestones, the solemn-faced girl with her long black hair hanging in tatty plaits clenched her fists tightly and yelled her support for her younger brother. It had been the talk of the playground for days. The gang from Colombo Street in Blackfriars had been threatening to come over to Howley Place and have it out and now they'd sent a kid built like a brick shithouse, wearing hobnail boots. Only Frankie Fraser was brave enough to face him.

A crowd gathered as word spread that a fight was on.

Workers spilled out from the London wastepaper factory around the corner and the women, still wearing sacking around their legs to keep the rats away, pushed to the front of the circle for a better view. They were the worst, those women; the toughest fighters, who would yank out clumps of hair, screech and scratch each other's eyes out to settle their scores. Eva didn't like them, with their loud-mouthing and cat-calling, but she wasn't afraid of them either and right now, they were in her way.

7

Eva elbowed her way forward as Frank and his opponent were pulled to their feet and told to fight properly, not scrap on the floor. They'd already done a couple of rounds. With two adults sparring, these things could go on for hours – twenty rounds, until one of them was knocked out cold. With kids, it was usually over much more quickly – the spectators liked a bet but they didn't want the lads doing permanent damage to each other. The local bookmaker shortened the odds on the lad from Colombo Street winning the fight. He had fists like hams and legs like tree trunks, for a start.

Blood was pouring from a gash on Frank's head but as his eyes met Eva's, he wiped it away on his vest, spat on the ground, and raised his fists once more. As his opponent swung a punch, Frank ducked and then slid in and hit him hard in the ribs. It was payback for the fat lip Frank had received earlier when he took one right in the kisser. The Colombo Street kid staggered backwards but the Howley Place onlookers thrust him forward into the makeshift ring – a patch of waste ground at the top of their street, the scene of so many fights. The murky water of the River Thames, with its barges and wharves, provided the backdrop to this bloody sport.

Someone was usually posted to keep a look out for the cozzers, but to be honest, they tended to leave well alone. Scores would be settled every week with bare-knuckles on the cobbles and, in the eyes of the law, it was better than in the bar after a few beers. Men, women, kids, dogs and even rats – it was all fair game for a fight in Waterloo. If it lived and breathed, the bookies would take bets on it.

A bull terrier bared its teeth and was kicked into silence by its owner, as the crowd jostled and called for more: 'Finish him, Frank!' The odds were against him, but the locals were on his side and it spurred him on. Kathleen and Jim, his older brother and sister, were standing on tiptoe near the back of the crowd, peering over the tops of shoulders to catch a glimpse of the fight. They watched, stony-faced with disapproval.

Eva felt her stomach lurch at the thought of the belting Frank would get from their father when he found out he'd been fighting again. And her mother, well, she would tear a strip off Eva for allowing him to do it. Eva was supposed to make sure Frankie stayed away from fights, especially since the accident. He'd almost died when a lorry ran him over and his head swelled so badly the doctors had to pack it in ice.

But there was no point telling him not to fight. He might be the smallest ten-year-old in the street, his cheeky face framed by a scruffy mop of jet black hair, but he was the gamest, he was good with his fists and never gave up. Besides, every time his mother tried to wrap him in cotton wool it only made him more determined to fight his corner. What's more, Eva had bet their last penny on Frank winning and they needed the money to give to their mother to help with the housekeeping.

Frank took a couple more blows to the face but if the Colombo Street kid thought that was going to stop him, he was wrong. Frank's eyes blazed with anger but he smiled at his opponent, as if he was actually enjoying being beaten to a pulp. It unsettled the Colombo Street kid, who dropped his guard, for a split second: 'What are you laughing at?'

'I'm going to knock your fucking block off,' said Frank, matter-of-factly, and he lunged in a frenzy of punches, driven by some unseen force, the blood still pouring from the cut above his eye. It all happened in an instant; the Colombo Street kid was down on the floor and Frank was on him, still pummelling away.

The crowd fell silent. The sport was over but Frank didn't stop. The big lump from round the corner was now just a pathetic ball of mother-love on the floor, howling for mercy. One of the regulars from the factory pulled Frank off and held his hands aloft in victory, sparking a few cheers. He was patted on the head. Somebody lit a cigarette. Backs were turned. Money changed hands. Lunch break was over.

The Colombo Street kid picked himself up, whimpering, and limped away. Frank's scrawny frame heaved with the effort of his fight as Eva counted their spoils. The bookie had paid out and left to prop up the bar for a while longer. Frank's sister, Kathleen, came over with a bucket with some leeches in it, given to her by a neighbour. Frank winced as she stuck one over his swollen eye to suck up the blood. He'd have to clean up a bit before they'd dare show their faces at home, the whole street knew that much and no one would mention the fight to his parents. The state of his face would be telltale enough.

He managed to grin at Eva: 'How did I do?' His stomach was rumbling. It was hours since breakfast and that had only been day-old bread from the bakery up in Covent Garden.

'You were the best, Frankie,' she said, turning the coins over in her pocket. 'But we're still running a bit short.' She gave him a wink as she grabbed his hand: 'Let's go to the corner shop and see what we can find there to take home. I'll stand lookout.'

CHAPTER 1

BORN CRIMINAL

Frank Fraser didn't have to steal to live. But all those who knew him throughout his fifty-year career as one of Britain's most dangerous gangsters will swear to one fact: Frank Fraser certainly lived to steal. Although he gained notoriety for acts of violence as a henchman and hitman – in razor and axe attacks – if you ever asked Frank to describe himself he would say, simply: 'I'm a thief.' The illicit thrill of thieving began when he was only four, finding his way in the run-down streets of London's Waterloo.

Frank Davidson Fraser came into the world on 13 December 1923, delivered by his maternal grandmother, who walloped him on the backside and declared him healthy. The youngest of five children, he was born into a working-class family, living in a street so rough that policemen wouldn't venture down it, even in pairs.

For years, the poorest immigrants had settled beside the River Thames in Lambeth and many families could trace Irish or Italian ancestry. Frank's own family had a more startling heritage, which included Native American and Canadian on his father's side, as well as Irish and Norwegian on his mother's. None of it mattered to anyone in the neighbourhood; each family was simply as poor as the next.

His father, James, was a grafter, a workaholic in Frank's opinion. Frank never forgave him for it because he sweated so hard for so little money. Even at the end of his days, Frank would still say, with a wry grin on his face, that his father 'was a huge disappointment to me because he let me down by being the straightest person you could ever meet. I saw where honesty got people and I didn't think much of it. I was sure of one thing, I wasn't going to end up like my father.'

Toiling seven days a week, from dawn until dusk, James Fraser earned less than £2 a week as a wood sawyer at the local cricket bat makers, Stuart Surridge. It was a job he had been given due to family connections – his wife's father, Thomas, worked as a nightwatchman at the docks for the same company. Frank's mother, Margaret, had three cleaning jobs to supplement the family income. Twice a day – early in the morning and after teatime – she travelled across the water to Millbank, to clean the buildings at ICI. During the day she scrubbed the floors in a little hotel in Waterloo Road to earn a few shillings more.

James, who was born in 1885, was a military man. He had lived such a life; fighting in the war against the Spanish in Cuba when he was in the US Navy in 1898, providing emergency relief to the stricken city of San Francisco after the 1906 earthquake and then coming over to England from Canada on a convoy of food during the First World War. Margaret was working as a cleaner when she caught his eye at the Union Jack Club in Waterloo, just as the conflict was coming to an end. He had swept Margaret, then aged nine-teen, off her feet.

James, who was thirty by then, was a world away from the other lads she'd grown up with. They still seemed like boys next to him. He was a real man who had served his time before the mast and now wanted to settle down and be a good father. Margaret hadn't meant to fall pregnant so soon after meeting him. Her father, Thomas Anderson, had been furious and threatened to disown her. Thomas, who had been crippled fighting with the Black Watch during the Boer War, had a fierce temper but James Fraser managed to talk him round, promising to stand by his daughter.

Thomas's wife, however, was a different matter. She was a tall, forceful Irishwoman from County Kildare in Ireland, who worked as a cook at a hotel in Waterloo Road and took no nonsense from anybody. Off she went to the Admiralty to check that James Fraser didn't have another family hidden away in his home country of Canada, before she would give her blessing to the young couple. Only when they confirmed James was what he claimed to be, did the Andersons open their house to James and their pregnant daughter.

James Fraser and Margaret lived together under the Andersons' roof, at 101 Cornwall Road, while they got themselves sorted out. James and Thomas would sit together in the evenings, playing cards by candlelight, as Margaret sewed clothes for the baby growing in her belly. Her mother, who liked to be known as Nanny Day, was at her side. Now they were a family.

James was a solid and dependable man. He went away to sea with the Merchant Navy in the early years of their marriage, once coming home really sick with malaria, which necessitated a spell in the Naval Hospital at Greenwich. Before long, Margaret really did have her hands full, and so James left the navy. The couple's eldest child, Peggy, was born in 1918. The twins, Kathleen and Jim, came along in 1920, then Alice Evelyn – known as Eva – born in 1922 and finally Frank, just in time for Christmas 1923. Frank was to be her last.

Although all the children were born at Cornwall Road, they were raised a stone's throw away at the house round the corner that their parents had begun renting just after Peggy was born, in a little row of slum terraces known as Howley Terrace, later renamed Howley Place. But no amount of name changing could disguise the squalor. Home was a two-up, two-down with a scullery at the back. There was no bathroom in the house and no lavatory – that was in the yard. The bath was a tin one, in the kitchen, and that was rarely used because of the cost of heating water on the stove. Sometimes, the entire family might go down to Manor Place Baths to have a wash but, as that was expensive, in the summertime Frank and the other children would swim naked in the Thames, right where the Oxo Tower stands today.

The tiny house struggled to contain them all – Frank and Jim shared an upstairs bedroom at the front of the house, the girls shared the one at the back. Their parents used the living room as their bedroom. It was fine, unless there was a birthday party for the children. Then, they would just shove the bed in the corner while the kids played games like blind man's buff and pass the parcel.

The houses in Howley Place stood in a row, facing railway

arches that had doors underneath. Some of the arches were used to store scenery for West End theatres. Over the top of the arches, in Waterloo Road, was a row of little hotels. All the rubbish from the hotels was thrown down into the back-yards of Howley Place, which made the area a breeding ground for rats as big as cats. The locals turned this into a form of weekend entertainment, with bull terriers brought in to chase the rats. It was a vibrant street, full of excitement for an impressionable young boy such as Frank, who loved nothing better than seeing a dog catch a rat and throw it up in the air, to the cheers of the other children.

Row upon row of similarly grim, cobbled streets sprawled along by the river, punctuated by a grocer's shop on the corner, or a public house where James Fraser might occasionally indulge in a well-earned pint. He was not a serious or regular drinker – he couldn't afford to be with so many children to feed and clothe, and with her three cleaning jobs, there was precious little time for Margaret to keep an eye on the children.

James was very careful with their money; Margaret had to budget for everything and woe betide her if she ran short. She wasn't afraid of hard work, but would have liked to have a few more shillings in her purse. Every Monday, she took James's blue serge suit to the pawnbroker and put it in until Friday, when his wages came, just to be sure she'd have enough to tide them through the week. He had no idea she was doing it. She loved that suit, not just because it provided much-needed cash for the family budget, but also because he had married her in it, to make an honest woman of her, after she'd had the twins. James didn't get round to taking

Margaret up the aisle before the twins came along because he was often away at sea and the couple never seemed to have the time or the money to contemplate getting hitched.

Frank, Eva and the other children knew from a very early age that there were times when their mother bore the brunt of their father's temper. James would dish out a slap and once he even shoved her down the stairs. But their mother's approach in those early years was to pretend that nothing had happened and do her best to carry on as normal, shooing the children out to play while their father sat brooding at the little table in the scullery. That pretence made it a family secret in which they were all complicit. It was something shameful, not to be talked about, in case the neighbours found out. That stuck with Frank, even later in life.

Beverley, Eva's daughter, explained: 'At first Margaret saw it as just being part of her lot. She didn't like it but she tried to do better to please him and to keep the home going, for the sake of the children. Where was she going to go? She had five kids to look after and she loved him. Nanny Day's view was very much that she had made her bed by marrying James and now she had to lie in it.'

Margaret preferred her husband hitting her, rather than the children. James used his belt on them, the buckle end, and it broke her heart. She'd hear him shouting at them, in his Canadian accent: 'Goddamn you!'

Sometimes she sent the children around to Nanny Day's in Cornwall Road, just to give James a bit of peace and quiet. They would come back with funny stories about how their granny had gathered them to her skirts and warned them, in the broadest Irish accent imaginable, 'never trust the Irish'.

Frank only remembered his grandfather, Thomas Anderson, as a poorly old man with a wicked temper, but Nanny Day was a warmer character, who provided him and his siblings with care when his mother was out at work or when there had been a row at home.

Margaret felt that she wasn't as badly off as some of the poor loves on her street – they'd had to pawn their own clothes, and had to wait until dusk before they went shopping down the market in The Cut, just south of Waterloo Station, because they only had sacks to wear. Their husbands drank themselves stupid in the pub each night, spending the housekeeping. Yet the slaps over the housekeeping were just the start of a litany of domestic abuse that was to blight Margaret's relationship with James Fraser, and which she struggled to keep secret in the close-knit neighbourhood.

Curtains twitched in the street at an unexpected visitor – and everyone knew everybody else's business, living cheek by jowl as they did. There were regulars in the street – such as the coal merchant with his lorry, the muffin man, the jellied eel man and, of course, the tallyman. Margaret and the other housewives would buy clothes and household items from him and pay him back weekly, or on the 'never-never' – as they never had the cash to pay upfront.

Noise in the street was constant, with the rattle of the trains on the railway line nearby, the shouting of children, the barking of dogs and the comings and goings of the inhabitants, packed into the tiny houses like sardines in a tin. Motorcars were quite a rare sight, and the horse and cart was still seen plodding along even as lorries rumbled to and fro along the main roads to the factories and onwards to the docks. When James straggled home after an exhausting day, he would find the children playing out in the street, as the brewer's dray plodded past, or the tallyman departed with a wave over his shoulder. Margaret was never quite sure what mood he would be in when he came through the front door.

Frank preferred to gloss over the domestic violence he grew up with, seeing it as just the way things were done at that time. He never openly condemned his father for what he did but, tellingly, for all his violence, nor did he ever raise his hand to a woman, nor did he beat his children. His son, David Fraser, said: 'Our dad Frank was known as a violent man and when it came to it, in what he would call his business life, he could be when it was required and he was well known for what he did in prison, but he never hit our mother and he didn't like that sort of behaviour against women or children. He was very clear about that. He had standards about how children and women should be treated and he passed those on to us.'

Today, nothing remains of Howley Place, Frank's grandparents' home in Cornwall Road or the factories that provided the noisy, filthy backdrop to Frank's earliest years. The house in Cornwall Road was torn down to make way for the Jubilee Line extension in the 1990s and an office block stands on the site of Howley Place.

Further east, on the other side of Waterloo Bridge, in the streets where little Frank and his brothers and sisters used to run amok, stands the National Theatre, a monument to the 1960s and 1970s love affair with concrete. But before the heart and soul of the bustling little corner of Waterloo was destroyed, it had made a lasting impression on Frank and his sister Eva.

In the 1920s Waterloo was a tight-lipped community, not given to 'grassing up' one of its number to the police, and these codes of criminal conduct stuck with Frank and Eva their whole lives. Despite Frank's criminal tendencies, his family were not like others in the neighbourhood that spawned many notorious 'faces' from South London. There were no bar-room loafers among them and his father did not have to rely on casual work at the docks, which brought with it the threat of sudden unemployment and inability to pay the rent and the temptation to make easy money from illegal sources. There were no uncles who were career criminals, no burglars or pickpockets to show him the tricks of the trade.

The Fraser family home was small but was not the worst in the district, which had more than its fair share of desperate families housed in damp basements and bleak tenements. The respectable neighbours in their street were hard-working men like James Fraser – labourers and handymen. One even owned a car – a rare sight in Howley Place. For the majority of the other families, simply having a car parked outside would have led to inquiries from the police about where and how they had acquired it.

For many struggling to survive on their meagre but honest wages, the temptation to take 'a bit of crooked' from someone they knew down at the pub was hard to resist. The police knew it went on and were often prepared to turn a blind eye, as long as people didn't draw attention to themselves.

Frank's father was strictly against any kind of stolen goods ending up under his roof and was quite prepared to hand out a beating to Frank or any of his brothers and sisters on occasions when he felt they had transgressed. Frank's view of the beatings he received as a child was that they were all done 'for his own good'. Frank said of his dad: 'He was trying to teach me the difference between right and wrong. It was harsh but that was how it was back then. When we see things now, we see it through different eyes. I always think he must have had a tough time when he was growing up but he was a man of few words about it.'

Little is known about the family of James Fraser in Canada, but he told Frank that his mother was a Native American of the Cree tribe and his father was a Scot, also called James Fraser, whose family had come to Canada as fur traders and trappers. Baptism records provided by the Catholic Church in Canada reveal that James junior was born at Fort Hope, an outpost of the Hudson Bay Company situated on the mouth of the Fraser River, in British Columbia. James Fraser senior and his wife travelled to New Westminster – now Vancouver – to have him baptised two weeks after his birth, where they were recorded as 'Fort Hope indians'. Such marriages were common in the forts, and were even encouraged by the Hudson Bay Company to promote trade between the tribes and the traders, but racism was rife. Some Canadians who made such marriages were derided locally as 'squaw men'.

Frank's father ran away at the age of ten to join the US Navy. The children of European–Native American marriages were called 'Métis' or 'half-breeds' and it is likely that James Fraser suffered at least some racial prejudice, as in late-nineteenth-century Canada mixed-race children were seen as second-class citizens. Many tried to hide their backgrounds and schools refused to let them speak in their native tongue, and beat them if they did.

James remained tight-lipped about his reasons for leaving his family at such a young age and Frank knew better than to ask too many questions about it, for fear of provoking his father's anger. 'He just didn't want to talk about it and he made that clear to me,' said Frank. 'I can only think that he fell out with his parents or he got sick of being beaten and wanted to run away. I like to think he had a pioneering spirit about him, it was brave leaving home like that and I admired him for it.'

In order to join the navy so young, James Fraser would have had to lie about his age. Official records suggest that's exactly what he did. James Fraser served in the British Merchant Navy during the First World War. His medal cards and service record show he gave his birth date as 1881, while his death certificate gives his real birth year as 1885 – reflecting the lie he may have told when he first joined the US Navy as a young boy.

Another family story is that James Fraser fought in Cuba during the Spanish–American War of 1898, during which Guantanamo Bay was first claimed by the US. He would have been just thirteen at the time. The many years he spent serving in the Merchant Navy may well have contributed to James's strict view on law breaking. But, according to family legend, James found himself on the wrong side of the law as a young man in his native Canada and the memory of that never left him. 'My mother always said that he had killed a man in a fight in Canada and served eighteen months for manslaughter,' said Frank. 'Whatever the reasons, my father was terrified of the police. He was desperate for us not to be in trouble. I think I let him down in that regard. No matter how hard he beat me, it didn't stop me, not at all.'

Often, when James started to pull off his belt and signalled for Frank to step forward to take his punishment, Eva would hold him back. Eva would then look her father in the eye and say she had done it, to take the belting on behalf of her brother, who she tried to shield from physical harm at every opportunity. The reason why Eva was so brave may lie in the guilt she always felt about the terrible accident Frank suffered at the age of five, at the top of their street.

Her only surviving daughter, Beverley, now in her seventies, remembers her mother reliving the horror of it: 'They were both playing out in the street, games of chase, that sort of thing, and Frank ran to the top of the road where the big lorries used to go along to the London Wastepaper Company.

'Frank loved to collect his football cards from cigarette packets and he would often shout to the drivers of the lorries to chuck them out to him: "Got any cards, Mister?"

'Well, on this day, a driver had thrown some out for him and he had gone to pick them up in the road but he dropped his own ones in the street as he did so. He was bending down to pick them up when another lorry came along and hit him.

'Eva saw it but couldn't stop him. She ran screaming for him to step back but it was too late. Frank's little body was just left there in the road. The lorry ran over his head.

'Of course, it wasn't her fault but that feeling never left

her. He was her little brother and she always felt she had to look after him, just like her mother told her to.'

Frank was left unconscious and was scooped up by someone from their street and loaded on to the back of a lorry tailgate, with his sisters and brothers crying beside him. They all went to St Thomas' Hospital, while their mother was sent for from her cleaning job and his father came back from work early from the factory. Frank suffered a fractured skull, leading to weeks in hospital. His head swelled up so badly that doctors had to pack it in ice.

Frank then succumbed to meningitis, requiring further hospital care – giving his mother many sleepless nights. Frank's view of the terrible accident he suffered was that it was 'just one of those things' and it didn't stop him running about like the other kids and getting into trouble. 'In fact, in some ways, I think it made me more determined because I had been sick, so I had to prove myself more, to show that I wasn't the weak one,' he said. 'I was more daring than quite a few of the other boys in my street for that reason.'

Like so many of the poor children in 1920s London, bread was the mainstay of Frank's diet – bread and jam, bread and a scrape of butter, bread and dripping. Often, it was stale, as the only way that their mother could afford to buy the amount of bread they needed to keep them going was to get it cheaply from the bakery when it was a day old.

From the age of just three, Frank made regular two-mile round trips across the water from Waterloo to Godden and Hanken, the bakery in Covent Garden, clasping a pillowcase to fill with stale buns and loaves for a few pennies, accompanied by Eva and their Airedale terrier.

Joining them in the queue, at five o'clock in the morning, was a ragged line of children who could have come straight from the streets of Victorian London; some had torn clothes, others had bare feet and fingernails black with dirt. Frank and Eva were clean. Their mother made sure of that – scrubbing their faces with a dishcloth before they were allowed to set foot outside the house. Their father had no idea what they were up to and the shame of his children queuing up with the urchins would have earned them a beating.

The Covent Garden they knew then was one of flower-sellers in long skirts and straw hats, their woollen shawls pulled tightly around their shoulders as they set up their pitches, while drunks from the night before still lolled in the gutters.

On one of these trips, when they were running late and were last in the queue, an older girl with startling blue eyes and long blonde hair allowed them to go in front of her, so that they didn't miss out. She was ten-year-old Kate Wall, the eldest daughter of brewery drayman Danny Wall and his wife Rosina. Kate lived in a cramped tenement building in Southwark with her seven brothers and sisters. Years later, she would go on to marry Frank and give him three sons, all of whom would launch criminal careers of their own. Their shared background of grinding poverty helped them to form a close bond.

Meat was a luxury, bought to keep Frank's father going, as the working man of the family. Their mother would make a stew for the children once a week, which had to last for several meals. The children had stewed 'pieces' of meat – chunks that could be little more than gristle – served in gravy, always with potatoes, sometimes with greens if they were in season. A joint of meat would be the focus of the family's week, for Sunday lunch, if they could afford it. Suet pudding with treacle was a treat, milk was a rarity and they might get fruit from the farm when they went hop-picking in Kent for six weeks during the summer with the rest of the neighbourhood, but otherwise that was a luxury their mother couldn't afford.

It is little wonder that Frank started out stealing fruit and sweets – because like many of the children in the neighbourhood, he was a hungry little boy. 'I didn't see it as doing wrong,' he said, 'and to be honest, I loved the feeling of being able to do something for myself by nicking a bit of this and that. There was plenty of opportunity to get up to no good because we all had so much freedom then, we didn't have grown-ups around, watching over us so much.'

The thrill of stealing money and getting away with it soon followed. And that thrill never left him. A key moment in his childhood came when he first stole from the till at the corner shop, at the age of five. The idea, of course, was Eva's. With her solemn little face and secretive nature, she had relished the prospect of no longer being the baby of the family when Frank came along. She had a playmate to boss about at last, rather than being bossed by the twins, Kathleen and Jim, who she felt always ganged up on her. Being the leader and telling Frank what to steal was a role she excelled in. 'It was usually even stevens in the crime stakes between me and Eva, but in those early days, where she led, I followed,' Frank remembered. 'I would have followed her off a cliff. She was only doing what she had seen the older kids do. It was exciting for us and it also meant we had extra money, which was unheard of for kids like us.'

Eva stood guard and then created a distraction as Frank dashed around the counter and stuck his hand in the till, grabbing what he could. Sometimes, Eva would send the shopkeeper downstairs to look for something – such as a candle – and then say she had changed her mind when he reappeared, by which time Frank had scarpered.

The first time he stole money, he took £2 – a small fortune in those days. As Frank said: 'A man could go to work for £2 for a week and come home and feel proud, as my father did.' Clutching the money, he ran home to his mother, who was a staunch Catholic and was raising them in the faith, with regular trips to Mass. All the children were pupils at the local Roman Catholic primary school, St Patrick's in Cornwall Road. Instead of marching him off to the police station, or demanding that Frank tell her where the money came from, Margaret crossed herself and raised her eyes to heaven. 'Dear Lord,' she said, tucking the money into the pocket of her apron, 'thank you for giving me such a lucky, lucky child.' And she patted little Frank on the head and sent him out to play.

The domestic abuse suffered by Margaret was an unspoken motive for both Frank and Eva's earliest thieving. They wanted to help their mother, who stoically struggled to make ends meet. With one parent prepared to turn a blind eye and the other leaving him unable to sit down for several days for his transgressions, it soon became clear that the law of the street held a bigger sway over Frank than any kind of rules at home.

Frank and Eva's older siblings wanted no part of any wrongdoing and looked on their younger brother and sister as the 'wild ones' in the family, who were always ripe for getting into trouble but were loyal enough never to inform on them to their parents. There were good, honest hard-working people in the community, who would tell James and Margaret if they saw Frank and Eva getting up to no good. But there were just as many who would happily egg them on as they fled down the street with something they had stolen from the corner shop. It was seen as just part of growing up around Waterloo Road, as Frank recalled: 'We'd laugh about it afterwards. It wasn't as if we thought we were really doing anything wrong. Lots of people were bent in some way or had a bit of stuff on them that was nicked. It was a way of life when you had so little.'

The desire to have a new pair of plimsolls to wear while he was boxing was the drive behind Frank's first attempt at thieving something bigger than sweets or loose change from the till. His shoes were always full of holes. One of his earliest memories was of crossing one foot over the other, as he took Holy Communion, to cover a hole in his boot. 'It never occurred to me that other children probably had holes in their boots too, so it wouldn't have been an unusual sight. I just felt I was trying to be respectful, because my mother did bring me up with respect for the church,' he said.

Although he was no scholar, he excelled at sports and was captain of the football team at St Patrick's, so his boots and plimsolls were always wearing through. 'I knew I couldn't ask my mother for a new pair of plimsolls, because they cost 11 pence – which was a fortune to her. I didn't want to make her feel bad that she couldn't afford it but I was ashamed of the holes in mine. I really wanted a pair because I had a boxing match coming up – she didn't know about that either.

'So, off I went to Peacry's, a general dealer in The Cut, which used to have rows of plimsolls hanging up outside. I had worked out by looking at them which ones were most likely to fit, so I just jumped up and tried to pull them down. My plan had been to run off with them, but I managed to pull the whole bloody rail down on top of myself. The next thing I know, people are chasing me and I have got hold of these plimsolls and I am running for dear life. I was caught a few streets away. I got a slap around the ear for it and they took the plimsolls back but no one told my mother.

'I went off to the boxing match and my plimsolls just fell apart and I ended up boxing in my socks. I did really well – in fact, I won. The thing I hadn't reckoned on was the result being in the paper. My mum found out when people started congratulating her in the street – and she put an end to it. My head injury meant that boxing was the very last thing I should be doing. That's how my first serious attempt at thieving put an end to my boxing career.'

Their neighbourhood had more than its fair share of characters – who were either thieves or handled stolen goods – and it was among these people that firstly Eva and then Frank really learned their craft. One of the regulars around the pubs near Howley Place was Annie Daley, known as 'Dartmoor Annie'. Her husband had a pitch selling evening papers outside Waterloo Station, and she was known for her generosity to convicts coming back from serving time in The Moor.

The Moor was the infamous Dartmoor Prison, where prisoners were still flogged with the cat-o'-nine-tails – a fearsome whip made up of nine knotted strands of rope – and the walls ran with water, as they had done during the Napoleonic era when the prison was first built to house French soldiers captured at Waterloo. Prisoners coming back to London would step off the train at Waterloo Station, safe in the knowledge that Dartmoor Annie would give them £1 to keep them going until they could find work – which usually meant going out thieving again. Dartmoor Annie was also known as a reliable local 'fence' – who would dispose of stolen goods for a commission.

She was more than happy to sell things on for Frank and Eva, who took to 'creeping' in hotels. This meant sneaking into the cheap hotels along the Waterloo Road, looking for things to steal, sometimes finding easy pickings and sometimes almost getting caught. 'If anyone asked me what I was doing, I would say I was just looking for my uncle or I was lost, that sort of thing,' said Frank. 'It was risky, but worth it.'

Frank also used busy travellers as another means of making a few pennies, either by charging them to carry their bags, or – under the watchful eye of Dartmoor Annie – offering to take money from them to buy a newspaper and then running out of the station, cash in hand.

Liz English, known as 'Lumps and Bumps' because she was always being beaten up by the police when she was drunk and disorderly, was another helping hand on the road to crime. She ran the flower stall at Waterloo Station and would tip Frank the wink about any delivery vans that might have goods worth stealing in them. Her son, Johnny, could be hired as a local lookout but he was so useless at it that he was known as 'Mile Away' Johnny – because that is where he would be, instead of keeping an eye out for the law.

Lumps and Bumps was also very obliging when it came to relieving Eva and Frank of the suitcases they had stolen from travellers at the station, which was another favourite ruse. 'They'd offer to carry a case for someone and leg it,' said Eva's daughter, Beverley. 'Later on they'd find Lumps and Bumps outside the pub – she'd usually had a few to drink by then – and give things to her to sell on for them. Whatever she gave them in return seemed like a fortune to them. They were just poor kids.'

Lumps and Bumps made a big impression on Frank, not least because she was a large lady who was usually very drunk and who didn't wear any knickers. Beverley said: 'She was well known for her habit of going into the pub, hoicking up her skirt and warming her bum in front of the fire, one cheek at a time. That was quite some sight.'

Frank and Eva's first major theft, which made Lumps and Bumps realise their potential as more than just naughty kids thieving for a lark, came when they were aged ten and eleven, after they stole a cigarette machine from a hotel in York Road, about a half a mile from their home. As dusk fell, they dragged it to a local church. Beside the church, there was a temporary health clinic in a hut on stilts. The pair heaved the cigarette machine underneath and prised it open to get at the cigarettes inside. Laden with their booty, they contacted

Lumps and Bumps, who took a cut before referring them on to Peter Daley, husband of Dartmoor Annie, who relieved them of the cigarettes for a fair price.

They took the money home to their mother and once again recited their story of how they had found a pound or two. This continued for the next few weeks, with Margaret accepting their cash, no questions asked. Somehow – aided and abetted by Frank and Eva's contributions – Margaret managed to save enough from her household kitty to buy a second-hand piano for their elder sister Kathleen's birthday that year. She even convinced her husband James that she'd scrimped and saved for the piano by doing extra hours cleaning at the hotel in Waterloo Road, putting her further in cahoots with her thieving offspring. The family would gather around while Kathleen bashed out a tune and they would all sing along. For a working-class family who were so poor to spend cash on a musical instrument was almost unheard of – particularly when they struggled to feed and clothe the children.

For the same reasons, very few photographs exist of young Frank, who was always quick to point out the relative wealth of his old rivals, the Krays, 'who had loads of pictures of themselves growing up'. The only time the Frasers had a family portrait taken was when his father lost a finger in a work accident and received £100 compensation. This windfall was celebrated with new clothes for everyone and a holiday to Southend. Looking back at the photo, Frank said: 'We are all sitting there, spruced up in new clothes. I look a bit uncomfortable because I wasn't used to dressing up. Although we were always clean, my clothes were often tattered. Eva is showing off her new beret. My mother, for once, looks quite serene. We even look like quite a well-off family but the truth was nothing like that. I like to think my thieving in those early days made things a bit easier for us, even if my mum couldn't acknowledge it at the time.'

Frank idolised his mother, giving her the nickname Lady Margaret as a mark of the respect he felt for her. His father was not held in such high regard, not only because he was heavy-handed with his mother, but also because he was determined to bring up his children to respect the law. Frank's view of the police, even from a young age, was that they were all corrupt or could be corrupted – so, as he would argue: 'What was the point of respecting them? My dad would have had me take every penny I'd "found" down to the police station, where some cozzer would probably have pocketed it, so to me it seemed fairer that we kept it and it did some good. I wasn't born criminal, no, but I am glad it turned out that way.'

CHAPTER 2

IN THE GANG

By his tenth year, Frank Fraser had been taken under the wing of one of the big crime families of early twentieth-century London. The Sabinis were of Italian descent and had lived in and around Clerkenwell since the latter part of the nineteenth century. They had developed a fearsome reputation through their feud with a rival gang, the Birmingham-based Brummagems, with whom they fought pitched battles at racecourses around the country during the 1920s. The knuckleduster and the cosh transcended any difficulties the two sides may have had communicating with each other and jail sentences did little to deter them from fierce fights.

By the start of the 1930s, the Sabinis and the Brummagems had called an uneasy truce, with the Italians controlling the racecourses in the south and south-east, while Billy Kimber and the Brummagems held the Midlands and the north. To the bookmakers, it made no odds who was running the protection rackets – they still had to pay up.

Frank was introduced to the family through a school friend called Billy Murray, whose mother owned a flower stall at Charing Cross Station. Frank would help Mrs Murray take boxes of flowers to her stall and, as a favour, she offered to help him find some paid employment, though the fact that Frank's dark hair and tanned complexion, a result of his Native American heritage, often saw him mistaken for an Italian child may also have played a part in him getting the job. The Sabinis were struck by his good looks and cheeky grin and gave him the job of 'bucket boy' – wiping the odds off the chalkboards at the races. As an impressionable young boy, he 'hopped the wag' and went to the races, where he watched how the family ran their business. It was a humble beginning but it was an important entry into the underworld.

One of the Sabinis' tricks was to make the bookies pay for the services of the bucket boy and even for the chalk they used to write up the odds. As well as wiping the chalkboards, Frank's job was to collect this money, demanding half a crown from each of the bookies to hand to his paymasters: 'I thought it was brilliant because I got a day off at the races, without telling my parents, and I would come home with two shillings and sixpence.' Anyone who refused would find themselves hassled off their pitch, thumped or slashed by the razors of the Sabini gang's thugs.

From this early experience among gangsters, he learned how to walk, talk and even dress like a mobster, although he was too young and too short of cash to really look the part. These men were known as 'the Chaps'. 'I noticed the way that the Chaps tipped their hats to the women, opened doors for them,' said Frank. 'They dressed really smartly – a suit, tie and a trilby hat. No man would consider himself dressed without a hat. That was what being one of the Chaps was all about back then and I liked that.'

The Sabinis' influence was not confined to the racetracks. They also ran protection rackets throughout the clubs and shops of Soho, as well as running illegal gambling dens, called 'spielers', which were open all hours and added to the allure of the West End, where the aristocracy slummed it with hoodlums. This made the leader of the gang, Darby Sabini – Darbo to his friends – a man not to be messed with. Frank was struck by the reverential way in which the leader of the gang was treated.

Darby – so called because 'darby' was a slang term for being left-handed in the boxing world – had a fearsome reputation as a boxer and a hardman, who could easily knock someone out with a single punch. He didn't need to rely on his henchmen to back him up in a fight – which made him all the more heroic in Frank's eyes. 'He was never menacing to me, in fact, I thought he was a nice bloke,' said Frank. 'He would pat me on the head, hand me my money and tell me to take it home to my mother. I had heard his men calling him "Darbo", so I'd copy them and say "Thanks, Darbo". That always made him laugh, because I was rather cheeky.'

Frank's new contacts in the racing world also helped him at school. For once, Frank, who was not an academic child in any sense of the word, passed his maths and English exams and almost came top of the class. Giving racing tips to one of the teachers meant he was rewarded with a copy of the forthcoming exam papers.

When he wasn't at the races, he was back in Waterloo with Eva, his sister and partner in crime. And they were getting more daring by the day, graduating from 'creeping' in hotels to crossing the water and stealing from offices. It was on one such expedition that they stole a packet of insurance cards, thinking they were nicking cash. When they got the packet home, they discovered they had acquired documents of some kind and, not knowing what to do with them, hid them behind a picture on the mantelpiece. Fortunately for them, their mother – and not their father – found the packet.

Margaret Anderson realised that her children had broken into an office and decided to take action of her own to protect them from their own stupidity. She crept out of the house at night, went several streets away, and threw the cards down the drain. The children knew she had covered for them and she told them not to do it again – but, of course, that was not the end of their thieving. In many ways, they were just getting into their stride.

As Eva and Frank's criminal activity stepped up a gear, so did the slaps their mother received from her husband. James seemed to have little understanding of the difficulty of raising five children on barely any money and when their eldest daughter Peggy left home, he docked money from Margaret's housekeeping. This made it even harder for her to balance the books. Behind closed doors James would throw the occasional punch and neighbours couldn't help but notice a bruised cheek or a black eye from time to time.

As Frank approached his teenage years, Margaret started to find a voice for her anger about the way her husband treated her. 'She would tell James Fraser that once the children were fourteen and could leave school, she'd be off,' said Eva's daughter, Beverley. 'She was biding her time and working out how to get away because he treated her so badly. It was hard in those days. There wasn't an easy way out and she had the kids to think about.'

By the time he was twelve, Frank's days as a bucket boy were over. He was no longer cute enough to pull in the punters and, overnight, he found his services were no longer required. To keep earning, he stepped up his stealing, with Eva at his side. Knowing that he and Eva could not take their loot home to their parents' house, the pair turned to their old friend Lumps and Bumps for help. She was a well-known fence around Lambeth but her associates spread as far as the Elephant and Castle, home to two powerful and inter-related local gangs.

They were the Forty Thieves, an all-female gang of shop-lifters, and the Elephant Boys, a loose association of burglars, thieves and thugs, often with sisters, girlfriends or wives in the other gang. The Forty Thieves had achieved almost legendary status by the early 1930s for their daring and dangerous exploits in the shops of the West End. Newspaper reports from the 1920s reveal how they terrorised upmarket stores including Selfridges, sometimes 'steaming' through in a big gang and grabbing everything in sight, before making off in getaway cars that were parked outside with their engines running.

By the 1930s, the operation had become more sophisti-cated, moving away from the 'smash and grab' approach, to highly organised and well-trained groups of four or five girls working their way through particular stores. The gang was headed up by the Queen of the Forty Thieves – strapping, five foot eight inch-tall Alice Diamond, who was born into a criminal family in Southwark in 1896. She wore a clutch of diamond rings, using them as a knuckleduster when required. The police knew her as 'Diamond Annie' and were warned that a blow from her fist could cost them an eye. When arrested, she put up a fierce fight and she had been known to dish it out to members of the Elephant Boys and other Forty Thieves when she felt they had transgressed or challenged her authority. She ran the show and her male drivers were kept in much the same way as a pimp keeps a prostitute.

Lumps and Bumps introduced Frank and Eva to Alice, and the Queen of the Forty Thieves was delighted to meet them. She took them under her wing, offering them a place to keep their stolen goods – for a cut, of course – a listening ear and a cup of tea. Eva and Frank used to love to hear stories of her most daring thefts and close shaves with the law. They sat wide-eyed as troops of Alice's 'girls' came into the house laden with goods stolen from Selfridges and Marshall & Snelgrove on Oxford Street and Whiteleys in Bayswater and unloaded their shopping bags. Furs, jewellery, leather goods and silk underwear were their speciality. They were stunned at how much loot these girls could hide about their person; inside hats and muffs, in the linings of specially tailored coats and most usually, down their drawers – a practice known as 'clouting'.

Alice's second-in-command, who was being trained to take over the role of Queen, was Maggie Hill, also known by her married name of Maggie Hughes. She was a hard-drinking girl, born to Irish parents in the Holborn area of London, one of twenty-one children. Her father was an inveterate gambler and drinker and her mother gave wild parties, which frequently brought the family to the attention of the local constabulary – and that was before they got on to Maggie's criminal exploits. Maggie was blessed with angelic looks, which belied her wicked temper. She went by the nickname 'Baby Face' but had already taken out a rival's eye with her hatpin. Eva was in awe of her and, in turn, Maggie began to regard the young teenager as her protégée.

One of Frank and Eva's favourite stories involved the time when, as a young woman in the early 1920s, Maggie had run into a jeweller's store and grabbed a tray of diamond rings. She darted out of the shop but was immediately apprehended by a passing policeman. When the case came to court, she received a custodial sentence. Her outburst as she was sentenced became part of Fraser family folklore and Frank loved to recount how, as the judge intoned, 'Take her away', she replied: 'You didn't say that last night when you were making love to me!' Maggie showed a total lack of respect for authority and Frank admired this greatly.

Despite her fearsome reputation, Alice was kind to Eva and Frank and her door was always open to them – although, it had to be said, she knew she'd usually do well out of a visit from the young Frasers. Eva looked up to Alice and wanted to learn from her. Before long, Alice was passing on her skills as a 'hoister' – a shoplifter – to Eva in training sessions in her scullery, like a latter-day Fagin. Eva soaked it all up, determined to excel at this new skill, which would allow her financial independence beyond her wildest dreams. As Frank said: 'Any girl with her head screwed on around the Elephant in those days was a hoister, but the Forty Thieves were the cream. They could pull in around £100 a week. It was a bleeding fortune and they could indulge themselves, buying the most beautiful clothes and things. For girls who had been raised with next to nothing, this was almost too much to resist.'

Eva never wanted to stop thieving with Frank, who she saw as her partner in crime for life, but she knew that she needed to branch out if she was going to make it on to bigger and better things. Alice Diamond and Maggie Hughes showed her how to 'screen' – using a bag or a dress on a hanger to disguise the fact that she was stealing a dress with her other hand, and how to 'clout' – shove the desired item into her knickers. This was not ordinary underwear: the Forty Thieves wore voluminous silk drawers for shoplifting, with elastic pulled in at the knee.

Eva learned how to roll furs, particularly mink, on the hanger and stuff them down her silk shoplifter's underwear. Specially tailored flared coats, hats with secret pockets, big silk knickers or sometimes large muffs were used to conceal everything from clothes to jewellery, watches and even china – although that rattled a lot, so it wasn't a popular choice for the hoister. Speed and agility were essential and the rolling had to be tight to maximise the amount that any girl could get on the hoist.

'Alice would make them practise over and over until they got it right, rolling the clothes from the bottom up, towards the hanger, then stuffing them down these ridiculous bloomers that had been specially made-to-measure for them,' said Beverley. 'Too slow and you risked being spotted. You had to keep a calm look about you. It involved a great deal of daring,' she added. 'Eva would have one fur coat between her legs, and one down each leg to the knee. And Maggie Hill –

she could literally make a fur coat disappear and you didn't know where she'd put it.

'Sometimes women had to waddle out of the shop because they had so much stuff hidden about themselves. Some people called them the Forty Elephants, and not just because they came from the Elephant and Castle, it was the way they walked when they were carrying. Other times they would stuff things in their handbags and pass them on to a "booster" in the shop. That girl would then swap bags and take the stolen stuff out to the car outside.'

By the age of thirteen, as a member of the Elephant Boys, Frank was treated to his first suit by the older members, which was seen as a rite of passage. 'I went down the East End with them and they took me to a Jewish tailor, Max Cohen, who made it. It cost a hell of a lot – about thirty shillings – and we had to put down a pound deposit. When it was ready, I stepped out of there feeling like I was one of the Chaps for real. It was a brilliant feeling and that has never left me. Whenever I put on a suit, I still think about those early days and how good it felt. It was nothing to do with my parents, it was my friends putting in for it, and my own hard work – well, thieving.'

Another key skill he learned at this time was how to fight using a knife, or a cut-throat razor. There were regular turf wars against rival gangs from Peckham and Blackfriars and Brixton. When he was younger, these spats would be settled with fisticuffs, but now the threat of serious injury was heightened. Frank said: 'A lot of the business of carrying a razor or a knife was the fear it put up them; they knew you could hurt them, to get them off your turf. I was light on my toes so, of course, I was good with me 'chiv' and word soon got round.

'When you are a young kid, it is easy to get into a row about nothing and I never backed down in them days. That added to my reputation. Some great lump of a kid came up to the Elephant from Peckham and was starting it, waving an iron bar around. I was ducking and diving and pulled me knife and stuck it right in him, in the leg. He went down. He didn't die – but I never saw him round our way again.

'I preferred the razor to be honest because you could make your point quite nicely but they were not going to die from it. There was still hanging and I was too clever for that.'

Despite his new suit and skills as a street fighter, as his fourteen-year-old sister Eva's star was rising as a shoplifter, Frank's luck started to run out. He was caught for the first time, stealing three packets of cigarettes from a corner shop near his home. As it was his first offence, the court let him off, but the second time they were not so lenient. He was caught breaking and entering at a warehouse, and this time the game was up: he was sent to a Catholic approved school. 'I never got there because I managed to run away,' said Frank. 'So, I was sent to another approved school and this one was much worse.'

Frank's memories of Arndale in Grays, Essex, were that it was a very bleak place, run with almost military strictness. This was just the beginning of a long career in detention and it did not start well. 'I ran away and was caught again, so I was given the cane by the headmaster. It was more humiliating than painful – bending over and getting hit on your bare backside. I didn't cry – I wouldn't give them the satisfaction of knowing they'd hurt me. After that, I decided I wouldn't stay long. I got away again and this time I was out for a good month on my toes. That is when I got my first real job.'

Frank worked at Boots the Chemist as a delivery boy, riding around Soho on a bicycle with a big, heavy basket on the front after getting the job via Patsy Fleming, one of his pals from the approved school. The clients he delivered to included the famous nightclub singer Leslie Hutchinson, who was a favourite of the Royal family, and even Winston Churchill. But the job was not to last. 'I couldn't resist nicking stuff for Eva,' said Frank. 'I got her make-up; things she'd like, and took them home to her. I knew they'd realise things were going missing at some point, so I didn't hang around in that job and I got another one.'

This time, Frank became a delivery boy for Odhams Press. 'This took me into offices and, once I'd delivered what I had to, I'd sneak back in and go thieving,' he said. 'I had standards – I never stole from women's handbags. That was for lowlifes. I only ever nicked from safes and cash boxes. I loved Soho, it was where I really grew up.'

Around this time, in late 1937, the rows between his parents had escalated, possibly because of Frank being in trouble with the law. Beverley said: 'Margaret always had to struggle for cash and that is why she was so grateful to Frank as the years went by, because although he was bringing it in illegally, and she knew that fully by now, she needed that money. By the time Frank got to fourteen and he was getting into trouble, she'd had enough. Kathleen and Jim, the twins, and Peggy had all left home and were living locally. One day it all got too much and she walked out.'

Margaret stayed with a friend at first and then rented a flat above a shop in Walworth Road, while her husband stayed in Howley Place. Eva and Frank lived there with her and found themselves in the bosom of their new gang friends, the Forty Thieves and the Elephant Boys.

A week or so went by and James Fraser became depressed and desperate. He sent word to Margaret that he needed to see her and the pair met on Waterloo Bridge one evening. 'He pulled a wodge of cash out of his pocket and thrust it towards her, begging her to come home,' said Beverley. 'He said he was really sorry, he wouldn't ever raise his hand to her again and he couldn't live without her.

'Well, she'd had enough of him. She grabbed that money and threw it back at him, saying: "You're fourteen years too late."

'She walked off that bridge and out of his life.'

CHAPTER 3

WAR

The lead-up to the Second World War saw Frank cement his friendships with other Elephant Boys in ever-more daring burglaries and smash and grabs. But once war was declared in 1939, things got even better. The blackout was like a thief's charter for Frank and his best friend Patsy Fleming. 'I never had it so good,' said Frank. 'We used to go out in the blackout and nick a car, break a window and take what we could from the shops. The darkness was our best friend. Rationing meant people were more up for a bit of crooked than ever before. Everyone was at it in some way. You had to, just to survive. For the average person, war was a very hard time and those little luxuries, like tea, sugar or a few petrol coupons, meant a lot.

'Before, they might have been too honest to want to take something stolen but now it was a case of making life more bearable, so they put that honesty to one side. The shopkeepers we sold stuff to were in on it too. I loved it. It was a real thieves' community. Material was hard to come by, so we started to nick bolts of cloth from shops to sell on, which was very profitable.'

Going out after dark was made much easier because cars were only allowed to have one headlight, with the other one blacked out. This made it virtually impossible for the police to spot a number plate. A favourite ruse for Frank and his other great friend from around the Elephant, Jimmy Robson, whose wife Toni used to shoplift with Eva, was for one of them to dress up as an air raid warden. One such raid was carried out on a tailor's shop, to steal suit lengths. 'He got the hat from somewhere – nicked it I suppose,' said Frank. 'We went up to the tailor's shop in Hanover Square, smashed the window, and I yelled at the people standing around that there was an unexploded bomb. All the while, I had the tin hat on with "ARP" on it.

'I was saying, "Stay back! Stay back!" while Jimmy was grabbing stuff. At one point, people were helping us to load up the car. It was unbelievable but people had such respect for uniforms. We laughed all the way back to South London.'

The war also changed Soho for good, in terms of the gangsters who were running it. 'All the Italians and half-Italians were literally rounded up overnight and interned,' said Frank. 'Most of them couldn't even speak Italian but because Italy had joined the war with the Nazis they were seen as a threat. On the street, there was a lot of anti-Italian feeling. These were people I had grown up with and been to school with, so it was hard to see them put away like that.'

A number of the Sabinis found themselves thrown in jail, the powerbase they had so carefully constructed through years of thuggery and having coppers 'straightened' – in their pay – was swept away by Home Office powers against undesirable aliens. The void was quickly filled by a rival gang from King's Cross, the Whites, who had been in an uneasy alliance with the Sabinis, and never quite managed to topple them. Now, they saw their chance. 'I felt sorry for the Sabinis because I liked them and they had been good to me as a boy but now they were finished. I was basically working freelance in those days but alongside the Elephants, so I wasn't scared of the Whites when they moved in,' said Frank.

Part of his time growing up in Soho was spent in the spielers, playing cards with the other Chaps but Frank, by now seventeen, also used to like to stop in at the Windmill Theatre to catch one of the racy revue shows. The Windmill was one of the few theatres that stayed open for the duration of the war – its motto was 'We Never Closed'. 'Or, as the Chaps used to say, "We Never Clothed,"' said Frank.

He graduated from being a boy who used to yell abuse at the prostitutes along the Walworth Road – just so they'd pay him a penny to bugger off – to a young man with a real interest in the female form. 'They really were the dregs, the brasses in Walworth,' said Frank. 'We used to shout at them – "Fucking brass!" – just to be horrible to them but the West End girls were something else.' And Frank preferred blondes.

'Most boys my age hadn't seen a naked girl before and there was no sex education other than what your mates might have told you,' he said. 'So, seeing those girls starkers was a bit like paradise. Today, it would seem really tame but back then it was very daring. The girls had to stand still in these poses, with maybe a couple of stars covering their modesty. If you got right up to the front of the theatre you could get quite an eyeful. They had comedians on as well – big names started out there, like Peter Sellers and the rest of the Goon Show. The punters weren't there to see them, though.'

In his teenage meanderings through Soho, Frank learned to be charming to girls, taking them out for drinks to see where it might lead. Some were suitably impressed with his reputation as a bad boy and a gang member. 'There'd be stories in the paper about who was the leader of the Elephant Boys. My name was usually up there. It's fair to say I had a lot of influence but there was no clear boss of the Elephant. It didn't work like that,' he said. 'If there was trouble, we'd band together to fight another gang. If not, we would work in small teams, or maybe on our own. We knew we had back-up when we needed it.'

In the early days of the war, as storm clouds gathered over Europe, trouble was also brewing on the home front in Lambeth. Despite being separated from his wife, James Fraser was determined to make his influence felt. He was still in contact with his older children, Peggy and Kathleen, who often popped in to Howley Place to see him, although Frank and Eva remained loyal to their mother and tended to stay away at first.

Kathleen, who was nineteen, had fallen in love with a local boy, Albert Ives. They wanted to get married but, as she wasn't yet twenty-one, she had to get her father's permission. He refused to give it and no amount of pleading from Margaret would change his mind. Beverley recalled what happened next: 'Eva had had enough of him dictating what they could and couldn't do. She'd had enough of him knocking their mother about for all those years while they had to watch. Now he was going to spoil Kathleen's chance of happiness, it just wasn't on. Eva went round to see him and found him in the kitchen. They started rowing. Then Eva spotted a pan of potatoes on the side, ready for cooking. She picked it up and tipped it over his head, to make her point. He gave his permission for Kathleen to get married after that.'

Standing up to her father was just part of Eva's new-found confidence. Even with the war on, Eva and the other Forty Thieves were treated almost like celebrities around the Elephant. Beverley said: 'The Forty Thieves idolised film stars like Rita Hayworth and they loved to dress up like them, really taking care of their hair and make-up, always wearing high heels and furs.

'The best hoisters didn't want to wear what they had stolen. They preferred to sell it on and then buy their own stuff. They would spend quite lavishly because they could, just for the fun of it. When you think they came from nothing, you can see why. Those war years were really depressing and so for them, drinking, having a laugh, nicking a bit of stuff, was a way to get through all the hard times.

'Many of them had brothers away in the forces, like Eva and Frank's older brother James, known as Jim. They were worried sick about him. Everyone was dreading a telegram arriving with bad news.'

Jim joined up at the outbreak of war and saw active service in campaigns in Africa, Italy and France. He rose to the rank of sergeant and was decorated for his efforts for King and Country.

Eva, meanwhile, poured all her energy into becoming the best hoister in town. She worked in a team of three or four girls, perfecting a lightning-quick bag switch within the shop and at other times handing stolen goods to her driver, who was handily parked outside the store, before going back in for more. 'She had to work the same shops, week in, week out and get away with it, it wasn't easy,' said Beverley. 'The shops had started to employ people called walkers, who were like an early form of store detective. She had to learn how to spot them, without being spotted herself.'

Alice Diamond was by now in semi-retirement and Maggie Hill had taken over as Queen. But Maggie had a fiery, quick temper and it was to prove her downfall. 'Maggie Hill liked a drink as much as she liked to hoist and Eva was never like that. She liked to keep a cool head on her when she was working,' said Beverley. Although she could be very feisty when pushed, Eva was slow to anger and preferred to think things through before acting.

Maggie Hill was arrested for shoplifting in 1939 and again lashed out with her trusty hatpin during the incident, stabbing a policeman in the eye. She got four years' penal servitude for her crime. Even in jail, Maggie had a terrible reputation – she would rant and rave, attacking the prison guards. The only person who could calm her down was the Roman Catholic priest. She was no stranger to the inside of a prison cell but this was to be her final sentence and it seemed to break her. On her release, she sank into alcoholism. She ceased shoplifting and the only work she could find was as a prostitute's maid – it was a terrible fall from her days as Queen of the Forty Thieves.

Shortly after Maggie was jailed, Eva got caught for the first time, stealing a dress, in 1940. She was out of town, in Kingston, which meant there was premeditation. Even though it was her first offence, she got a jail sentence. 'Maybe it knocked her confidence,' said Beverley. 'Maggie had always been such a strong leader and then she was gone. The girls had to find their own way and there were the usual petty arguments and things. People got careless and then they got caught.' Eva was given a six-month sentence in London's Holloway Prison, following in the footsteps of many of the Forty Thieves.

Holloway was a forbidding place, a Gothic monstrosity designed to resemble a medieval castle, complete with battlements and turrets, a harsh regime and poor conditions for the inmates. However, the governor, Mary Size, was a reformer and had softened some aspects of the regime to make life more bearable for its inmates, repainting the walls in calm tones of cream and brown, putting lights-out back to 10 p.m. and allowing pictures and family photographs in the cells. Prisoners were given lessons in home hygiene and childcare and there were handicraft classes and even an annual exhibition of their works.

As luck would have it, Holloway Prison was relocated in the early years of the war and the prisoners were evacuated to Aylesbury, still under the command of Mary Size, and it was there that Eva served her sentence. Despite the reassurances of older members of the Forty Thieves, being locked up came as something of a shock to the previously carefree Eva. Many of the women in Holloway were repeat offenders for crimes such as prostitution and drunkenness. Thieves such as Eva regarded themselves as a different class of criminal and in any case her nature was to keep herself to herself. However, in order to survive in prison she did make friendships.

'She regarded getting jailed as a hazard of the profession but she didn't find being locked up as easy as Frank,' said Beverley. 'She tried to just get on with it as best as she could and keep out of trouble.'

The clanking of keys in the locks, the slamming of doors, bells to signal the time to get up and lights-out, the rules on making her bed, 'slopping out' the chamber pot in the morning, lining up for exercise and chapel all became part of her routine. 'But I don't think she found it particularly hard going that first time. The main thing she talked about from that sentence was the cocoa,' said Beverley. 'It was apparently very tasty. Once she got out, she carried on as if nothing had happened. It was business as usual. If she struggled at the time, she didn't like to show it because that was seen as being weak.'

Shortly after this, perhaps gripped by the desire to do something for her country, Eva decided to join the Land Army and travelled north to dig for victory. It didn't last long. 'She couldn't bear all that digging in the cold and the dirt,' said Beverley. 'She ran away and ended up dressing up as a mermaid telling fortunes on Blackpool Pier to earn her train fare back home. She looked a lot like a gypsy, with her long, black hair, which was due to being part Native American, so that came in very handy for her. She just wanted to get back to London, which was where she belonged.'

Frank and Eva's mother, Margaret, was now living with her lover, Patrick Duhig, a tall, kind-hearted man who embraced her children as his own. He worked as a fireman during the war and would go on to work as a postman, bringing home a regular wage for Margaret. Meanwhile, Frank had a good sideline as a wartime spiv – selling goods on the black market – but he needed to keep pace with demand, which entailed constant breaking and entering. His stolen goods were secreted away in Soho basements or warehouses. Sometimes they were literally sold off the back of a lorry.

In 1941, while he was trying to steal a consignment of ladies' stockings from a shop in The Cut in Waterloo, he was caught. Still only seventeen, he was sent to borstal in Feltham. 'Of course, escape was on my mind,' he said. 'So when the chance came, I took it. Me and a couple of the other boys were coming back from the chapel one day when we decided to try to get over the wall. It was about twelve feet high but I was pretty fit and so were the rest. We got over but the screws caught us and there was a massive fight. That was my first experience of the punishment block and then they moved me to Borstal in Rochester, which was a hole.'

Once there, he got into trouble for assaulting a prison officer in the bathhouse. Frank felt that the officer in question was a pervert who kept walking in on him while he was taking his first bath in weeks. 'He was having a good look at me and he kept telling me to hurry up,' said Frank. 'I'd only been in the bath about ten minutes. Now, I realise he was kinky and up to something. Back then, I lost it and swore at him. He was a big bloke – well over six feet – and gave me a right hook.

'That was it. I was stark naked but I flew at him and got his head under the bathwater. A couple of the other prisoners, who had worked their way up – or should I say grassed their way up, to being "leaders", with special privileges – came in and jumped on me.

'Other screws arrived and I was beaten to a pulp with their sticks and put into a punishment cell. After that, I was put on bread and water and given the birch for what I had done. Assaulting a prison officer was a very serious offence indeed, not that I regretted it for a minute. He had it coming.'

The birch was sanctioned for use in the penal system for punishing younger male inmates until the late 1940s. Worse than the cane, it was a fearsome bunch of birch or alder twigs, over a metre long, which had been soaked in brine, to make each stroke inflict more pain and deeper welts. Being soaked in salty water also lessened the likelihood of infection in the cuts it left on the prisoner's behind.

Frank was transferred to Maidstone Prison to receive his punishment. 'You never got to see who was giving it to you, because you were marched out of your cell into the workshop and there was a wooden triangle frame waiting. After I took my clothes off, they handcuffed me to it by my wrists at the top, facing the wall. My legs were cuffed to each side of the frame. I knew there was a fair crowd of screws who came to watch.

'And if you were getting it for assaulting a screw, they really made you pay. There was an element of humiliation in it, because it was on your bare backside and everyone got to see it. It just wasn't very manly, being made to strip like that.

'Those birch twigs made a big "swish" as they went through the air. The screw would count "One", and so on. I was no stranger to corporal punishment, but the cane felt like a tickle compared to this.

'The birch really cut into me and the screw put all his strength behind it, to make me suffer. But I didn't scream or cry even though my skin was cut to pieces and I was in agony. The worst thing was after the first one or two, he paused to let it sink in and I knew ten more strokes of that birch were coming.'

Although it was seen as the system's strongest sanction against unruly boys, for Frank, getting the birch improved his status. 'The others looked on me as hard case now. I had done that screw and I had had the birch and I didn't complain about it. What might I do to them if they crossed me? It was a good place to be, it gave me a leg-up. I looked like I didn't give a damn but, bloody hell, I couldn't sit down for a week.'

Afterwards, Frank was transferred to Portland borstal in Dorset, where he staged what turned out to be the first of many protests in his career on the inside. Prisoners were supposed to sit in a little cubicle, pounding flint-stone into dust, from dawn until dusk. It was a Victorian punishment, designed to break the spirit. Each prisoner had to fill a box with flint dust and if they failed, they had to keep pounding until they had done so. 'I just refused to do it, I wouldn't come out of my cell,' said Frank. 'It was an inhumane punishment. There was no point to it because the screws would throw away the powder. Your arms ached, your elbows ached from it and it was freezing cold. It wasn't as if we were sewing mailbags or making brushes or something that could be used. So, I sat in my cell and told them I wasn't coming out. They really didn't know what to do with me.'

He was sent to Wandsworth Prison to be dealt with by the adult system, in the hope that the stricter regime would knock some sense into him. 'It was strict,' said Frank. 'The rules were petty. You couldn't have your bed down until 8 p.m., the blankets had to be neatly folded. Anything other than that, you were on report, which meant more punishment, bread and water and so on. I was on report quite a lot.'

After a few weeks in Wandsworth, he was transferred to Chelmsford. Had the prison authorities known what was to happen next, they might have thought more carefully about sending young Frank Fraser, embittered and thirsting for more criminal knowledge, to that particular jail. There he would meet a criminal mastermind who, apart from his beloved sister Eva, had arguably the biggest influence on Frank's life, raising him up from a bit player on the streets of South London, to a serious gangland 'face'.

For behind bars in Chelmsford plotting his next move was the up-and-coming Soho gang boss, Billy Hill, younger brother of Maggie Hill, Queen of the Forty Thieves. While Maggie had carefully nurtured Eva Fraser in the ways of becoming a top hoister, Billy now took young Frank under his wing. And it was from Billy that Frank would go on to learn what he really wanted to know – how to become a gangster.

CHAPTER 4

BILLY

Billy Hill's first visit to prison was as a young boy, wearing a sailor suit, carrying an aspidistra plant. Buried in the plant pot was enough snuff to make sure his sister Maggie was a lot more comfortable in Holloway Prison. The warders were so taken with this charming little lad and his gift that they let him in without searching him or the plant pot. For Billy, it was mission accomplished and the first lesson in dealing with screws – always be nice to them, even if you secretly hate them, because it can make life on the inside more bearable.

Born in 1911 into a family where the chief topic of discussion was how much the stolen goods in the parlour were worth, Billy was always headed for a life of crime. He claimed to have been a native of the infamous Seven Dials area of Covent Garden, which was notorious as a thieves' kitchen, but he was actually born near St Pancras. His family probably lived in the Covent Garden area for a time when he was growing up before moving to a street off Tottenham Court Road.

He had so many brothers and sisters – twenty in total – that he could not remember all of them, but he was particularly close to his older sister Maggie. Like Frank, he graduated from nicking bits of fruit to house burglary and theft. But Billy had a liking for his 'chiv' – a five-inch knife he used to scar the faces of those who crossed him – and he soon found other criminals looking up to him as some sort of a leader.

He dressed the part – with slicked-back hair, natty suits, trilby hat and tie. With a handsome face and a toothy grin, he looked a bit like Humphrey Bogart, who happened to be one of his favourite movie stars. When he was at work with his chiv, Billy tried to avoid cutting arteries, because massive blood loss usually meant death and, for the perpetrator, the hangman's noose. So, he was content instead to inflict scars on, and lasting psychological damage to, those who crossed him around the streets of central London.

By the late 1930s, he had assembled a tough gang of robbers and thieves who were willing to join him on lucrative criminal escapades. His gang of faithful followers had improbable nicknames, such as Franny the Spaniel, Teddy Odd Legs, Horrible Harry, Tony the Wop, Scarface Jock, Taters, Mutton and Birdie, to name but a few.

When Frank first met him in 1940, Billy had already made good money robbing post offices but was serving two years for conspiracy, for a bungled smash and grab on a jeweller's in Conduit Street in the West End. Like so many robbers in the 1940s, the unreliability of the motor car he was supposed to be escaping in proved disastrous. After one of the getaway cars stalled, the gang were forced into another car, which then had its windscreen smashed by a truncheon lobbed by an enterprising policeman. Billy fled while his two companions were grabbed by 'have-a-go' heroes. Billy tried to brazen it out, walking back through the crowd, but the public were having none of it and pointed him out to a police officer, landing him with a prison sentence.

He was working as the prison barber in Chelmsford and had heard about this newly transferred upstart prisoner, Frank Fraser, who was constantly badmouthing the screws and refusing to fit in with the system. Billy's way was to have a screw or two 'straightened' with payments from his relatives, making life more comfortable for himself, securing the cushiest jobs and ensuring he had extra little luxuries. 'He took me into the cell they were using as a barber's shop and had a chat with me, very friendly. Billy's view was that with doing bird, it was better to just get on with it – because there would be more chance of getting back on the outside more quickly that way. He told me: "Frank, you've just got to keep your head down. You're no use to anyone in here. Think about what we could achieve on the outside."'

With that in mind, Frank did calm down and he got himself a job as a cleaner. 'There was something special about Billy; the way he talked to me. It just made sense,' he said. 'I knew he was a very respected thief but to meet him, you just felt that you were listening to the guv'nor. He had brains and he had style. You could just tell he was a different class of Chap to the rest.'

Billy Hill filled the role of the wiser, older brother who had already trodden the path on the wrong side of the law. Frank wanted to follow in his footsteps. It was an echo of what had happened several years earlier with Maggie Hill, who was like a big sister to Eva when she joined the Forty Thieves.

Frank's new job as a cleaner gave him the chance to move around the prison and drop in on Billy Hill from time to time. Part of Frank's job was to go around with a bucket of hot water for the prisoners to have a shave in the mornings and then return to the kitchen with it. The kitchen prisoners usually saved him a bit of bread and cheese or meat, which he happily took off to share with his new mate, Billy. 'That really was how we got to know each other,' said Frank. 'Yes, I admired him and so I shared what I had. That is how it worked in prison.'

Billy Hill and Frank made a pledge to look each other up once they had left the nick. There is no doubt that Billy recognised that Frank was a force to be reckoned with. Beyond liking him personally, he saw violence in him that he wanted to harness for his own ends. Billy was an extremely shrewd operator, and there was no way he was going to let someone like Frank – who reminded him of a younger version of himself – slip through his fingers, not least because he didn't want to come up against him in any street turf wars. 'I did have a reputation already,' said Frank. 'I was young but I was tough and I think Billy knew that. I respected him hugely but I guess there is always the thought of "What if he sets up against me?" in our world. I was loyal to Billy from the outset. Not foolishly so, but something in me liked him a lot, so he needn't have worried.'

Meanwhile, Eva was caught pilfering from shops for a second time and was sent to Holloway for her second six-month sentence. The prison had moved back to London and she had to get used to life in a tiny cell, housed along a series of landings, which radiated from the echoing centre of the

Victorian jail. When Eva arrived, the prison was abuzz with news of the arrival of the famous and hated fascist couple, the Mosleys. Diana and Oswald Mosley had been interned as unrepentant fascist sympathisers. He was leader of the British Union of Fascists – the Blackshirts, as they were known – and she was a huge admirer of Adolf Hitler, who had attended their secret wedding at Joseph Goebbels' home in 1936. The Mosleys were housed in a little cottage in the prison grounds and were afforded special privileges because of their social status, such as the right to grow their own vegetables, play music and even to sunbathe in their garden; the sight of Oswald's toned chest as he sat outside, shirtless, caused palpitations among the sex-starved female inmates.

Diana socialised with the prison community and Eva was among those she spoke to on a regular basis. 'Eva always spoke very highly of her, in fact she wouldn't have a word said against her,' said Beverley. 'She didn't care for Diana Mosley's politics but she knew that this privileged woman was just trying to make the best of it in prison. Eva respected that.'

On her release, Eva was ready to go out and have fun again with her best friend, Gladys Say. Early one morning, nursing a hangover in her mother's flat on Walworth Road, the air raid sirens went and her mother rushed in to tell her to get up and come down to the Anderson shelter – the tin air raid hut at the bottom of the garden, which was shared with three other families. Eva refused with characteristic bluntness, pulling the blankets over her head, saying: 'I am not leaving this flaming bed for Adolf bleeding Hitler.' It was a decision that might have cost her life, as days later the flat was destroyed by a German bomb.

Fortunately, Eva had taken to hanging out in the snooker hall over the road and bedding down under the tables, accompanied by Gladys. This was daring, as Frank pointed out: 'Girls did not go into snooker clubs in those days but Eva was fearless. She preferred it to the Anderson shelter which was dank and horrible and smelled of piss.' The family were re-housed in Munton Road, just east of the Elephant and Castle, but this too was bombed, so they moved to Chaucer House in Tabard Street, off Long Lane, in the Borough. The building was a red-brick tenement hastily built by the council during the First World War.

While he was still in borstal, Frank had met up with another local lad, Jimmy Brindle, who had been arrested for petty theft and was serving a short sentence. As contact with the outside world was very limited, Frank asked Jimmy to go and look his mother Margaret up, once he was back on civvy street. Knowing that the Brindles were cut from the same cloth as himself, Frank felt he could trust Jimmy to deliver the message that he was doing fine to his beloved mother. She had married her lover, Patrick Duhig, without bothering to get a divorce from James Fraser. She had used her maiden name, Anderson, but her bigamous union was an open secret in the family, who didn't blame her for turning her back on the wife-beating James Fraser.

The Brindle family were well known around the Elephant and Castle. Jimmy's older brother, 'Tom Thumb' Brindle, was a friend of Billy Hill and was a popular bookmaker. It was a straight business, although he had to pay his dues to those in the gangs in order to operate his pitches, as his father had done.

Tall and good-looking, with fair hair and twinkly blue eyes, Jimmy sauntered around to Margaret's flat in the Borough. Eva opened the door. 'She invited him to stay for a cup of tea and that was that, really,' said Beverley. Eva was bowled over by his easy-going nature and charm. 'She knew that Frank would approve of her choice, because he had sent him around in the first place. I don't think Frank was deliberately playing cupid but he was very happy for him to be with Eva. Jimmy was his pal in borstal and he remained his lifelong friend. He always joked that it was the most expensive message he had ever delivered in his life.'

By the time a nineteen-year-old Frank came out of prison in January 1943, Eva was already pregnant with her first child. Beverley was born in the bed of her grandmother, Margaret. As Eva lay recovering, Frank and a few friends arrived to wet the baby's head. 'They had a bit of a knees-up,' said Beverley. 'They all took turns in holding me, calling me "little Eva". It was very early in the morning when I was born but that didn't stop everyone celebrating with a drink.'

Shortly after this, Frank's call-up papers arrived. 'My mother opened them,' he said. 'Then, she threw them on the fire.' While Frank's brother, Jim, was serving King and Country, his mother made it clear she had other ideas for her youngest. Margaret Fraser had no intention of both her boys becoming cannon fodder. She had seen what the Boer War had done for her father, for a start. 'I didn't want to join the Kate Carney anyway. All that square bashing wasn't for me but my mum's decision cemented it, really,' said Frank. 'After that, I knew it was just a matter of time before the authorities caught up with me, so I decided I would give them the runaround. I'm proud to say that I did quite a good job.'

He was picked up by the police a few weeks after his call-up. They spotted him and some accomplices acting suspiciously in a van near the Oval. After delivering him to the barracks at Norwich, the policemen might have thought that was the last they would see of Frank Fraser for a while. They were wrong. After being left alone in the barracks, Frank ran away and caught a train back to London.

He was on his toes for another three weeks before he was picked up again as a deserter and this time he got three months in a civilian prison. Once again, after he had served his time, he was taken to Norwich to join the army but at the railway station, he managed to slide out of the old-fashioned cuffs, hitching lifts back to London. Avoiding his usual haunts – and the chances of being picked up by the law for deserting – he went on a night out in a pub in Kennington with some of the Chaps.

He might have lost a small fortune at cards if he hadn't been distracted by a blonde bombshell, who stood nearly five foot ten inches tall in her high heels.

Instead, he lost his heart.

CHAPTER 5

KATE

Kate Wall stepped into Frank's life on a night out during the darkest days of the Second World War, just a few weeks after his release from prison. He was struck not only by her blonde hair and beautiful, blue eyes but her kind and easy manner. She met Frank at his most charming – smartly dressed, with slicked-back hair and a wallet stuffed with notes from his ill-gotten gains. Kate knew he was gaining notoriety as a 'face' around the Elephant but that didn't put her off. Once they started chatting, Kate and Frank realised that they had shared the same Covent Garden baker as children and that Kate had once let him go ahead of her in the queue for second-day bread.

He was completely infatuated with her, particularly as she had developed her own sense of style, topping off her outfit with a silk jockey cap, which made her stand out from the crowd even more. She, in turn, was more than happy to let this good-looking young Chap with a great sense of humour buy her a few drinks, especially as money was tight.

Kate Wall came from a family with a criminal pedigree of its own, in the backstreets around Drury Lane. It was an area so notorious for thieving and prostitution that her relatives used to joke about being 'the whores of Drury Lane'. Kate's mother Rosina was born Rosina Woods in Holborn, the daughter of a printer's compositor, with seven brothers and sisters.

The Woods family lived in cramped, rented rooms in Lamb's Conduit Street and then Red Lion Street, just off High Holborn. By the time Rosina left school at fourteen to work as a printer's assistant, her older brother Jim was already making his way as a bookmaker, with several pitches at race-courses throughout the south-east and serious connections with gangland figures. Her younger brother, Bob, was regularly thieving from the markets near their home. Rosina's only surviving daughter, Maggie, now aged ninety-two, remembers seeing her uncle Bob tied to a handcart after one such expedition ended up with him being caught. 'They strapped him down to the cart by his arms and legs and were wheeling him up to the police station, with him effing and blinding. He got penal servitude at Dartmoor, which was no joke in them days. While he was there, he got the cat-o'-nine-tails. It seemed to do something to him because when he came out, he was a sort of reformed character. He had learned to sew – mailbags, probably – and when he come out he decided he wanted to be a tailor, so he got that as his trade. He wasn't a hundred per cent straight after that, nobody was, really. But it changed him.'

During the early years of the First World War, Rosina married her sweetheart Alfred Willoughby, an engineer's labourer, also born in Holborn. The couple settled in Dodson Street in Southwark, and she quickly fell pregnant before he went away to fight in France. She had a baby, also named Rosina, known as Rose, in 1916. In September that year she received some devastating news. Alfred Willoughby had been killed in battle, leaving Rosina a widow at nineteen, with a young baby to care for.

It wasn't long before she caught the eye of twenty-five-year-old Daniel Wall, who drove a horse and cart for the iron foundry and lived a few streets away. Although he was several years older than her, the couple fell in love. Rosina needed a father for little Rose and Daniel was happy to raise her as his own. When Daniel proposed, grieving Rosina said 'yes' and their first child Kathleen Lydia Wall – known as Kate – was born in 1918. However, Rosina never forgot her first husband and proudly displayed his medals on their bedroom wall. Little Rose bore the surname Willoughby all her life and was sent to a different school from the other Wall children, to avoid her being teased for it.

The new couple moved into Jubilee Dwellings, tenement flats in Gerridge Street, Southwark, just around the corner from Daniel's fearsome mother, Maria Wall, known in the family by her maiden name, Nanny O'Mahony. She and her husband, Thomas Wall, had come to London from Cork in the late-nineteenth century, like so many other poor Irish immigrants. Thomas, a scaffolder, died in the early 1900s, leaving Maria and Daniel to fend for themselves. Nanny O'Mahony found work 'skin-pulling' – yanking fur from the carcasses of dead rabbits with the aid of a blunt knife, before they were turned into fur coats, muffs and stoles. It was relentless and hard physical work done in the family home –

a dank basement flat in Webber Row – which invariably stank of decaying rabbit and was covered in bunny fluff.

Rosina went to work in a candle-making factory to bring in extra money, while Daniel found a job driving the dray for a brewery near Drury Lane. Before long there were eight children: Rosie, Kate, Mary, Danny, Maggie, Jessie, Albie and Maureen. Maggie remembers their tenement flat – which only had two rooms and a scullery – being crammed to the rafters but full of laughter, with Danny always finding time to play a joke on his children. He had nicknames for all of them: Rosie was 'Dyed Hair' because she bleached it once; Mary was 'Cock Eye', on account of her squint; Danny, her brother, was 'Dopey'; Maggie was 'Soapy' because she needed a wash; and Kate was 'Key Hole', because she was always listening at doors. Jessie and Albie were 'Gertcha' – meaning 'get out of it' – because they were always into everything and Maureen was 'Baldy' because she lost all her hair as a baby due to shock – her sisters had dropped her in the Serpentine when they took her out in the pram one day.

They slept top to toe, four to a bed. Kate was the quiet, easy-going one who always took the rap for every wrong-doing and rarely complained about anything, just like her father, Danny. The family was so poor they regularly had to go to the parish church to get extra food and shoes. 'Kate was always given the parish boots, for some reason,' said Maggie. 'I remember when we had a photograph taken my mother was telling her to get to the back because of the shame of those boots she had to wear. They had a special ticket on them, so you couldn't pawn them if things got really bad. They knew poor folk like us would sell anything we could get our hands on. Poor Kate, she just put up with it but we refused to wear them. She was very kind hearted and that is how she was her whole life.'

Unlike her sister Maggie, who was very bright and passed her 11-plus exam, Kate rarely attended school, struggling academically, preferring to 'hop the wag'. This meant that when it came to finding work after she left school at four-teen, she found it hard to stick at anything and was always up for a lark, which often ended up with her getting the sack. A series of dead-end factory jobs provided little reason for her to change her ways. Maggie remembered: 'She got a job with our brother Albie in a cheese factory, the ones making the little triangles in silver paper. Her job was to get all the damaged ones, pick the silver paper off and chuck the cheese back in the machine, so they didn't waste anything. She got so bored by it, she just chucked everything in the machine, silver paper, the lot. She got fired on the spot. She did have a laugh about it later.'

When Kate was seventeen, tragedy struck. Her beloved father Danny suffered a burst ulcer and died at the age of forty-two, leaving the family with little income. 'It was a huge shock to all of us and we never really got over it,' said Maggie. 'Suddenly he just wasn't there anymore. I was eleven and I was going to be going to high school because I had done well in my exams but there was no way that could happen once he died. The burden fell on the older kids, such as Kate, to help my mother provide.'

As a mark of his popularity in the neighbourhood, there was a huge turnout for his funeral, with his coffin pulled on the brewery dray down Drury Lane. All the men came out of the pub as it passed by to sing 'Danny Boy', as the family followed his coffin with tears in their eyes.

A few months later, having now turned eighteen, a still-bereft Kate fell into the arms of her twenty-five-year-old neighbour, George Wickenden, and very quickly found herself pregnant. Although he had a good job as a motor fittings assembler, it was not a love match. Their son Antony, known as Tony, was born later that year. 'She felt she had to marry him,' said Kate's sister Maggie. 'He wasn't really her type but after losing our dad, it gave everyone a focus to have a big event to look forward to.'

The wedding was a huge family occasion, a chance for happiness to fill the rooms at Jubilee Dwellings after so much sadness over Danny's death. 'I can still remember seeing a huge bowl of peaches and going to get one and my mother giving my hand a slap,' said Maggie. 'They were for Kate's wedding. We had a right old knees-up that day, with everyone in the building popping in and wishing them well. The party spilled right out along the landing and down the stairs.' But without Kate knowing, her new husband George was also involved with her sister, Mary.

When the Second World War broke out, he was among the first to sign up and Kate was relieved to see him go, because their relationship was already strained. When letters came home from George addressed to both Kate and Mary, the game was up. Maggie said: 'I'm not sure if Kate actually confronted Mary about it because that wouldn't be her way. She got a letter and she went around to Mary's house and there was one lying there on the kitchen table from George. Maybe Mary left it out on purpose for her to see. I think Kate'd always had her suspicions that something was going on between them but this proved it.'

Mary moved on and married someone else but she still kept in touch with George Wickenden. Kate made it clear that they were no longer together and was glad to see the back of him. She set about enjoying herself, going out to pubs and clubs again, while her sisters babysat little Tony. Although the split was permanent, because divorce was so expensive they did not actually legally end their marriage until the late 1940s.

It was on one of those nights out that she met Frank. The attraction between them was instant. 'They sat talking to each other, flirting, holding hands,' said Beverley. 'Frank could be a real charmer and he certainly was good at spoiling the ladies. He knew how to impress Kate and she loved that. She'd had a tough time with George Wickenden. She had a little boy at home. All of a sudden, here was a man who was a bit like a local celebrity and he was courting her. It felt like the world was opening up to her once more.'

But when word reached George about Kate's dalliance with Frank, he was furious. 'George didn't want his son anywhere near Frank, who already had a list of convictions as long as your arm,' said Beverley. 'George was away fighting for King and Country and Frank, well, he wasn't.' In a move that still shocks, more than seventy years later, Mary and her new husband persuaded Kate to give up her son to them. 'Mary couldn't have children, for whatever reason, she just couldn't,' said Maggie. 'They made a good point that they had a stable home and they would love Tony. It broke Kate's heart really but she gave him up.

'She felt she had to make the choice because Frank was her only chance of happiness. He wasn't too keen about having another man's child in his home and Kate felt she had to consider that too. Mary was a forceful character who was determined to represent George's interests, even though she had moved on from him.'

Kate and Frank's son David Fraser remembers his half-brother Tony Wickenden visiting often as he was growing up and still calling Kate 'Mum'. 'He grew up to be a very nice guy, who died a few years ago. To give them their due, Mary and her husband did a great job of raising him. But my mum never got over it.'

CHAPTER 6

IN THE FAMILY WAY

In 1943, Frank had the dubious honour of being one of the first thieves to be caught out by a burglar alarm. He had only just been released from a three-month sentence for shop-breaking and larceny in March of that year and was back thieving the moment he set foot on the outside. He was breaking through the wall of a backyard store to get inside a clothing shop in Southwark with two accomplices when he came across a set of electric wires and thought nothing of it. Unfortunately for Frank and his accomplices, the wires were part of an alarm system connected to the local police station, and while they were inside the shop, the law arrived. Frank managed to squeeze himself under a sink to hide but was eventually found. He got fifteen months in prison and was sent to Wandsworth.

His name appeared on the charge sheet as Francis David-son Fraser, although his real name at birth was just plain Frank. He had got into the habit of telling the authorities his name was Francis whenever he was in trouble because it sounded more formal than Frank or Frankie and it was the name he was called by his mother when he misbehaved.

Kate proved her devotion to him by writing him letters every week. But without the calming influence of Billy Hill to guide him on how to make life easy for himself on the inside, Frank was back to his old ways, with his motto being: 'Do Them, Before They Do You'. This applied to every member of the prison service and it was during this sentence that questions were first raised about his mental health, as Frank set about roughing up every prison officer he came into contact with.

After a psychiatric assessment – the first of many – prison medical officers thought electric shock treatment might help him. 'I didn't know much about medical stuff but I did know that with my head injuries as a kid, it would probably do more harm than good. I was worried about it, but what could I do? I was a prisoner and they could basically do what the hell they liked with me,' said Frank. 'That was partly what giving them aggravation all the time was about. I knew I was powerless so I just wanted to cause trouble for them, to make their lives difficult, just for the hell of it. I wasn't going to go quietly.'

Frank's prison mugshot from around this time shows him with his trademark stare, looking every inch the hardened prisoner. Although he was only a small man – standing no more than five-foot six-inches tall – he was powerfully built, a skilled street fighter and, when riled, appeared to gain immense strength that could overpower men who were much bigger than him. He already had a fearless reputation from his borstal days, and his continuing violent behaviour was a cause for concern among the prison authorities.

Frank was transferred to Wormwood Scrubs, with the

prospect of weekly trips to Banstead Hospital in Surrey for ECT – Electroconvulsive Therapy. He hadn't been in the Scrubs long before he made friends with the entertainer, Ivor Novello. Their friendship was a brief highlight in an otherwise bleak stretch for Frank. Novello was serving an eight-week sentence for misuse of petrol coupons, after an adoring fan stole them from her employer and gave them to him as a gift. Even though he hadn't stolen the coupons, the courts found that he was guilty of rationing offences. He had even tried to bribe the police officer who arrested him to avoid going to court, which made matters worse.

In jail, he was treated as a celebrity, with prison officers fawning over him, but he still found the whole experience shattering both physically and emotionally. 'He was a very charming man,' said Frank. 'He was intrigued by all the villainy I had done. We came from completely different worlds. I had no idea he was a raving poof; no one did back then. He clearly wasn't cut out for prison and I felt a bit sorry for him.

'He'd had a very showbiz life and was used to the finer things, yet here he was slopping out with the rest of us and eating the awful prison grub. He wasn't happy but he put a brave face on it. We used to talk about the war, what was going on on the outside, just to pass the time. I knew he wasn't ever going to make any trouble and he never did. In fact, he got out after four weeks.'

In the end, the dreaded ECT never happened, because Frank got into a fight with a prison officer, after smashing up his cell in an act of sympathy for a Canadian airman who was about to be hanged the next morning. Frank was put on a diet of bread and water and was made to serve out every day of his fifteen-month sentence. When he was released, the army came for him again, taking him to Bradford to try to get him to serve. He promptly escaped. When he got back to London, Frank took his girlfriend Kate around to meet Eva.

The two women struck up a lifelong friendship. Kate adored Frank and Eva approved of that wholeheartedly. In Kate she saw a woman who would be as devoted to Frank as she was. 'Kate recognised something in Eva – maybe it was that Eva was daring, whereas Kate would just go along with things,' said David. 'Kate loved a bit of crooked but she never had the bottle to nick it herself. They got on brilliantly. When Beverley was a baby, her mum would drop her at Kate's so that she could go out hoisting and she'd nick something nice to give to Kate as a thank-you.'

As for Frank, he was delighted that the two most important women in his life were getting along famously, although he did upset them both once by stealing identical mink stoles, which they both wore at the same time, on a night out at the pub. 'Frank had to nick something for both of them or there would be hell to pay,' said Beverley. 'It did used to annoy Kate that he would get them both the same thing. He was just trying to show he cared and, like a typical bloke, wasn't sure what they would like, so he tried to cover all bases with the same thing. Eva used to like to wind Kate up a bit if they both had the same stuff. It was a bit of a laugh for her.'

Before long, Kate found herself pregnant with Frank's first child and they set up home together in a tenement building in Mason Street, Southwark. 'I knew I had responsibilities and so I was always out thieving,' said Frank. 'This was probably the busiest time of my life in terms of pure criminality. I was constantly at it. I knew I had to put food on the table and I took my job very seriously.'

Using tips he had picked up from Billy Hill in prison, he started to venture further afield for smash and grabs, out of the West End and over to suburban Ealing. Billy was one of the leading lights of the smash and grab in the years leading up to the Second World War and Frank had soaked up all the knowledge he could from him while they were in jail together. There had to be an element of surprise and daring, and Frank took it to new heights. In the middle of Ealing Broadway, in broad daylight, he drove on to the pavement, smashed the windows of a jeweller's shop with an iron bar, and made off with trays of diamond rings. 'I abandoned the car and stuffed the tom into my jacket pockets and took the tube back to central London,' said Frank. 'It was a sweet job.'

Kate's family connections put him on to a nice little earner down at the docks, which continued for years. When consignments of goods came in, one of her relatives would cream off a bit for Frank to sell, in return for a small commission. He kept this ruse going until the docks closed, providing him with a small but regular source of income. It was a closely guarded secret known to only his closest relatives, because Frank would by nature share what he had stolen, but he didn't want anyone else to get a look-in on this. To him, it was a bit like having a thief's pension, a little nest egg to fall back on if times got hard.

'I was a big spender,' he admitted. 'I liked to treat people and buy them drinks. There are quite a few people who I went out on jobs with around those early days who put their money to work and went straight and made good businesses out of it. I was never one of them. I never drank a lot myself, I just liked everyone to have a good time.'

He was also building on his reputation as a man not to be messed with. When his friend, Jimmy Robson, along with his wife Toni, a member of the Forty Thieves and a friend of Eva's, were badly beaten up in December 1944, Frank took it upon himself to track down the five perpetrators, one by one. 'It took me a while, but I did them all. I had my knife and I wasn't afraid to use it. Billy Hill had told me in prison how to use it to the best effect, drawing the blade down the face to slash them, rather than up, which could cut an artery and end up with them dying. I was trying to scar them, to give them a reminder that they had crossed the line, not kill them.

'Once I got it into my head to do something, I did it. They hurt my friend and Eva's pal and I made them pay. I'd find them in a pub or a spieler or sometimes in broad daylight going down the street; it made no difference to me. They had it coming.'

Part of the code of honour on the street was that if you took a beating, you didn't go to the police about it. Frank said: 'That was just our way. Anyone who did would be known as a grass for the rest of their life and in a tight-knit community like ours, it could make life difficult. So if I gave someone a clump or slashed their face, they knew better than to go squealing to the cozzers about it.'

Around this time, Frank also used to go drinking with Charlie Kray, father to a young pair of boys, Reg and Ron, who liked to call him 'Uncle Frank'. He knew the legendary Kray twins as little boys, eating beans on toast at their mum

Violet's house in Vallance Road, Bethnal Green. That image of them as kids never left Frank, even when he faced them down as grown men. Plus, their bona fides as criminals were of a lower order than Frank's, according to the codes of the time. 'Their dad, Charlie, was what we would call a thief's ponce,' he said. 'That is not to be disrespectful to the twins' father but he was never one to do the actual thieving.

'Officially he was a scrap gold dealer who was always going on the "knocker" – going from door-to-door selling gold and silver jewellery – but he liked to ponce off other people who had, sell it on, take a bit for himself, whatever. In the pecking order of the criminal world, being a thief's ponce is not as respected as doing the actual thieving yourself.

'So, the twins would call me "Uncle Frank" and I would see them sometimes when the pubs shut around 3.30 p.m. and we would go round to Violet's for some tea and chat about boxing and the like until the pubs were open again in the evening. The twins liked to hear about what I had been up to but I was careful not to tell them too much. Children are innocent, that is how I see it, and they have to be protected from the harsh realities of life. Let's face it, the Kray twins found their own way without too much assistance from Uncle Frank.'

Meanwhile, on one of their many shoplifting trips in the West End, Eva and her best friend Gladys Say were caught. Because Gladys was only eighteen, she got borstal and was quickly spirited away over the wall by her boyfriend, never to return to serve her sentence. 'In fact, she was on the run for the rest of her life,' said Beverley. 'Gladys and Eva used to have a cup of tea and laugh about that. The authorities just never came after her. I suppose with the war on, they had better things to think about than a teenage hoister.'

However, Eva suffered a heartbreaking six-month separation from Jimmy and baby Beverley, who went to her nanny Margaret in Tabard Street to be looked after when Eva was sent once more to Holloway. Frank and one of his mates, Dickie 'Dido' Frett, who was also a criminal accomplice on many break-ins, decided to take baby Beverley up to Holloway to visit her mum. This was no mean feat, as Frank was still on the run from the authorities as an army deserter. But such was his loyalty to Eva, he was prepared to risk everything for her. He was able to visit his sister that day but prison officers would not let the baby in, so she had to wait at the gate with Dido. 'It was disgusting, inhumane, not to let a mother see her baby but that's how it was. I was still on me toes, but I didn't care. I would have done anything to let Eva see her baby. Beverley wasn't even a year old,' said Frank.

As 1944 drew to a close, Eva missed Frank's twenty-first birthday party, tucked up in Holloway with only her prison cocoa for company. Down in the Borough, Frank's mother, Lady Margaret, and her husband Patsy gave Frank a night to remember with crates of beer and a party so raucous that the revellers threw up all the way down three flights of stairs in Chaucer House. The beer was provided with the help of Darbo Hicks, father of legendary entertainer Tommy Steele, who used to run barrows down at the market and was on friendly terms with the Frasers.

With her youngest son now of age and about to become a father, Margaret felt a contentment that had been missing all her life – even if Frank was openly breaking the law at every opportunity and Eva was in and out of jail. Beverley explained: 'Nanny Margaret loved a bit of crooked – a fur stole, a nice handbag. Frank gave her things she never could have afforded. She'd gone from crossing herself and thanking the Lord to just thanking Frank. She knew it was nicked, of course she did.'

Just after New Year in 1945, the day before Eva was due to be released, Frank went out thieving to make sure he could give her something nice as a welcome home gift. Charles Henry 'Harryboy' Jenkins, who was a fellow member of the Elephant Boys gang and already had a fearsome reputation for violence, came along with him to rob a jewellery shop in Bond Street.

Harryboy, who liked to be known as the King of Borstal, would later find infamy at the end of the hangman's noose, after being found guilty in 1947 of shooting Alec de Antiquis, a bystander who had tried to foil a robbery at a jeweller's in Charlotte Street. Harryboy's sister was married to Kate Wall's brother Albie, so Frank looked on him as family and always spoke with some sadness about his execution. But when it came to it, although Frank could be violent, he was always very careful about who it was aimed at. If members of the public were involved, it wouldn't be Frank who was waving a gun in their faces. He was much too clever for that. 'Harryboy was the gamest of the game but killing a straight person in the street was something I would do anything to avoid,' Frank said. 'Yes, I would give someone a clump if they got in my way while I was working, but nothing serious. I carried a cosh but it was rubber. It wasn't designed to kill anyone. I wouldn't use my knife on them; that was for the villains.

Back then the hangman's noose was a serious threat. You got done for murder; you could get topped. It was sad when Harryboy went. It was a hazard of the profession and the threat of it didn't stop me working, not for a minute, but I was careful.'

Frank's robbery in Bond Street was called off at the last minute because the police appeared to have had a tip-off. Ever the opportunists, he and Harryboy used their iron bars to hold up a van selling cigarettes – a precious wartime commodity. Frank sold the proceeds of their robbery and was very pleased to be able to take Eva out shopping the next day to buy some new clothes 'without her having to nick them, for once'.

Just weeks later, the long arm of the law caught up with him once again, in a pub in Clapham, where he was arrested as an army deserter. This time, just as it seemed that army boots and a short back and sides were inevitable, he dived headfirst through a window at the barracks in Bradford to escape. He was caught again. Frank was taken to prison in Bradford and from there was sent for psychiatric assessment after smashing up his cell.

Without him even having to appear, he was court martialled and given two years' hard labour. The military doctor who conveyed this news to him then went on to say that owing to his mental and physical condition Frank was deemed not fit to serve; he was discharged and sent home. There were rumours that he had faked mental illness to get of military service but Frank and his sons insist that this was never the case.

His son, Patrick Fraser, said: 'He had fractured his skull

when he was run over as a kid and that had led to meningitis, so they didn't want him on medical grounds. It is likely that his behaviour in prisons, attacking the guards, didn't do him any favours in the eyes of the army either but he didn't fake anything to get out of serving. He didn't want to serve at all but he didn't pretend to be mentally ill to swing it.' To his mother's delight, she was even sent money by the army to look after him.

While his brother, Jim, was still busy fighting the enemy, Frank had got out of the army without even putting on a uniform. 'To be honest, I couldn't believe my luck,' he said. 'I never felt there was anything wrong with my mental health but I was quite happy to get a medical discharge.'

Although it seemed he had won the battle, Frank's war against the system was far from over.

CHAPTER 7

PRISONER 536648 FRASER

When the war ended, on 7 May 1945, Frank was among the few who found little to celebrate. 'I don't think I ever forgave Hitler for surrendering,' he said, with typical candour. 'The war years were a boom time for villainy and I never saw anything like that again.'

Gone was the blackout, the night-time cloak of darkness, which made a thief's life so much easier. However, rationing was to last into the mid-1950s, which meant the black market was booming and with everyone's spirits lifted, people wanted luxury goods even more. Trying to capitalise on this demand led Frank and five accomplices to set off on an ill-fated trip to a town hall in Essex, to try to steal clothing coupons that were stored there.

In an almost comical turn of events after the break-in, the police gave chase and the robbers' motor car ran out of petrol in the Rotherhithe tunnel. Three of the gang fled on foot and evaded capture, but Frank, 'Spindles' Jackson and Charlie Ransford were caught. Frank was granted bail at the Old Bailey and managed to renew his acquaintance with Billy Hill in Soho.

Billy, who had been released from prison in June 1945, made it clear he wanted Frank to work for him. Frank was flattered to be asked and also knew better than to turn down the invite because with the Sabinis gone, Billy's star was rising in gangland. Billy Hill and his mob were also highly organised. Their cars didn't run out of petrol because he had a lucrative petrol coupon racket and they didn't tend to break down either, because Billy had got himself into the second-hand car market and made sure that all his getaway vehicles were properly maintained.

This level of planning impressed Frank, who at this point was still essentially a freelance; he would do a bit of work here and there with his mates, including Franny 'the Spaniel' Daniels, Jimmy Robson, Dido Frett and Jimmy Essex. Frank also knew that Billy liked to pay his men fairly, even when they were in prison. In fact, he made a point of ensuring that their families were looked after. That was a very attractive prospect for Frank, who had a baby on the way. But before he could keep his promise to work for Billy, Frank was sentenced to twenty months hard labour for the clothing coupons robbery and sent to Shrewsbury jail, where his violence superseded anything he had done in prison so far.

For the first time in his prison career, Frank attacked the governor. 'I suppose the nearest thing you could liken it to, would be attacking the prime minister or the Queen. In the prison, the governor is like God. His word is final,' he said. Frank justified his attack by saying that he had been fitted up by a prison officer and put on a report, for a completely fictitious offence. The rules were very strict: prisoners had to slop out their chamber pots by 7 a.m. then return to their cells for breakfast of porridge – 'like cement' – before going off to the workshops to do menial tasks, such as sewing mailbags or making brushes. The wooden cell bed had to be up against the wall straight after breakfast and prisoners could not put it back down until 8 p.m.

Prisoners on hard labour, such as Frank, were not even given a mattress for the first fourteen nights – they had to sleep on bare boards. If prisoners didn't complete their jobs in time, they could be put on report. Sometimes they would be allowed to take mailbags back to the cell to work in the evening by gaslight. Even then, the mailbags had to be sewn eight stitches to the inch and if that was not done correctly, they would be put on report – which meant bread and water and a trip to the punishment block, where they might get beaten up as well.

When the prison officer complained that Frank wasn't sewing his mailbags correctly, it seemed to him that the system was out to get him. 'One thing about me is, if I am going to do something, I do it well. I am neat and tidy and I was neat and tidy with my sewing. If they thought I was going to be picked on by them, they had another thing coming,' he said. 'If they were going to fight dirty, I would fight dirtier.'

Frank saw himself as being at war with the whole of the prison service and it was a fight he continued for the majority of his time on the inside. 'It's hard for people who haven't been in prison to imagine what it's like and especially what it was like back then,' he said. 'They were pretty much the most evil, spiteful bastards you could imagine and so I saw it as my duty, like a soldier's duty, to have them whenever I got the chance. In fact, my brother Jim always said I would have made a good soldier because I was so single-minded. It was me or them, even though I knew I would get a belting for it.'

His son, Patrick, added: 'From the moment he first done a screw when he was in borstal that marked his card. The screws' view, every time he wound up in prison, was "Who is this cocky little Cockney cunt, then?" They were out to get him and so he was out to get them back. They would wind him up and he would just go for it.' When he was brought before the governor, Frank put in his complaint but it was dismissed, so he told the governor that he would attack the prison officer in question when he got the chance. The governor barely had time to respond – 'I think my officers can look after themselves, Fraser' – before Frank had launched himself across the table, grabbed a little wooden truncheon lying there and whacked the governor over the head with it.

He was beaten unconscious and woke up in the punishment cells, naked except for a body belt, which handcuffed his wrists to his sides. 'I knew I was for it, it was just a case of when,' said Frank. 'They could make life uncomfortable for me for a while and they did.' He was robbed of the most basic dignity; he had to urinate on the floor as requests to go to the lavatory were denied. 'If you wanted to do anything more than pee, you had to bottle it. If they knew you wanted to go, they wouldn't let you. I tried not to give them the satisfaction of having to ask. They kept me like that for a few days. Eventually, I was given a shirt but put back in the body-belt.'

Frank's mother and his brother Jim came to visit him and protested to one of the daily newspapers about the conditions in which Frank was being held, but there was little interest in campaigning on behalf of a criminal. When he was brought before the visiting magistrates, he was sentenced to be flogged and transferred to Liverpool Prison to receive his punishment.

The build-up to getting the cat was worse than the birch because the prisoner was not told when it would happen and knew he could wait up to a fortnight to receive it. The psychological torture of hearing the heavy footfall of prison officers' boots along the landings and then the keys rattling in the lock was hard to bear. When it did happen, Frank had prepared himself mentally to withstand the pain. He had already gone through days of hunger on bread and water as part of the punishment. 'It was better than the birch because you only had to strip from the waist up and it was a more manly punishment in that sense,' he said. 'The wooden tripod was the same but this time you had to put your head through a slit in the canvas and there was a sort of leather belt around your back to protect your kidneys. You were fastened up by your wrists so it stretched you.

'The cat had knots on the end of the rope and it cut into you. By God, it hurt. I had eighteen strokes of it. Afterwards, no one said anything but they just put ointment on your back, which was cut to pieces, and you were sent back to your cell to just get on with it, back on bread and water.'

Once out of the punishment cells, Frank found that the other inmates looked at him differently. 'It was a bit like an exclusive club, getting the cat. I'd had it and seemed OK. There was no trouble for me from anyone. It sort of gave you a status, more than the birch, which was for kids, really. Being flogged was a grown man's punishment.'

While he was in prison, he missed the birth of his first son, Frank Junior, in September 1945. Like Beverley, Frank was born in Nanny Margaret's bed in Tabard Street. Kate managed as best she could, with the support of Eva and Margaret, but she didn't find it easy with Frank being away. She would write letters often, coordinating with Eva, so that Frank always had some interesting news to read. Letters were a lifeline in prison and even though the news of home may have been mundane, it kept Frank going through the difficult times, which by his own admission, he had largely brought on himself through his refusal to toe the line.

Eva was by now pregnant with her second child, Shirley, who was born in 1946. At this point, Jimmy Brindle begged her to stop hoisting for the sake of the kids and married her. 'He couldn't bear her to be away in prison again,' said Beverley. 'He also made it clear that he wanted to provide for her, so that she didn't ever need to go out hoisting. She always felt a responsibility to contribute, to make her own money. Maybe it was because of the poverty, the way she had been brought up not having anything. She liked to be her own woman. But she loved Jimmy. He was a kind and caring man, a real provider. She agreed to stop working for the Forty Thieves, although she kept up her friendships and she and Gladys used to meet up once a year and go out hoisting, for old time's sake. And, of course, she did go out and treat herself to a new handbag now and again, and she always nicked Frank's shirts, so that he didn't have to buy them himself. She knew exactly what to get – he was a seventeen-and-a-half-inch collar back then.'

When Frank came home from Liverpool Prison in late summer 1946, he went straight back to work with his gang of shopbreakers and smash-and-grab artists. Frank loved little Frank Jr but, like many men of the time, he couldn't be described as a hands-on father. In fact, he couldn't wait to get out of the house to see the Chaps for a 'meet' to discuss business. It became a regular excuse not to be home in Mason Street. On one occasion, Kate, who was several months pregnant with their second child and suffering from a bad back, caught him out. She was lying on the floor to try to get rid of the pains and, to her astonishment, heard Frank's laughter coming up through the floorboards from the flat below, which was used by prostitutes. Instead of going out for the meet as promised, he had simply gone down to their flat and was enjoying a drink with them. Furious and in agony with her back, she crawled down the stairs and hammered on the door until it opened – and a very sheepish Frank emerged.

Shortly after this, Frank got another twelve months after being caught equipped for burglary, and he was only out of prison for just over a week before he was caught again. His next arrest was, by all accounts, one of the funniest in his criminal career. Frank was not a man who suffered from too much pride – in fact, he got a kick out of putting himself down when things had gone wrong and he'd got caught. He loved to tell the story about the bungled jewellery raid in Oxford Street, with his accomplice 'Dodger' Davies.

Dodger was so-called because he was brilliant as a get-away driver, able to wiggle down side streets and drive up pavements to evade the law. Frank said: 'We pulled up right outside the shop but there were a lot of people window shopping so we waited and I pretended to read my paper. There were a few cars going past, lots of background noise. I thought I heard him say – "Go on, Frank" – so I got out of the car, smashed the window and grabbed an armful of tom and got back in the car. He was sitting there looking really pale. I asked him what was wrong and told him to get going. He just looked at me and said: "I told you, the car won't start!"'

By now, the car was surrounded by people banging on the windows and trying to yank the doors open. Frank held on for dear life; for what seemed like an eternity. Eventually the pair decided to make a break for it but were easily apprehended. 'We were up in court the next day. We looked like complete idiots. It was hilarious. I got two years and he got twenty-one months. It was no less than we deserved, really.'

He missed his second son David's birth, in May 1947, and his name did not even appear on the birth certificate. Frank was sent to HMP Pentonville, where he was to meet the man who was to be his nemesis, Governor Lawton.

CHAPTER 8

LAWTON

Pentonville Prison in North London, known as 'The Ville', is where Frank almost met his end. For reasons he could never fully explain, Frank decided to slash his arms as a 'sort of protest', leading him to require nearly eighty stitches in one arm. 'Kids still do it today, cutting themselves, and it was no different back then,' he said. 'We tried to make trouble by drawing attention to ourselves. It seems silly now but I was young and rather foolish.'

While he was in the hospital cells, he received a visit from the governor, a man named Lawton, who he had known as a vindictive prison officer at Wandsworth. When Lawton came into his cell, Frank flung the contents of his chamber pot over him. 'To say I didn't like the man is an understatement. He was a sadistic screw who took great pleasure in making life hell for the prisoners. It was me against him, so, of course, I gave him a little present he wouldn't forget in a hurry.'

Frank's version of events is that in order to save face, Lawton declared that Frank must be mentally ill, and so ordered that he be put under medical observation. As a punishment, he was put into a straitjacket and prison officers stuffed wet blankets down the back of it, to make it heavy and even more uncomfortable. He was slung into a cell with mattresses on the floor and left there overnight. 'I was only twenty-three and fit, but the weight of those blankets pushed me down into the mattresses, so I was suffocating in the night,' said Frank. 'It became a battle for survival.

'I couldn't lie on my back for long because it was so uncomfortable. It was like having a great big hump on my back. So, I turned on to my stomach and I was lifting my head to breathe. It was exhausting. At that point, the spyhole in the cell door opened and I heard Lawton say that I was tiring and it wouldn't be long, I'd soon be gone.'

This thought gave Frank the strength to carry on. 'If I had died they would have said I just passed away by accident or I could have been found hanging in my cell, who knows? In those days, screws could get away with just about anything. The family would only be told afterwards and there would be no inquiry into it, just a cover-up,' he said. 'I thought about Kate and the babies. I thought about Eva and Jimmy and I wanted to live. They wanted me to die. The system wanted me gone because I was too much trouble, but I wasn't going to give them the satisfaction of going how they wanted me to.'

At 7 a.m., the cell door was unlocked and he was helped to his feet and allowed to drink some water. He had survived.

Almost immediately, he was transferred to the hospital wing at Wandsworth, which – because of bomb damage – consisted of nothing more than a few cells in one of the blocks, where he was kept under medical observation. His medical discharge from the army and earlier concerns about his mental state from Wormwood Scrubs, where he was supposed to have had ECT, had followed him. Now, with the attack on Governor Lawton, there were serious questions being raised about his mental health.

It was there that another prisoner gave Frank the idea that he should try to get himself certified insane, by making the regime at mental hospital sound like a holiday camp compared to prison. Frank realised he would be assigned to the mental hospital in his home county, so there was no question of being transferred miles away, and when the prisoner said that the patients were allowed to play football, that clinched it for him.

It is clear that he always felt a certain amount of shame about being sent to a mental hospital. He admitted: 'It wasn't really great for your kids to be teased about having their dad in the nuthouse and I was very aware of that. It wasn't so much what others thought of me, it was the effect on my family that I was bothered about.' To this end, he preferred to take control of the act of being certified, claiming that he had tricked the authorities. It is certain that he played the part of someone suffering psychosis very well on this occasion and the prison system was glad to be rid of him. But medical records from later on in his prison career show that he was diagnosed as a psychopath several times by qualified doctors.

'Even back then, proving I belonged in the nuthouse still wasn't going to be that easy,' he said. 'I had to put on a bit of a show, so I did.' He began by smashing up his cell and singing to the rats that were always running about, calling them his friends, which landed him in a strong cell in the punishment block in a straitjacket. He kept this charade up all weekend, even thinking up names for the rats and staring at the walls for hours on end. 'When the medical officer came in, I asked him if he had met my friend Winston Churchill,' said Frank. 'It seemed to work because they took the jacket off me and brought me my tea and just left me to it.' He had even defecated in his cell to keep up the appearance of lunacy. But, true to his nature, even that was left in a neat pile. 'I couldn't smear it up the walls like other people did,' he said. 'I was just too tidy. I did it just to make them think I was mad.'

Visiting magistrates and a prison doctor came and certified him the next day and a week later he was transferred to Cane Hill Hospital in Coulsdon, South London. Before he left, he received an unexpected visit from Eva and their brother, Jim. Frank immediately let her know he hadn't gone mad, with a wink. 'As soon as she saw it, I could see that the fear in her eyes was gone,' said Frank. 'She pretended to cry into her handkerchief, just as a show for the screws, but I could see she was smiling. She winked back at me. We both knew after that, I would be fine and I knew she would let Kate know she didn't have to worry.'

When he arrived at the hospital, Frank told the doctors he had been acting mad to escape the inhumane conditions in the jail. Whether they believed him or not remains unknown, but he certainly was allowed a lot of freedom in the hospital and even joined the football team – until he became their star goalscorer. 'I realised when we beat the team from another hospital that if I was too good at it, they might never let me go, so I pretended to have hurt my leg to get out of it.'

On the outside, Kate was struggling financially, with no regular income and the money that Frank had given her before he was jailed running out. Eva came up with a rescue plan – she got her mother to look after all of the kids, while she and Kate went out to work in a textile factory. The factory foreman was wily enough to check everyone's handbags on leaving at the end of the day, just to be sure that no one had made off with anything, particularly because they were handling expensive silks from time to time. But he hadn't reckoned on the ingenuity of Eva and her Forty Thieves' determination to fiddle. Frank's son, David Fraser, said: 'Most days Eva managed to shove a whole bolt of material into her bag or even down her drawers – she still had her shoplifting ones. She'd nip into the loos with Kate, tell her to take off her dress and wrap the material around and around her. Kate would waddle out of the factory looking like Tutankhamen's sister, desperately praying the material wasn't going to slip down. They kept that up for quite a few months – sometimes it was silk, sometimes just cotton. It provided the family with much-needed income while Frank was away. It was amazing how everyone in the neighbourhood seemed to have curtains cut from the same material for a while.'

While Frank was inside, his grandmother, Nanny Day, who had delivered him safely into the world as a baby, died at home. Beverley remembered her body being laid out in an open coffin at Margaret's flat in Tabard Street: 'It was quite something getting the coffin up three flights of stairs,' she said. 'I can remember being fascinated by it. Everyone was crying but I was only a little kid and I didn't understand. I went into the bedroom while the grown-ups were all talking and I peeked up over the edge of the coffin and saw her body. She had pennies on her eyes. I was trying to nick them before someone caught me. I didn't know any better really. I just wanted to see whether her eyes were open underneath.'

Kate and her two boys escaped from the sweltering heat and dirt of London that summer by going hop-picking down in Kent. It was a big tradition among families from London to decamp en masse – Kate's own family, the Woods of Holborn, had been hop-picking in the same part of Kent since Victorian times. Whole streets would pack up and go together, staying in rudimentary wooden huts on the farmer's land in return for picking the hops, while the kids had a bit of a holiday, running about the fields and woods.

Kate's sisters Maureen and Maggie came with her and the boys, as well as Eva and her two kids and all their friends from around the Elephant and Castle. David recalled those yearly trips from his childhood: 'We would all pile on to the train and go down to Beltring in Kent, there'd be all the adults and the kids crammed into the carriages. When the ticket inspector came along, the shout would go up, "Quick! Hide!" and dozens of kids would be shoved under the seats, hidden under coats and even chucked up into the luggage racks. There was no way we could afford to pay fares for all our family. When we got to the other end, the grown-ups would gather all the belongings and the kids would scarper through the station and down the lane before anyone could catch them and make them pay.'

The Frasers, Brindles, Woods and Walls all stayed at Bell Farm in Beltring where they spent six weeks hop-picking. When David was only a toddler he used to have to be tied to the hop-picking bucket to stop him biting the other children. 'I was a bit naughty,' he said. 'I just used to take a chunk out of some of the other kids and so my mum thought it was safer to keep me with her.'

Kate's sister Maggie remembers Kate always being left with the washing-up: 'There was loads of it but she never complained. We'd all eat outside at these big trestle tables, whole families sitting together, the kids running about. We loved it. It was a very healthy way of life for people who came from the city. The farmer would let us have eggs and fruit and we'd buy bread in the local bakery. It was a happy time for everyone.'

Women would bring a few home comforts and some even brought curtains to put up in the huts – with the material courtesy of Eva and Kate's textile factory fiddle, of course. David said: 'Hop-picking really did bring people closer. The whole community would go – people you knew from round the corner would be out in the country with you, sharing the fresh air and the good times. It seems unimaginable to do such a thing today, but back then it was a way of life, and my family had been doing it for generations, going back to the 1840s on my mum's side.'

When it was time for Frank to come out of Cane Hill Hospital in 1949, his faithful sister Eva and her husband Jimmy went to pick him up. 'I will always remember Eva standing there at the gate, smiling. After all I had been through in that sentence it was just marvellous. Throughout my life she would always be there when I came out. She never let me down,' said Frank. 'If I could rely on one person in my life, it would always be my sister.'

CHAPTER 9

THE BOSS OF SOHO

In the late 1940s, Soho was a seething mass of seedy spielers, bars, nightclubs and theatres where people could get sex, drink and fun – but at a price. For many, the collective sigh of relief that the war was over started as a night out swilling beer and spirits at exorbitant cost in private drinking dens and ended as vomit splattered in the greasy gutter, with a week's wages spent.

The White family had moved into Soho after the Sabinis lost control, and not everyone in gangland was happy about it. Topping the list of disgruntled 'faces' was Jack Spot, a former Sabini henchman who helped them control pitches at racecourses around the south-east. Jack, whose real name was Comer, was born in Whitechapel in 1912, the son of Polish immigrants. He was known as 'Spot' because, as he liked to say, he was always in the right spot when trouble occurred.

Spot was no stranger to using a razor to make his point and his trademark was to slash his victims on the buttocks with his 'chiv', so that whenever they sat down, they split their stitches. During the war he had played his cards carefully, assiduously building up protection rackets in the East End, while keeping an interest in the racecourses and, tentatively, in Soho. He was no friend of the Whites and disliked their attempts to take over what he saw as his rightful inheritance – post-war clubland. But he was clever enough to know that he could not oust the Whites on his own and was also wary of the powerbase Billy Hill was building. Spot did not intend to spend a single day of his life behind bars and he was clever enough to make sure that his hands were always clean. He knew the importance of having the right people working for him, to secure his position.

Spot befriended Billy and the pair set about beating the living daylights out of the Whites to drum them out of Soho for good. Frank was away in prison at the time, or he certainly would have been at the forefront of the battle. In his memoirs, Billy claimed that Jack Spot was challenged by the Whites and a turf war erupted, with a few reprisals, including an attack on one of Billy Hill's gang. Billy said that Spot asked him for help and he called in his 'army' – gangs from south of the river including the Elephant Boys and some from Brixton, plus hoodlums from Notting Hill, Paddington and Kilburn. When the Whites heard what was going on they tooled up and went up to Camden to find Billy, who was already in the West End looking for them. In Billy's version, he burst into the Whites' flat in Islington and tortured their leader by holding his face close to the fire until he agreed that Billy was now the King of Soho. Closer to the truth is that Jack Spot was the man in charge at this time and he coordinated all his troops – which then included Billy Hill's muscle – to thrash the Whites in a series of bar-room brawls, ending up in a fight in a nightclub that left one man with a life-threatening slash wound across his throat.

Much to Spot's concern, Billy was also already forming alliances with a new generation of Italians, the Dimeo family, known as the Dimes. Albert Dimes was a second-generation Italian immigrant born in Scotland who had served in the RAF during the Second World War before he deserted. Dimes was seen as the natural heir to the Sabinis. His family owned shops around Soho and he was involved in protection rackets and pitches at the racecourses. He was not known as a thief, but was a big presence on the streets who could be called on for muscle when required, although he preferred diplomacy to get his way.

Frank had looked up to him when he was a teenager pedalling around Soho on his errand bike and was delighted to find himself taken under Albert's wing after he came out of jail. Detractors said Dimes was a loudmouth but Frank was having none of it. 'He was a big bloke, standing well over six-foot two-inches tall, good-looking and kind-hearted with it. When I come out of the nick I was up for anything and he and Billy sort of took me under their wing a bit. I learned a lot from Albert about dealing with people day-to-day in business, running clubs, that sort of thing. Until then, I had been all about the smash and grab and I would still say I was a good thief but there was more to it. Albert taught me about people.' Albert became firm friends with Frank's mother, Lady Margaret, and was a regular fixture at parties at her flat in Tabard Street.

For the Soho Chaps, days were largely spent drinking, hanging around in spielers, scouting out post offices and banks to be robbed or waiting for work orders to come in from Billy. One club, The Log Cabin in Wardour Street, acted as an unofficial labour exchange for villains. Another, The Cabinet Club, was run by Billy Hill's wife, Aggie, a fiery Glaswegian, who liked nothing better than to ask Frank to buy her a drink, ring it through the till and not take a drop. 'She'd stare you out, waiting to see if you would say anything,' said Frank. 'I never dared.'

Aggie also ran the Modernaires Club in Greek Court, off Old Compton Street, which was a favourite haunt for villains and showbiz people alike. Darbo Hicks used to run the cloakroom there. Billy had Captain Mark Hewitson, the MP for Hull, on his books. Hewitson enjoyed a pension from the club, free drinks and free women when he felt like it and in return he put his name down for the club's management to ensure that there were no problems getting a licence. The head of the Flying Squad, Ernie Millen, was a regular visitor to Billy's clubs and even his flat and it is beyond doubt that Billy's contacts in Scotland Yard and in parliament were invaluable to his crime empire.

Billy had all but separated from Aggie but she still worked for him and they enjoyed a business relationship, while he wined, dined and plotted crime with his seductive moll, Gypsy Riley. Raven-haired Gypsy had a temper worse than Aggie's. Growing up in Essex, she had learned how to fight from Arthur Skurry, the King of the Gypsies, who was a close friend of her family.

Once provoked, Gyp was quick to start laying into anyone who crossed her. She spoke the didicoi dialect – a mixture of Romany and cockney – which made her something of a target for teasing, although anyone who did so lived to regret it. Legend has it that she became Billy Hill's lover after one such incident, which led to them both beating up her tormentors in a Soho street battle. Afterwards, they were so consumed with mutual desire that they fell into bed together.

Several years later, Gyp found herself in court for beating a woman unconscious with a chair leg and glassing her husband in the face, taking out an eye, after the pair made derogatory remarks about her appearance. It looked certain that Gyp would go to prison but the victim changed his story after a visit from Billy Hill and told the prosecution he was now unable to identify Gyp. The case against her was thrown out.

Billy had his hands full keeping Gypsy out of trouble and the two women in his life apart. Although Gypsy knew she had the lion's share of Billy's attention, her need for him in those early days was all-consuming and Billy didn't like being tied down. His mob knew better than to question his complicated domestic situation, especially when he upped the ante between his women by having numerous dalliances with showgirls who took his fancy. As Billy used to say, it was all part and parcel of being a crime lord.

Frank was a flirt – particularly with hoisters, who he felt were the 'best, fun girls' – but was still faithful to Kate. David Fraser said: 'It was part of the image. All thieves like to have a bird on their arm and my dad was no different.' His only real love affair at this time was with his work and the money it brought in, which he spent at an alarming rate. He reckoned that he spent around £30 or more a day just on buying rounds of drinks, eating out and showing his face around town.

Billy put him on a weekly retainer of about £50 a week – a small fortune back then. But for this, he was expected to do his bidding and that included some disposing of the corpses of people who had crossed his boss. In his later years, Frank used to like to tease journalists that he had murdered up to forty people. Privately, he admitted this was nonsense; although he would not be drawn on the exact figure, he signalled that it was probably no more than a handful of lowlifes, who were neither mourned nor missed.

Billy Hill had a crematorium worker in his pay and Frank was called on to drive a corpse or two to be incinerated. 'It was a case of good riddance to bad rubbish,' he said. 'They were people from our world who had it coming. Did I regret it? Not for a minute. I'm not saying whether I did or I didn't do things but what I will say is that when there were bodies to dispose of, ash don't tell tales. I looked on doing what Billy asked me to do as work, nothing more, nothing less. I was still primarily a thief.'

Despite being in the big league in Soho, Frank couldn't resist stealing something just to get one over on someone who had annoyed him. The tallyman, who provided household goods 'on tick' – and charged interest – was still a way of life for many families, including the Brindles and the Frasers. Frank saw himself as something of a Robin Hood character and didn't particularly like their local tallyman, who was 'a nasty sod', so when he popped around to Eva's house one day and found the tallyman's van parked outside it was an opportunity not to be missed. 'I knocked on the door and Eva told me she was in there having a cup of tea with him. He was bragging about how his van couldn't be broken into now, because he'd had new locks fitted. I told her to keep him talking,' said Frank. 'He was right. It couldn't be broken into, so we had to tow it away. Eva said the look on his face when he opened the front door was priceless.

'He went down the local police station to report the theft and when he said whose house he had been in at the time, having a nice cup of tea, the desk sergeant practically fell off his chair laughing.'

One day, while he was out and about in the West End, Frank spotted his old enemy, Governor Lawton from Wandsworth Prison, on his way to attend a conference about the abolition of capital punishment. 'That put an idea into my head,' said Frank. 'I wanted to have him and so I did. Back then, the governor always had a house next door to the prison, so I just observed him for a few evenings and saw that he always took his dog out for a walk about 8 p.m. One night I put a stocking mask over my head and jumped on him, knocked him about and then strung him and his dog up to a tree. They didn't die – the branch bent and I hadn't done a great job of it, but I made my point. He must have known it was me but there was nothing in the papers about it the next day. I expect it was all hushed up. It wasn't the sort of thing the powers that be wanted reporting. I felt better for doing it. I was sorry about hurting the dog though.' He later claimed that this was the first incidence of a crook pulling a stocking over his head as a mask to distort his features.

Frank being out all hours was a way of life Kate accepted – she knew what she had got herself into with Frank and he was bringing home money and treating her to nice furs and handbags again, but she did get lonely. Their home in Mason Street was a grim tenement block, built in 1801, which was a complete firetrap, with wooden staircases leading up three floors. Each floor was home to two families and each flat had a tiny living room, one bedroom and a small kitchen – but no bathroom. The only water available was cold and came from a single tap in the kitchen sink. The lavatory on the landing was shared with another family and if anyone wanted a wash, it was either a cursory wipe over the sink or, once a week at most, out with the tin bath – just as their great-grandparents had done in the previous century. The family still frequented the public baths down at Manor Place, just as Frank had done as a boy.

David remembered: 'My mum and dad slept on a fold-out bed in the living room and us kids shared the one bedroom. There wasn't much privacy – not that we noticed or cared.' The rudimentary accommodation was completely at odds with the spick and span, suited and booted Frankie Fraser who went out up in Soho. Kate worked her fingers to the bone to keep everything clean and pressed.

When she found herself pregnant with baby number three, Frank did the decent thing and decided to make an honest woman of her, taking her up the aisle, before the long arm of the law could put him away again. On the marriage certificate he described himself as a 'general dealer' – he omitted to add that his dealing was in stolen goods. But even marrying Kate couldn't disguise the cracks that were beginning to appear in their relationship. 'There were arguments a few times, I can remember,' said David. 'It was just the usual stuff about him being out and her needing him to do stuff with us kids. We didn't question why he was never around much. We just thought our life was normal. We never thought about what Daddy was doing – he was just going out to work.'

Concealing weapons in their tenement in Mason Street was just part of life for Frank, who had by now started the Friday Gang – a wages scam which involved him and his team holding up clerks as they made their way to offices with the weekly pay. Frank and his team would scope out a get-away route and then take turns to follow the clerks to the bank to see how much money they were taking back to each company they were going to target. 'It was a case of scoping out the timings and lying in wait,' explained Frank. 'I'd carry a shooter but never planned to use it. It was more a case of giving them a clump around the head and shocking them into letting go of a bag of money. Sometimes it worked, sometimes it didn't. I had one fellow who simply would not let go of the bag. In the end I had to let him keep it because the cozzers were coming. I wasn't up for killing anyone and having a stocking on your face made it harder for them to ID you. I was always getting put on identity parades around this time so I thought it was a genius idea.'

Five-year-old David Fraser had already got a cowboy gun from his grandad James Fraser, who still worked down at the cricket bat factory. 'It was a proper one, all the way from America, I have no idea how he got it but it was bloody brilliant. It was miles better than anything else the other kids had. I felt like I was a real cowboy,' said David. 'Me and my older brother Frank were playing in the bedroom and one of us looked on top of the wardrobe and there was this shotgun lying there.

'It was a sawn-off shotgun but to us it just looked like fun. We pulled it down and had a closer look at it. We loved all the cowboys and Indians films, so this was like a dream come true. We didn't stop to think about why it was there. We found the cartridges for it in the cupboard. It was big and heavy but somehow I held it while Frank pulled the trigger and a bullet shot out and blew the lock off the bedroom door. We were thrown backwards against the window. If it had been open, the force of that would have sent us flying through it.

'I can still hear the sound of that bullet and my mother's screams as she came running in, followed by my dad, who grabbed the gun and then grabbed us. My mother was hysterical. They were too shaken to be really angry with us but my dad told us never, ever to touch guns if we saw them in the house.'

It didn't occur to the boys to ask why their father had a sawn-off shotgun on top of the wardrobe. They were too young to realise that the ricochet of gunfire was an omen of things to come in the Fraser household as the 1950s unfolded.

CHAPTER 10

GET CARTER!

Feuds are a feature of gangland life but Frank Fraser managed to sidestep many with a mixture of personal charm, backed up by the fact that he was not a man even hardened gangsters wanted to cross. 'I was friends with a lot of people from so-called rival gangs, right from being a youngster,' he explained. 'I was in South London but I was across the water with the Italians, because of the Catholic thing. I was in Soho, but I also used to drink in Clerkenwell.

'I made it clear I was not out for trouble, unless it came to find me. People knew not to cross me. There was always a sense that people wanted to have me inside their tent, pissing out, rather than outside the tent, pissing in,' he said.

But when another South London crime family, the Carters, attacked Bobby and Whippo Brindle – both brothers of Eva's husband, Jimmy – Frank knew he had to act. It was a feud that was to bring trouble to his front door in Mason Street.

The background to the bust-up between the Brindles and the Carters went back to the previous decade, during the Second World War. The Carters had started out running protection rackets in south-east London and, alongside the

Brindles, had been members of the Elephant Boys, before they graduated to operating pitches at the races. But the two families had fallen out and Jimmy Brindle's older brother, Whippo, had smacked Buey, the eldest Carter, around the head with a starting handle and went to jail for it. After that, it was open season between the Brindles and the Carters, with numerous reprisals.

Frank had been friendly with Johnny Carter, but after Bobby Brindle was sliced, Frank stepped in, warning Johnny Carter off hurting Jimmy. Despite Frank thinking that they were still friends, a row developed in a bar during which Johnny jumped on Frank and stabbed him in the face. 'That was it; it was war,' said Frank.

To complicate matters further, Johnny and Harry Carter had formed an allegiance with Jack Spot, while Frank was clearly Billy's man. Relations between Billy Hill and Jack Spot were outwardly cordial but Billy was vying for suprem-acy. Spot put up the money for jobs and took a huge cut, but didn't get his hands dirty. He'd never been a thief, having made his way up on the racecourses. Frank and other thieves, encouraged by Billy, looked down on this, seeing him as only one step up from being a ponce. It was inevitable that the feuding among the lower ranks of the organization would come to the attention of the bosses – and the police – and it did.

Billy Hill told Frank to keep the fighting out of Soho, or the law would come down on Billy's club ventures like a ton of bricks. Frank agreed that he would do his best not to spill blood in the West End and keep the fight south of the river, but he would not be swayed from his quest for revenge.

On Christmas Eve 1951, as Kate was preparing everything at home in the hope of having the perfect family Christmas, Frank and Albert Dimes caught up with two of the older Carter brothers – Buey and Harry – leaving a pub in the Old Kent Road. Buey, who was at least ten years older than Frank, was slashed to pieces and ended up in hospital, but his brother Harry got away. Frank hung around the hospital hoping that Johnny Carter would pay a visit but it didn't happen, so he returned home to Mason Street to celebrate the big day with Kate and the boys.

They certainly had a houseful. His youngest son, Patrick, had been born in January that year. It was the only one of his children's births for which Frank was at home, although, as was the way at the time, he kept out of it, pacing up and down the communal hallway while a prostitute from downstairs helped Kate through the labour. Patrick said: 'It was all going well until my head got stuck and the brass had to call an ambulance. My mum had to be rushed off to the hospital to get the doctors to help deliver me.'

On Christmas Day 1951, Patrick was just learning to walk and David, five, and Frank, six, were two excitable, cheeky little boys who woke up at the crack of dawn to see what Santa had left under the tree for them. Frank had made sure his boys had plenty of presents to open. Later on Kate pulled out all the stops and laid on a full turkey roast with all the trimmings. After lunch and a few glasses of sherry, Frank went for a lie-down, as he was planning to meet up with the Chaps later that evening to plan their next move on the Carters. Patrick was trying to walk and David was playing happily with his best Christmas present, a toy train, on the communal stairs, when a shout went up that Johnny Carter had arrived. Frank swiftly roused himself from his slumber. He sprang out of bed, grabbed the loaded shotgun he had stashed underneath it, and ran onto the landing. David Fraser said: 'I was sitting there playing with my toys when Carter came up the stairs, pointing a pistol at my dad, who was standing at the top, with a shotgun.

'I was caught right in the middle of it. It played out in slow motion. My dad pulled the trigger; it clicked and didn't go off. Carter ran up the stairs, past me, still pointing his loaded pistol. My dad tried to fire again and again and still it didn't go off. After we had played with it, his mate had fixed it so it couldn't be tampered with and for some reason he couldn't get the safety catch off. Carter was at the front door now and so my dad turned his gun around and smashed him in the face with the butt.'

Carter reeled backwards down the stairs, almost falling on top of David, who was frozen in terror, as the fight went on. Carter made off, just as an Irish neighbour grabbed Frank's gun and got it working. 'The Irish guy also had a knife and he came halfway down the stairs and grabbed me, bringing me into his flat, for safety,' said David. 'Frank ran out after Carter, who had a getaway driver, and shot at the car as it screeched around the corner.'

It certainly was a Christmas Day to remember.

The police came and arrested Frank for firearms offences but he was released without charge because none of the neighbours would say anything. 'In fact, the whole incident turned our street against the Carters,' said David. 'A day later, a shout went up that they were back again. A car pulled up outside our tenement building and the whole street fell silent. All these guns appeared from the windows, pointing at it. A lot of people had weapons after the war and the whole thing with Carter coming in and us kids being involved made a lot of people very angry.

'I don't remember who fired the first shot but the car was peppered with bullets and there was smoke everywhere. Very slowly, the door opened and a prostitute staggered out, waving a white handkerchief. It wasn't Carter after all but just one of the women on the game who lived downstairs.'

Growing up with prostitutes as neighbours was seen as an opportunity for David and the other kids in his block to get up to no good. The building had a shared attic, which you could crawl along inside, from one flat to another. David, his older brother Frank and few accomplices liked to crawl on their hands and knees to go and muck about with various bits of old junk stored up there. This was great fun for their little gang until David slipped and started to fall through the lath and plaster ceiling into the flat below. 'I can still remember the look of shock on the prostitute's face as I appeared,' he said. 'The punter was on top of her and he jumped off and pulled his trousers on, sharpish. They were all covered in plaster from the ceiling. My brother Frank had hold of me by an arm and a leg and I was just sort of hanging there. She screamed at first and then started laughing. She was naked and we were all peering through the hole in the ceiling having a good look.'

Frank Jr and David were real bomb-site kids, playing in the rubble and the ruins left by the Second World War. David said: 'We'd use it as a backdrop for our own war games. I can remember my dad laughing as we all came charging down the road waving wooden swords, wrapped in lino we'd nicked from the ruins. We were using it as armour to have a war. We were the Mason Street Gang and we used to fight the kids from the street around the corner.'

It was on one of these escapades that David fell onto a piece of metal and slashed his chin open, leaving a deep scar, which is still visible. 'I don't suppose it has done me any harm over the years to have it,' he said. 'It looks like I might have got it in a fight, but it was just mucking around on a bomb site in south London.'

The bombed-out buildings of the Blitz also offered an opportunity to earn money, and they would nick the lead from the roofs to sell to local scrap merchants. David said: 'There wasn't a lot left to nick but we were always scouting for it. Once my brother Frank and his mates tied a rope around my waist and lowered me down from one roof onto another to see what I could get.'

Patrick added: 'Another time, when we were older and my brother Frank was about fourteen, we were still scavenging about the bomb sites and a fella came and told us to hop it because he was hoping to take whatever lead he could find. Frank went over to him and this bloke squared up to him. They traded insults and were about to fight. This fella said he would take his jacket off first and he was just shrugging it off his shoulders when Frank punched him twice – bang, bang – right in the face. The bloke just keeled over. I remember thinking it was such a smart move. Reggie Kray used to do a similar thing with a cigarette. He would offer a cigarette and then as they were lighting it, he'd lay them out with a punch.'

Just three days after the shoot-out at Mason Street, Frank was arrested for stealing cigarettes from a warehouse in Bedford. At his trial, Eva did her best to nobble the jury, bringing David, Frank Jr and Patrick along to sit in a cafe where the jurors were having lunch. The kids were primed to start crying as the jurors looked on. Eva told the children: 'Don't worry, your dad is innocent and he will soon be home.' The trick didn't work and Frank got three years and was sent to Pentonville, where he got into trouble for punching a prison officer. He was transferred to Wandsworth, where he came face-to-face once more with his nemesis, Governor Lawton.

When the governor saw Frank he just eyeballed him and said: 'Back.'

This sentence was the first in which David realised his father had gone away and could not just come home. 'One minute he was there and then he was gone and the grown-ups would be saying this word "prison",' he said. 'It was said almost in a whisper, they tried not to let us hear, but we understood he had gone away somewhere and it was a bad thing.'

Frank knew he was going to be in for a rough ride, but that didn't deter him from trying to settle old scores when Johnny Carter began a two-year sentence in Wandsworth for assault. The first chance he got, Frank hid a lump of lead from the prison workshop and bashed Carter around the head with it. He was sent to Dartmoor for a time and Kate was driven to visit him in one of Billy Hill's cars, with David and his older brother Frank in the back.

On the way to the Moor, there was a terrible accident when the car swerved off the road. Kate hit her head on the dashboard. 'I don't remember too much, just crying and then a farmer coming with a big shire horse to pull us out of the ditch,' said David. 'My mum hit her head quite hard and we didn't know it at the time, but she had done some serious damage to her eyes.'

David still recalls the visit to Dartmoor Prison in vivid detail. 'That was when I really realised what prison was all about,' he said. 'We went in to the visiting room and there was this big table, with wood going across it, dividing it, to keep us and my dad apart. There were two screws behind us on one side of the table and two behind him, on the other side. It seemed as if he was miles away and as my dad and mum were talking, I reached over and tried to touch him.

'Well, the screw didn't like that. He said: "No touching!" My brother Frank and me were playing and messing about but we wanted to hug our dad and we couldn't. That was very hard for young kids to understand.'

Frank was transferred to Durham but not before a kindly prison officer had warned him that the wardens at Durham would seek to break him, as he was seen as such a trouble-maker within the prison system. From the moment he arrived, he was beaten up by the staff and left with head wounds so severe he required stitches. While a young medical officer tried to stitch him up, a prison officer continued to slap him around the head with a wet towel, reopening the wound.

He spent the majority of his sentence there down the punishment block on bread and water and when he came out, set about evening the score, assaulting every prison officer who had attacked him. In the end, the prison doctor had him certified insane, telling him it was for his own good. Frank was horrified because he knew that he would be going to Broadmoor. 'I told him I wasn't mad and he agreed I wasn't but he said it was the only way I would ever get out of prison the way I was behaving. I can't say I agreed with him. The night before I went, a screw opened the little hatch to my cell and told me that if I didn't behave in there, I wouldn't get out alive.'

He had already heard from other prisoners about the regime at Broadmoor, which involved new arrivals being stripped, frogmarched naked across a courtyard while all the inmates jeered at them, before being put into a punishment cell with a shirt made of canvas so stiff it could stand up on its own.

The authorities at Broadmoor had two other surprises in store for its new arrivals, both of which went into their food: one was known as 'the shitter', because it induced symptoms similar to dysentery, and the other was called 'the sleeper', because it made the inmate docile. 'If they really disliked you, you got the shitter *and* the sleeper. I only got the sleeper and the next morning the governor came around and told me that I had to behave myself because they could do things to me here that they couldn't in prison. I understood him perfectly. If I didn't behave, I probably wouldn't see my family again. I did behave myself and I never had any trouble. They knew I wasn't mad; I had just got too much for the prison system to cope with.

'Those were not my best years. I can't say I wanted to be in the nuthouse. I was thinking about my family and the effect on the kids of having a dad banged up in there, rather than myself but this is what it had come to. Once you are in Broadmoor, you just have to keep your head down and get on with it and pray they let you out. I wasn't out to make friends in there, or enemies for that matter.'

He added: 'Mind you, I did have some fun. There was a fella who thought he was a light bulb. Well, it was too good to miss, I used to sneak up and whisper in his ear that I had pulled his plug out, just to upset him. It was one of the few laughs I got in there.' The other inmates Frank got to know were hulking great blokes who had been done for murder but declared insane. He watched them crying as they fought over each other's cigarettes. 'It was a pathetic sight to see men reduced to that,' he said. 'I made damn sure I behaved myself so that I could get the hell out.'

While he was in jail, wodges of cash used to arrive every week at Mason Street for Kate and the kids, courtesy of Billy Hill, who kept up his tradition of looking after his men's families when they were inside. David said: 'We lived in a tenement but we were the only ones to have a television and we had a big radio set as well. We didn't tell anyone at school about my dad being in prison. It came as a shock years later to find out that their dads were in the nick as well.'

While Frank was inside, the police burst into the flat one day looking for him. The incident still shocks, decades later, as David recalled seeing his mother pistol-whipped by an officer of the law, as she tried to explain that Frank wasn't there. 'He smacked her around the face with the gun several times,' said David. 'She was trying to shield us from it but we were all screaming and crying. If we didn't hate the police before, we did after that.'

Billy and Albert Dimes also passed money to Eva when required. Sometimes she would organise payments to people from Frank, for services rendered on his behalf while he was inside. At other times, Albert and Billy would make sure that Frank's share of any business interests they had – usually protection rackets – was handed on to Eva for safekeeping, To evade the police, she used to send her children, Shirley and Beverley, over to Soho in a taxi to collect it. 'I used to like going because Albert would buy us an ice cream or a bottle of pop,' said Beverley. 'I can remember sitting in the back of the cab and peeking into the box and seeing piles of cash, so much of it.'

Kate was also given a helping hand by her sisters who worked in a grocery shop in The Cut in Waterloo, in return for helping them to steal goods from the store. David said: 'Whenever the owner's back was turned, my aunt would have a box of stuff she'd nicked under the counter and we would carry it out for her. She'd let us have some of it, but she had a nice little earner going flogging things to people she knew. The whole family was at it in one way or another in those days. It was just a way of life.'

She also had the support of her neighbours: 'Black' Albert – who was Indian – and his wife Betty, who was white but known as 'Black' Betty. Their daughter, Jean, was an un-official mother's help to Kate. She, in turn, stuck up for Jean whenever she encountered racism. David said: 'The signs in the pubs in those days used to read "No Gypsies/No Irish". We were all Irish anyway, so it was ridiculous.

'Anyway, one day my mother Kate and Jean from downstairs went to the beer garden of our local pub on the corner, The Bell, to find us kids and have a drink. Jean went to the bar and the landlord points to the sign saying "No Gypsies" and tells her she can't come in. We were all in there, larking about. Jean was still only a young girl then. My mum stood up and said, "If she's a gypsy, I'm a gypsy" and slammed her drink down and walked out. At that point, the rest of the people in the beer garden stood up and said, "We're all gypsies, then" and followed her. Someone ran into the pub and told the drinkers inside, and they all slammed their pints down and walked out. The owner was speechless for a minute and then he called everyone back, including Jean. He knew he couldn't get away with it. We were all as poor as each other. Racism didn't come into it.'

The family was broken up for several months when Kate suffered detached retinas in both her eyes and nearly went blind as a result of the car crash on Dartmoor. She was sent to Moorfields Eye Hospital on City Road in London, where surgeons performed pioneering surgery to save her sight. She was the first person in the country to undergo a new method of treating detached retinas, which became standard procedure after that. David was sent to live with his maternal grandmother, Rose Wall, who was 'a mean old cow' to him: 'You could leave your eyeballs on the table and she would have pawned them by the time you came back,' he said. He couldn't wait for his mother to return.

Frank Jr went to his aunty Kathleen's, Patrick went to Eva and Jim's for a while before he lodged with his godparents, who bought him a violin and taught him how to play it. 'We started a sort of skiffle band after that,' said Patrick. 'It was basically begging but we all looked quite cute so it worked. We'd go up the West End with our gear. We'd have my brother Frank on the guitar and David bashing on the tea chest and I would sing and dance about and collect the money.

'We couldn't sing and we couldn't play either but Tommy Steele's family lived on the corner next to our block and we knew them all, so it must have inspired us. Well, that and the thought of making a few quid. If we did well, we'd get a taxi back home.'

As Frank languished in Broadmoor, Billy and his girlfriend Gypsy went on holiday to the South of France with Jack Spot and his new wife, Irish girl Rita Molloy. The trip had been Spot's idea – he was keen to live up to the image of a wealthy gangster – but it served only to underline the cracks in his relationship with Billy. The two women didn't get on either, which made the trip something of a disaster. While Gyp posed in her bathing suit and looked like a film star, Rita refused to be parted from her long black trousers and her headscarf, even in the heat of a Riviera afternoon, giving her the appearance of an extra from *On the Buses*. Gyp undulated along the Promenade des Anglais and flirted expertly at the bar in the Hotel Martinez. Rita simply longed to put her feet up and have a nice English cup of tea, which was impossible to find in the South of France.

To make matters worse, Gypsy made it clear that she felt that Billy was the senior partner in the crime relationship with Spot, whispering in Billy's ear that he did not need Spot at all. She warned her man that he was foolish in drink, noting that Jack Spot barely touched a drop, which made Billy cut down his alcohol consumption to keep his wits about him.

Billy capitalised on his stay, befriending the Corsican mafia, which had moved into casinos along the Riveria. It fired an interest in high-stakes gambling, where the cards were marked, which Billy was to bring back to London with him, targeting the aristocracy.

On his return home, Billy decided to plan a major robbery, without telling Jack Spot. Until the Great Train Robbery in 1963, the Eastcastle Street job was known as the most successful raid in Britain, and Billy Hill got clean away with it. He had been keen to rob the Royal Mail for several years, knowing that their vans were poorly guarded, but rather than risk getting caught stealing bags full of money in the street, he decided to steal the entire van. Post Office contacts tipped him the wink about cash from South Wales and the West Country coming in to Paddington Station each day and being driven across London to the sorting office. Police contacts told him that roadworks in Oxford Street would last for seven weeks during early summer 1952, meaning traffic was being diverted down Eastcastle Street, which had two mews where cars could be hidden in preparation for the ambush.

Billy played his cards close to his chest and only briefed his gang the night before. The team included Gyp as a getaway driver. A postman had been paid off by Billy to disable the alarm on the van the day before the robbery.

Just after 4 a.m. one morning in May, as the van turned into Eastcastle Street, the driver found his way blocked by a black car. Another car boxed him in from behind and before he knew what was happening, the doors to the van were yanked open and he was dragged into the road. His passenger was also pulled out of the van and coshed while the gang got busy with the keys, to get to the guard, who was also assaulted and left in the road. A police constable came running just as the van sped off towards Goodge Street and on up to Camden, where Billy Hill was waiting to inspect his haul.

They took eighteen mailbags and loaded them on to a fruit lorry, leaving a further thirteen in the van. The lorry was taken to Spitalfields before heading to a farm in Essex where the money was divided up. Each man who took part got a £15,000 share. The entire haul was worth over £230,000 – more than £6 million in today's terms. Billy and Gyp returned to London and booked a suite at the Dorchester Hotel, where they set about laundering their money – quite literally, some of the notes were filthy. Billy summoned Jack Spot to give him a share. Choking with humiliation, as he realised Billy had outwitted him and pulled off the biggest robbery in living memory, Spot accepted a wodge of notes. In doing so, the power balance between the two men had shifted irrevocably.

Billy was now an unstoppable force in crime and in 1954, he pulled off yet another spectacular raid. This time he made off with £40,000-worth of gold bullion. Billy had discovered through contacts in Ireland that a KLM plane had crashed at Shannon airport and it was loaded with bullion and diamonds. The bullion was making its way to London via a KLM lorry and Gypsy was among the drivers who tailed daily deliveries to the KLM offices in Jockey's Fields in Holborn. One evening, as a KLM lorry parked in what is a narrow, quiet street, a van backed up and the lorry driver was assaulted before the thieves made off with two boxes loaded with gold bars. It all happened in the blink of an eye.

Word of the Eastcastle Street job and the KLM raid reached Frank in Broadmoor. He was gutted not to be in on them but Billy was still looking after his family for him financially and the success of jobs served only to further Frank's admiration of his boss. 'They were beautiful jobs, because no matter how hard the police and the Royal Mail tried to pin it on Billy, they couldn't,' said Frank. 'He was the greatest. The planning that went into it showed Billy had brains. His methods went on to inspire generations of thieves; the Great Train Robbery, the Brink's-Mat bullion raid, they all owe a lot to the technical planning of Billy Hill.

'There has never been another criminal mastermind like him. Billy had done his time and now he had proved he was the boss of the underworld because on these biggest jobs of his career, he didn't get caught. He was untouchable.'

CHAPTER 11

RAZORS AT DAWN

When Frank got out of Broadmoor in 1955, after three years inside, he did his best to make up for his absence as a father by bringing home the biggest Christmas cracker he could find to give to his boys. 'It was about three feet long,' remembered David. 'And I can still picture him and my mum arguing with each other as they tried to hang it on the wall before Christmas. It was filled with presents and we kept trying to get our little fingers in it to pull them out.

'We were glad to have him back home again and no one mentioned Broadmoor. He didn't seem any different to us, there was no change in him, he just went straight back to work for Billy Hill.' Frank added: 'I never looked back or got down about being inside or being sent to the nuthouse. Why would I? I was out and I had plenty to keep myself busy.'

Billy Hill helped Frank to secure an interest in his first West End club. It should have been a nice little earner – giving Frank a wage of around £50 a week for doing very little – but life in Soho was about to get very complicated. It went without saying that Billy expected Frank to pick up where he left off in terms of doing his dirty work for him.

The days of Frank being a 'freelance', who could sidestep gangland slights and vendettas and flit from one side of the river to the other were, to all extents and purposes, over.

Tensions between Billy and Jack Spot had reached boiling point in the years that Frank was inside, partly fuelled by a public relations war, which would not look out of place in today's gossip columns. With Billy as his boss, Frank now had to choose which side he was on.

Billy had the *Sunday People* crime reporter, Duncan Webb, eating out of his hand. Billy made great copy and Webb had secured the scoop in which Billy outed himself as man in charge of Britain's underworld. But Webb also had personal reasons for getting Billy on his side. He had fallen in love with a former nightclub hostess, Cynthia Hume, the divorced wife of murderer Donald Hume, who was doing a twelve-year sentence. Police hadn't been able to prove Hume had murdered a car dealer from London's Warren Street, chopped him up and put the body parts in the English Channel, but they had managed to secure a conviction for being an accessory to murder.

Cynthia had divorced Hume and married crime reporter Webb, who feared their marital bliss would be short-lived. Webb was terrified of what Hume would do to him when he got out. Billy played on Webb's fears and need for protection and Webb gave Billy the column inches to help secure his position as the King of Soho, by belittling the importance of Jack Spot in print whenever he got the chance.

Frank played a key part in winding up Webb to suit Billy's needs. He used to sit with him at Billy's flat in Barnes, waiting for his boss to idly muse: 'You were in prison with Hume, weren't you, Frank?' At the allotted moment, Frank would look grave and murmur: 'Yes, and I'll tell you one thing, Bill, he never forgets a thing.' Webb would wring his hands and wince. Billy would then pat him on the knee and say: 'Don't worry, Duncan, we'll see you right.'

Jack Spot was left to tell his story in a rival rag – the *Sunday Chronicle* – and Webb had infuriated him further by declining his offer of an exclusive interview. Webb let it be known that he was penning a book with Billy Hill, *Boss of Britain's Underworld*, documenting the gangster's life of crime. Spot, seething with anger, could only watch his reputation and his empire crumbling around him. He had developed a particular enmity for Billy's new best mate, the affable Albert Dimes. Albert had busied himself helping to run Billy's clubs, while expanding his own interests in the horse-racing world – which trod rather heavily on Spot's polished brogues.

Albert ran a successful betting shop, A. Barnett, in Frith Street, and would buy fruit every day from a little corner shop nearby. Spot knew this and was ready for a fight one bright August morning when he bumped into him. Insults were traded and the brawling pair fell into a delicatessen shop in Old Compton Street. Spot grabbed a knife that had been left on a sack of potatoes and stuck it into Albert, who yanked it out of his bleeding thigh and plunged it into Spot. The shop was splattered with blood as the men grabbed at the knife and took turns in sticking it into each other. The fight was only stopped when the shop owner picked up a set of cast-iron scales and walloped Spot around the head with them.

Both men staggered out into the street and were whisked away to hospital by loyal henchmen. The police were soon by their bedsides, charging them both with grievous bodily harm and affray. Spot suffered eight stab wounds and Dimes had wounds to his thigh and stomach, as well as a cut in his forehead requiring twenty stitches. Frank was quickly despatched to Brighton to nobble Spot's main ally there, nightclub and casino owner Sammy Bellson. He was tasked with extracting money from Bellson to pay for Albert Dimes' defence lawyers. It was a shrewd move designed to send a message to Jack Spot that he was becoming even more isolated.

When Frank turned up on his doorstep and made it plain that Billy wanted funds, Bellson readily complied. He later told friends: 'I knew what would happen if I told Fraser to fuck off. I did what Billy Hill wanted me to, like any sensible person would have done.' Frank remembered: 'He put up quite a good sum – about £500, I think. It was most welcome. He wasn't Spot's man any longer. Funny, that.'

Billy wanted Frank to stay down in Brighton to keep an eye on Sammy Bellson, to prevent any of Spot's cronies from seeking reprisals. Sammy provided a flat for his new minder, in Marine Parade – the same one that Spot used to stay in when he had a day at the races. Unwittingly, Billy had set the stage for the next big romance of Frank's life, because it was there in Brighton, in the dry cleaners, that he met his future wife, Doreen. The only problem was, he was still married to Kate.

Frank's three-year absence at Broadmoor had weighed heavily on the family but Kate had stood by him. When he disappeared off to Brighton, she'd just about had enough. In the weeks after his release, he had increasingly lived the life of a single man and she suspected he was up to no good, entertaining good-time girls up in Soho. He put in the occasional appearance at home and Kate was torn between wanting to yell at him and desperately needing him to be around for the boys. She kept silent to maintain the peace between them.

When times were hard at the beginning of their relationship, they pulled together but when Frank had money he was increasingly a ladies' man. There was a sense of him trying to live the life Billy Hill wanted him to after his release from prison. Frank didn't bother coming hop-picking with the family in Beltring that year either. Perhaps it had been too much for Kate to expect him to. He had work to attend to up in town. As Kate later discovered, that included a dalliance with a local married woman, Maria Callaghan, who was the wife of a thief from the Elephant. Patrick remembered his father turning up for the day in Kent that summer 'in his best suit and trilby. He was one of the Chaps all right. He didn't want to hold me when I was little in case I threw up all over his best threads,' he added.

Now, he dumped his family without so much as a backwards glance and it was more than Kate could bear. It was an episode that was to shame him later in life but at the time, he saw nothing wrong with escaping the demands of his children and his nagging wife. Furthermore, Doreen's uncle was a friend of his old gangland hero Darby Sabini, who had retired to Brighton years earlier, which seemed to make it right.

While Frank wooed Doreen, Billy Hill got busy up in

London, picking off Spot's henchmen one by one. The majority of them switched sides. Those who didn't were given such beatings that they wished they had. But when the Spot-Dimes fight came to trial, Spot launched his secret weapon: a dodgy vicar. The Reverend Basil Claude Andrews, then in his eighties, was wheeled out to reveal that he had witnessed everything and, on his word as a man of the cloth, Dimes had started it. Spot was acquitted and Dimes was released shortly afterwards after the prosecution withdrew its evidence. Despite stabbing each other in a frenzied attack in broad daylight, both men got away with it.

The Rev. Andrews then, incredibly, gave interviews to the daily papers, saying he was beginning to remember things that had previously slipped his mind. The press went into a feeding frenzy about 'The Fight That Never Was'. Spot's wife Rita was arrested for perverting the course of justice. The vicar was called to court and there were gasps from the public gallery as he revealed how Mrs Jack Spot had paid him to lie for her husband at the trial. She got off with a fifty-pound fine but three of her co-accused – Spot's henchmen – were all jailed. It was not Spot's finest hour.

Late in 1955, Billy Hill's book was launched in London and Frank was among the many 'faces' who attended the party, along with the gossip-column favourites Lord and Lady Docker. Lady Norah was allegedly seduced by Billy Hill in an upstairs bathroom during the soiree at Gennaro's in Dean Street, now home to the Groucho Club. 'I knocked on the door and opened it and found Billy giving her one,' said Frank. 'You had to admire the man.'

Meanwhile, Spot languished in the shadows in one of his

dwindling number of spielers and was furious. He hatched a plan for revenge and several weeks later lured Duncan Webb to a hotel in Tottenham Court Road with a fake phone call, pretending that Billy Hill was in trouble. When Webb arrived he jumped on him, hit him with a cosh and broke his writing arm, saying: 'I'll give you Billy fucking Hill.' Webb shopped him to the police and Spot got a fifty-pound fine but Webb was not satisfied. He sued for loss of earnings and was awarded £700, which bankrupted Spot – who never paid a penny of the damages he owed.

All the while, Frank's need to seek revenge on Johnny Carter still festered. Frank hadn't let the matter go, in fact, he had brooded on it during his time in Broadmoor and was still hell-bent on getting even. But Frank was never one to rush into action; he preferred to wait for the right moment, at which point he would act decisively and with terrifying brutality. And in the case of Johnny Carter, he did just that.

He found him one evening, just as last orders were being called in a pub down Lambeth Walk. Carter sprang over the counter and into the public bar to make his getaway. With Frank hot on his heels, he ran through someone's garage and into their house. Frank pursued him, believing the home-owner in his shirtsleeves to be a Carter ally, and gave him a beating for good measure. When the owner's Alsatian dog jumped on him, Frank slit its throat. He made his way upstairs and found Carter hiding in the bathroom. 'I cut him to pieces,' said Frank. 'I stopped counting how many times I slashed him. He was cowering in the corner with his hands up but I kept going until I was satisfied I had paid him back. I had waited years to get even and seeing the claret spurting out of him felt really good. He was a bully boy who could dish it out but he couldn't take it.'

Carter was taken to hospital and it was only then that Frank realised that the homeowner had been a completely innocent bystander who had been caught up in the fight by chance. He immediately went round to the house, paid compensation and apologised. For all his violence, Frank had his own sense of right and wrong and when he felt he had done something to hurt someone by accident he did his best to make it up to them. Frank also heard that the police were looking for Johnny Carter because he had broken a man's arm.

Frank asked Billy Hill for help to ensure that Johnny Carter would not tell the police who had put him in hospital by offering the services of a tame QC, Patrick Marrinan. Marrinan lived in the same block of flats as Billy Hill and was paid handsomely for his legal services. The man who had his arm broken was paid off by Frank not to recognise Johnny Carter in court. Carter, in turn, would get the services of Patrick Marrinan, QC, for free, plus £750 for not naming Frank as the man who cut him. It was a typical gangland deal.

But there was one problem: Johnny Carter did not stick to his side of the bargain and named Frank to the police, putting him on his toes. From that moment on, Carter was a marked man and suffered severe reprisals in the years that followed: he was mown down by a car in Peckham and beaten up no less than three times by people who were either loyal to Frank or who had their own axes to grind.

Billy Hill, meanwhile, was quietly waiting to take revenge

on Spot for what he had done to Albert Dimes. He bided his time for a year. All the while, Spot knew trouble was coming and made several trips to Paddington Green police station to ask for protection. He even asked the young Kray twins, who had previously looked up to him, to keep an eye on some of his racing pitches. By now they were in their early twenties and beginning to explore the seamy world of protection rackets, run from their snooker club in Bethnal Green. When they did help Spot out, it was a half-hearted affair – the boys pretended to snooze on a bench, rather than doing any minding. The message to gangland was clear – Spot was no longer a man to be taken seriously. If the Krays wanted to emulate anyone, it was Billy Hill. The final straw came when Spot paid some young hoodlums from Paddington to shoot Albert and Billy. It was an ill-judged move, as Spot no longer had the backing of serious players, other than the Carters, who were themselves increasingly marginalised. The would-be assassins got cold feet and word of Spot's treachery reached Billy's ears, particularly after Frank had worked one of them over. Billy called a council of war at his flat in Barnes, with Frank and his other trusted henchman, Ginger Dennis, who sold used cars in Warren Street. When Billy asked him to 'do' Jack Spot, Frank readily agreed.

In many ways, Billy was the father figure Frank never had: he praised his talents as a thief, he utilised his violence and paid him handsomely. Frank felt he belonged in Billy's gang. It was a family in which crime paid and it paid very well. Billy was quite clear in the orders he gave. Frank was not to kill Spot. It was far more humiliating for him to be badly beaten up and survive, with lasting scars for all the world to see.

Frank was armed with his trusty chiv, his cut-throat razor, but in a scene reminiscent of *The Godfather*, Billy also handed over a shillelagh – a cudgel – for Frank to strike Spot with. It had been a gift from Spot to Billy in the early days of their criminal union, before their ill-fated trip to the South of France. Billy Hill's old gang member Billy Blythe joined Frank as the driver and lookout, but the attack was carried out by Frank alone.

It came late one evening in May, as Jack and Rita Spot were making their way home from the pub to Hyde Park Mansions. Frank pulled a stocking mask over his face and jumped out of the shadows. Rita screamed as Spot shoved her out of harm's way and he was felled by a blow from the shillelagh, wielded by Frank. Blows rained down on Spot, who lay sprawled on the steps to their mansion block. When Spot was down, Frank pulled out his razor and slashed away mercilessly at his victim's face. Rita managed to stagger inside and call the police, blurting that Billy Hill and Albert Dimes had attacked her husband.

By the time the law arrived, Fraser and Blythe were long gone and Spot was found badly beaten, repeatedly slashed and stabbed in the back. His wounds required seventy-five stitches and he was left with a seven-inch scar down his face. Frank slipped quietly away to Brighton and waited for the fuss to die down.

Billy Hill made his presence felt by sitting in a car outside the hospital while Spot was recovering, knowing this would get back to the man whose face had been cut to ribbons. To emphasise the point that Hill had taken retribution and the game had changed – putting Spot out in the cold – Ron and Reg Kray paid him a visit. Previously, they had done Spot's bidding, but now they smiled and asked him: 'Who did that to you?' It was a powerful message. Not only was Billy showing Spot that the Krays had switched their allegiance, the menace behind their concern would have been clear as day. They were also reminding him of the gangster code – to say nothing.

But Spot, the man who had slashed and stabbed his way to the top and had insisted that his victims stick to the criminal code of honour as far as the law was concerned, then did the unthinkable: he grassed up his assailants. Rita, by virtue of being a woman, might have been excused for her treachery but, as far as Frank was concerned, Spot could sink no lower. 'He'd been putting it on people for years and now he had gone bad on us,' said Frank. 'It proved he was the lowest of the low. Spot was never half the man Billy Hill was. He had no honour and he proved it by singing like a canary to the cozzers.

'I should have killed him.'

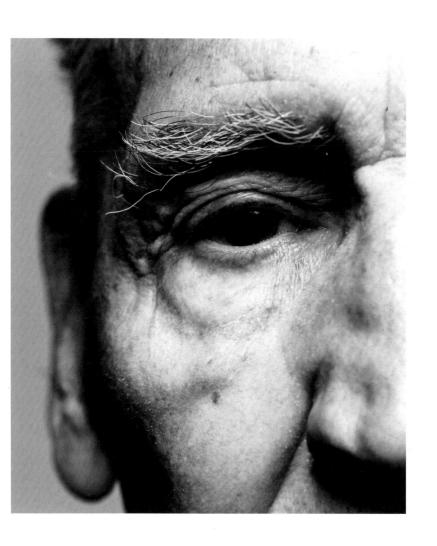

Original lost.
Renewal
N° 506024

A rare photograph of Frank's father, James Fraser,
taken from his Merchant Navy records.

This kind of squalid two-up-two-down terraced housing was typical
of Waterloo, and the Fraser family home in Howley Place would have
looked similar. (This is nearby Tabard Gardens.)

St Patrick's football team, with captain Frank holding the ball.

Chaucer House in Tabard Street, where the Frasers were rehomed
after being bombed out during the war.

The Fraser women about to set off on a beano (a trip to the seaside).
Back row, from left to right: Frank's mother Margaret, his sister Kathleen, his
girlfriend Kate Wall, Gladys Say (Eva's best friend) and his favourite sister, Eva.

Above left Gladys Say and Eva, leading lights in the Forty Thieves.

Above right Eva's husband Jimmy Brindle, a good friend of Frank's and a good man.

Frank with Albert Dimes behind him, about to play a charity football match. Frank looked up to Dimes.

Crime boss Billy Hill took Frank under his wing. Here Billy is
bellied up to the bar in one of his Soho clubs.

A sing-song at a party to celebrate publication of Billy's autobiography in 1955.
From left to right: Soho Ted, Bugsy, Groin Frankie, Billy Hill, Ruby Sparkes,
Frankie Fraser, College Harry, Franny the Spaniel, Cherrie Bill, a female journalist
and Russian Ted. Another journalist is on the piano.

Above left Jack Spot with his wife Rita after being acquitted of causing grievous bodily harm to Dimes. *Above right* Albert Dimes with his wife after being released. He had been charged with causing grievous bodily harm to Spot but the prosecution withdrew its evidence.

The Carters and Frank had a long-running feud. Left to right: Eugene Carter, his wife Tina and Frank's particular nemesis, Johnny Carter.

Frank's mother, Lady Margaret, and
her second husband, the kind-hearted
Patrick 'Patsy' Duhig.

Patsy holding Frank Jr, and a young
Beverley with Lady Margaret at Ramsgate.

Eva's daughters Beverley and
Shirley at Southend.

Frank Junior in the mid-sixties
at Bognor Regis.

CHAPTER 12

ROUGH JUSTICE

In May 1956, with Jack Spot naming just about every major player in Soho as his attacker, the police saw their chance to clean up the streets once and for all. Unfortunately for the Flying Squad, Billy Hill and Albert Dimes had been dining, very conspicuously, in the Mayfair Hotel on the night in question, so Spot's attempts to implicate them fell flat.

However, Frankie Fraser's name was at the top of Spot's list, he had no cast-iron alibi and was already on the run for the assault on Johnny Carter, so Billy Hill arranged for him to escape to Ireland for a time. Frank holed up in a house outside Dublin, which Billy had rented from a local doctor via Patrick Marrinan, QC. There he would have remained until the fuss had died down, if it hadn't had been for his sense of honour.

When he heard that the police had picked up two of his best mates – Dido Frett and Ray Rosa – in connection with the Johnny Carter stabbing, he felt he had to come back to London. Frank intended to quietly slip back into the country and see if he could get a copper 'straightened' with Billy Hill's help or try to persuade Carter to drop the assault charge. What he hadn't bargained for, as he was making arrangements with Billy Hill to return to London, was that the police were listening in, via a wiretap on Billy's phone.

The moment he stepped off the plane at London Airport, he was seized by a boys-in-blue welcoming committee, headed by the legendary Nipper Read of the Yard, and was taken straight to jail, where he was charged with the attack on Spot. After this fiasco, a scathing Billy Hill would tell anyone he did business with: 'I don't talk on the phone'. He went back to the tried and tested 'meet' instead and other gangsters followed suit. 'I couldn't believe it,' said Frank. 'We'd all heard about spies and the like having their phones tapped but none of us thought that we would warrant that kind of attention from the police back then. We were wrong.'

At the committal hearing, Billy Hill arranged for every 'face' Jack Spot had slashed or chopped to be present in the magistrates' court. They lined up, staring down at him. The message seemed to get through to Spot. When the prosecution asked him if he could identify who had attacked him, he changed his story and said he couldn't. But it was too late. The case went to trial anyway, and Jack Spot was made a hostile witness. His previous statements – which were numerous and quite detailed – were used and his wife Rita stuck to her story and named Frank Fraser and Ginger Dennis along with Billy Hill's old gang members Billy Blythe and Bobby Warren. She also threw Albert Dimes' associate Bert 'Battles' Rossi into the mix.

Frank insisted, to the end of his days, that Battles Rossi was nowhere near Jack Spot that night and neither was Ginger Dennis. Bobby Warren would have been, but he turned up late and just sauntered up after it had finished. What Rita did by naming them and putting them at the scene seemed to him an unforgivable act, because not only was she grassing, she was grassing up men who were innocent of the crime.

Such was the publicity and interest in the case, it was unlikely that anyone named by Rita would get off without a jail sentence. Dido Frett and Ray Rosa were briefly in the frame but because they had alibis for the night of the attack on Spot, the case against them was dismissed. They were not so lucky with the Johnny Carter slashing – and got seven years each, while Frank got away with it because he was charged with the Jack Spot slashing instead.

Frank said: 'Billy paid me for cutting Spot but, to be honest, I would have done him for free because I hated the man. His wife Rita naming everyone else was just pure spite. It was all about Spot trying to big himself up by saying there was a gang of us attacking him and his wife, well, she just was a nasty bit of work.'

Patrick Fraser added: 'My dad was quite clear he had done Spot on his own. All the other stuff was just nonsense. Spot wanted to make out it was a group of them because it was so shameful for it to be just one-on-one and he got cut to bits. Don't forget, he is a man who had used a lot of violence in the past to get his way and it didn't look good for him. Billy Blythe was the getaway driver and would have got involved if he had to but Spot put up no resistance and the razor went through him like a knife through butter.'

Billy Hill had Billy Blythe and 'Battles' Rossi spirited away to Ireland for a time but their stay was short-lived. Tommy

Butler, who later found fame as the police officer in charge of the Great Train Robbery inquiry, arrested the pair on the steps of the court in Dublin after a magistrate had thrown out an attempt to have them sent back to England, on the grounds that the warrant was flawed. As Frank put it: 'Butler grabbed them and had them bundled into a car and taken over the border into Northern Ireland.' From there, they were put on a plane to London, to face justice.

At the behest of Billy Hill, Marrinan went to their aid, without first being instructed by a solicitor – which was the usual procedure. As a result, the powers that be started to take a close interest in his involvement with the gangland boss, something that was to come back and haunt the lawyer in the months that followed.

Meanwhile, at Paddington Green police station, Rita identified Rossi and Blythe as her attackers. A police officer opened their cell door and Rita glanced at them momentarily, before saying: 'Yes, that is the man, officer.' Frank explained: 'It was totally unfair, but that is nothing new where the cozzers are concerned. The funny thing was that Rita had never set eyes on either Battles Rossi or Billy Blythe before. But the police never let the facts get in the way of a prosecution.'

At the trial in the Old Bailey, Rita was the star witness. Despite her recent fine for perjury in the case of the Spot-Dimes fight, and her admission that she was 'no angel', her weeping testimony persuaded the jury in her favour. Frank said: 'She made a big play about telling the court that Jack Spot had told her it was me, the little rat Fraser, who had done him. Well, she was right, of course, but I wasn't going to admit to that. The thing is, she then dragged everyone else into it. These were people who were not even there.'

Frank's weak alibi was that he was helping out a book-maker at the dogs on the night in question, with none other than Sammy Bellson from Brighton as his main witness. The prosecution started asking Frank some tricky questions about the fictional bookmaker's office, including what colour the phones were. Frank answered 'black, green and red', and Patrick Marrinan, QC – who was in court observing – helpfully slipped out to let Bellson know the colours Frank had come up with. Despite their best efforts, the prosecution drove a coach and horses through the whole story and the defence's only mitigation was that Frank was a 'mentally ill man' who had been 'used by greater forces to do evil deeds'. He ended up with a seven-year sentence.

Bobby Warren, who Frank insisted did not take part in the attack, got seven years as well. Frank's friend Battles Rossi, who was 'miles away' at the time, got four years, along with Ginger Dennis, while Billy Blythe got five. The men were split up, to ensure no camaraderie in jail. Frank was sent to Bristol, Billy Blythe went to Liverpool, Battles to Winchester, Ginger to Lincoln and Bobby to the Scrubs.

The judge had Billy Hill banned from the courtroom, fearing his presence would disrupt the proceedings, so he based himself in a cafe over the road, where he was to be found sipping tea as his runners darted back and forth with updates. The verdicts were a disaster, but Billy had bigger fish to fry. He hatched a plot to use the law against Jack Spot by framing him. Although such underhand methods were usually beneath criminals of Billy and Frank's calibre, they felt that this was justified, given that Spot had let his wife put so many of them away.

With half of his gang inside, it was left to Albert Dimes and Billy Hill to organise matters. Their first port of call was a Scottish villain and old-school robber, Scarface Jock – real name Victor Russo – who was asked if he would like another scar, and blame it on Jack Spot. He declined and returned to Glasgow, so another willing volunteer was selected, in the form of Tommy Falco, another 'face' from around Soho. Falco received a thirteen-inch slash to his arm, requiring more than forty stitches. He told police that Jack Spot was the perpetrator and had yelled 'This one's for Albert!' as he hacked away at his arm outside the Astor nightclub. The police were convinced by his story and brought charges. It was all going well until Victor Russo returned from Scotland and pitched up as a witness for Jack Spot, saying he had been asked if he would take a scar and blame it on Spotty.

The jury found Jack Spot not guilty of the charge and he was left to celebrate a pyrrhic victory. He found himself increasingly beleaguered, guarded by the Carters who were now engaged in a feud with another family, the Harrises. Before long, his last remaining nightclub was mysteriously burned down. He tried to emigrate to Canada but was sent back as an undesirable alien. His empire gone, he retired to Middlesex and lived quietly with Rita until she tired of him and left.

Back in south London, quietly getting on with the job of raising Frank's three little boys, was Frank's long-suffering wife Kate. Kate now found out from neighbourhood gossips about Frank's affair with a local woman, Maria Callaghan. In the months leading up to the Spot slashing, Frank had only put in the most fleeting appearances at home and most of the time, Kate had no idea where he was. At this stage, she didn't know about Doreen from Brighton, whom he had been secretly living with for the past two years. She couldn't understand why Frank had told visitors that his mother – rather than Kate, his wife – should be named as his next of kin. Eva and his mother certainly knew about what Frank had been getting up to and why he was seeking to put distance between himself and Kate, but had tried to protect Kate and the children from it.

They had been in a relationship for thirteen years but Frank had spent more than half of that time behind bars. Now, at the age of thirty-three, he was jailed again and once he was off the streets, local gossips – perhaps emboldened by his absence – got to work and Kate began to find out, drip by drip, the extent of her husband's betrayal. She wrote him a Dear John letter as he languished in jail, which reveals the full extent of her hurt. Despite her rage about what he had done, there is a palpable sense of sadness about him missing out on seeing his children.

Frank,
    I am writing to tell you that you need not worry about getting a divorce as I am going to get it myself, naming Maria Callaghan, as I have got plenty of proof that you were getting about with her before you was in this trouble.
    Different people have told me also that is the reason her husband left her. That is what he told people.
    Frank, you had a right game with me before you went

away and of course people wouldn't tell me when you was about but I have heard plenty since you have been in there. I wouldn't have wrote this letter but I am just about fed up with you running me down to different people who visit you, even if you don't do it, it is people getting at the mix about 'you don't want me for your next of kin, your mum is'.

Surely you don't think I would do any harm to you?

Also, Frank, you suppose to say you don't want nothing to do with your children unless people is getting at the mix but that is what I was told. After all, Frank, who has brought them up all this time? Only me – and they have only had my love, they didn't know what a father's love is. But I admit you was good to them when you were home.

I mean, Frank, little Frankie wrote you 9 times and you never answered his letters. Also, I had Patrick in hospital with a suspected TB hip but you never even found out how he was getting on. I have now got Frankie ill, I don't know if Eva has told you?

Don't think, Frank, I am trying to get round you because I'm not. I done everything for you and run about everywhere on my own. I never had nobody come with me. None of your friends who come to see you didn't want to know. I could tell you a lot.

Frankie I am writing this letter because this is between us, as plenty of people are making it their business.

Most touching, perhaps, is her final sentence before she signs off 'From Kate', in which she reassures him that she has been looking after his suits – such was the importance of expensive clothing in the gangster's world. Even as they were breaking up, she still couldn't help caring for him in a practical way; the little things that a wife does to show she loves her husband, without question. She wrote: 'I gave Eva the tickets of your suits, I kept them going right up-to-date.'

Of course, she was unaware at this point that his new girlfriend Doreen, who was already pregnant with his love child, had been picked up down at the dry cleaners, which was quite fitting for a man so concerned with his appearance.

Kate, pointedly, did not tell Frank that she had found a shoulder to cry on throughout her tribulations since he left her. Salvador Manzi, a half-German, half-Italian immigrant, who was some twenty years her senior and had been an accomplice of Frank's since the early 1940s, now offered, over a quiet cup of tea at the flat in Mason Street, to be a father to her three boys. Salvador – known as 'Dor-Dor' or 'Fred' – was an old-time thief from around the Elephant who had survived the Dartmoor Mutiny of 1932, in which inmates protesting about harsh conditions and appalling food, took over the prison. Taking part in this event undoubtedly gave him status among the criminal fraternity, as Dartmoor was known as the bleakest prison with the most punitive of regimes; many convicts were broken by hard labour there.

Salvador came from Frank's world but, because he was older, he seemed less likely to stray. Kate wanted stability and she needed someone who would help her provide for her boys and, as well as a nice sideline in housebreaking, he had set himself up as a bookmaker. Salvador, who could turn on the charm when he wanted to, was her man from that moment on.

Kate had admired Salvador as a man not to be messed with when she was just a little girl; she once saw him hanging his first wife, Anna Mary Manzi, out of a window by her ankles during an argument. She saw this act of violence against his wife as a sign of strength. It was something she would later live to regret. Although Frank had never laid a finger on her in anger, he was emotionally cruel with his cheating. Salvador provided financial stability but he also had a temper, which spilled into physical violence. Kate mutely accepted it. She had made her choice – rightly or wrongly – and she was sticking with it. Her children needed a father and although he hit her, he never once laid a finger on the boys. Salvador had also lost an eye in a street fight. He was winning until a woman glassed him in the face. He always told the Fraser boys: 'It's never the men you have to watch, boys, it's the women.'

Word soon reached Frank in prison about this new love tryst and he was incandescent with rage that Kate had 'betrayed' him with Manzi. What was sauce for the goose was not sauce for the gander in Frank's world. It didn't matter that he had betrayed her on numerous occasions. Frank felt that Kate had let him down badly and a bitter divorce was now on the cards. He and Salvador never spoke to each other again, despite the fact that Salvador had been a very close friend: he had accompanied Frank on shop-breaking escapades and had even cudgelled one of the Carter brothers in Walworth Road, when the feud with the Brindles was at its height several years before.

Salvador had always carried a candle for Kate and could never understand why Frank had left her. As it was, he had little compunction about making her his woman, even though it meant taking on the financial responsibility for her three boys. It was a mark of his strength of character that he was not in the least bit worried about upsetting Frank or frightened of any kind of retribution. And although Frank was furious, he directed his anger at Kate, rather than at Salvador.

Kate now only traded insults with Frank across the divorce court in Lambeth. When the case was heard in 1957, Frank had to be brought from prison, handcuffed to guards. Frank then denied that the children were his, just to spite her, something for which Kate never forgave him. He even told the court that Kate had already had one child by another man before they got together, to try to blacken her name. The divorce was as bitter as it could be and that was before she had even found out that his lover, Doreen, had already given birth to Frank's son, Francis, in the summer of the previous year. Frank's meticulous list of his correspondents in prison reveal he wrote a letter to Mrs D. Fraser in the Sussex Maternity Hospital in July of that year, to congratulate her on the birth.

David remembered sitting outside the court as a twelve-year-old boy, next to his aunt Eva and not really understanding what was going on. 'My mum came out crying and I only caught a glimpse of my dad, but from that moment we knew he had disowned us. I couldn't speak his name in the house and we never heard from him. He told Eva and Jim to stop seeing us and to turn their backs on my mum but they never did. When Frank was inside we used to be able to see them quite freely. When Frank was out, it became more difficult but we still stayed in touch. We were very much brought up with our cousins, Beverley and Shirley.'

Although Frank and Kate had split, their anger with each other never subsided. David and Patrick believe this was a sign that deep down, they still cared. David said: 'I believe that he still loved her, even then, because his anger about the break-up was so violent and she loved him because she was furious with him for cheating on her and leaving her with us kids.

'She knew Dor wasn't the best husband because he had a violent temper, but she needed someone and that was all she had because of the way Frank had left her. It wasn't as if their feelings for each other mellowed over the years and in their case, it was a thin line between love and hate.

'Their love had been a real passion and they lived through some very tough times together. They were young when they got together and as Frank got more successful, he got sucked into this gangster way of living, with the late-night drinking and the birds on his arm and Kate was just struggling with the kids.

'If he had apologised for his infidelity and begged her to come back at the start, she might have had him but because she had gone off with Salvador it was a bitter stand-off and it lasted the rest of their lives.'

At the time, the boys knew not to mention their father anymore and would tell people that they had an 'uncle' called Dor, who would now stay over from time to time with them in Mason Street. Patrick, who was just six, remembered very little of Frank and quickly came to accept Dor as his father. As a result, he had arguably the most stable upbringing of the three Fraser brothers. He was the baby of the family and was fussed over and shielded from much of the pain of the split, which was all too evident to his older siblings. 'Dor did all the things that dads do with their boys,' Patrick said. 'He raised me as his own and I am still grateful for what he done. I was too young to remember much about my real dad, Frank, back then.'

As the middle child, David was old enough to know things had changed forever and a quiet anger began to simmer inside him. He said: 'It was confusing because I looked up to my dad. One minute he was there and then the next, I wasn't to mention his name. My mum never did any character assassinations of him when I was young, she just never spoke about him and then Dor became more and more of a permanent fixture in our lives.'

David learned to hide his feelings of loss about his father and had to bottle up his anger about the way Salvador treated his mother. 'He was good to us but I never liked the way he was heavy-handed with my mother,' he said. 'Whenever we did something wrong, he would slap her because he didn't want to lay a finger on us. I think he knew that our mum would never have stood for that.' Despite Frank's orders to Eva to abandon her nephews, Patrick had the fondest memories of going up to see Eva and Jim every weekend 'to get my pocket money'. 'They used to give me half a crown, which I was very pleased with,' he said. 'She was a brilliant aunt to me and Jim was a wonderful uncle. Of course, it was ridiculous for my dad to say we weren't his. We all look like him, for a start.'

Kate packed up their things and moved out of Mason Street, just as the council decided to tear the place down. She was ready for a fresh start with Salvador and the boys and managed to find a council maisonette in Brixton. 'It was like moving to the country for us after that tenement block,' said Patrick. 'Every thief worth his salt wanted to move to Brixton, which was seen as quite posh. It was a step up for us.'

Frank Jr, who was already a serious, secretive child, became more insular and more determined to succeed as a result of his fractured childhood. With only sporadic contact with his father from a very young age, he had looked to his mother and his aunt Eva for guidance. Beverley remembered her mother Eva's motto: 'Don't say nothing and they won't have nothing on you.'

'We were always polite to neighbours but were all brought up just not to talk about our business. It was always "Good morning" and "Good evening", but never invite them into your home and don't tell anyone what you are up to,' said Beverley. 'God knows, my mum wouldn't like society today with all this Facebook and telling people everything. She'd think it was like being the grass of the class.'

Patrick added: 'Eva was a woman of very high principles. She hated the police, hated the screws and loved her family. She was like her brother Frank in female form. They really were like peas in a pod those two.'

Frank Jr was fourteen at the time of his parents' divorce – the same age as his father had been when his parents split up. Frank Jr was bright but he was already getting into trouble at school. One day David heard a commotion in the class-room next to his and realised that a teacher was hitting his brother with a cane. With his father gone, David became even closer to his older brother and would stop at nothing to protect him. 'I rushed in and jumped on to the teacher to get him off Frank,' he said. 'I don't know what he had done or was supposed to have done but Frank wound up getting expelled. The headteacher, Mr Rosarti, was a wonderful man, an ex-boxer, who told my mother not to worry about what had happened and no matter that our dad was away in prison, I could stay. He got both me and Patrick into boxing and was something of a mentor to us, which I will never forget.'

Frank Jr was determined to make his own way in the world and his thoughts soon turned to thieving as a way of making easy money, with his younger brother David as his willing accomplice. David said: 'I was still going to school but that didn't stop me and my brother Frank going to work together, literally, as kids. Brixton was like a goldmine. We had never seen such big shops and big houses and we went out thieving whatever we could.'

With their dad Frank gone from their lives, the regular handouts from Billy Hill had ceased and it became harder for their mother to make ends meet, despite Salvador's earnings as a bookie and his forays into housebreaking. 'We were poor, we weren't the poorest, but I had holes in my shoes,' said David. 'Thieving was just a natural thing to do. It was the next step; everyone was at it in our school. I knew my dad was a thief, my stepdad was a burglar and I knew my mum's relatives were on the fiddle, so it was only natural that I would want to go out stealing.'

The stage was set for the next generation of Frasers to enter a life of crime.

CHAPTER 13

A LONG STRETCH

Frank embarked on a seven-year stretch, his longest prison sentence to date, in a bullish manner, spoiling for fights with the prison officers. But the system was ready for him. He was frequently moved and, when he caused trouble, he was treated harshly, locked up, beaten up and then kept in solitary confinement for months on end.

He started off the sentence in Wandsworth but was quickly transferred to Bristol, before being sent to Pentonville, where he pulled off a major security breach by working out how to jam all the locks in the prison using shirt buttons. Frank and a mate managed to steal thousands of buttons from the prison workshop and distribute them to the cleaners, who could move freely from cell to cell during the day. New locks had just been fitted to all the cells and Frank worked out that by slotting the tin buttons into the locks, he could jam them. Once the cell doors were closed and the buttons put in, it was impossible to open them again, meaning that the prisoners could not be locked up. The ruse was rumbled during the afternoon, when someone went sick in the workshop and had to be returned to their cell, which wouldn't open. By then, the cleaners had disabled some 300 cells, causing a major incident. Although the governor couldn't prove that Frank was behind it, he had his suspicions and so he was moved to Wandsworth, before being transferred to Lincoln.

'I would have stayed there a while, except I got into trouble. It was the usual story, fighting a grass and giving a screw a belting at the same time,' said Frank. 'I was put down the strong cells and given bread and water. It was probably no more than I deserved but in a funny way it helped me, because while I was in there the *Empire News* ran a story about me saying I had given a statement to the police grassing up Billy Hill and Albert Dimes.' For Frank, being named as a grass in a newspaper was a disaster. It was also potentially very dangerous, not only for him, but his family. 'I could prove that I hadn't said anything because I was down in the punishment block in isolation at the time,' he said. 'It was totally malicious, a lie.'

The newspaper story concerned Billy Hill's attempt to fit up Jack Spot with the stabbing of Tommy Falco. Police sources said that they had interviewed Frank and he was helping them with his inquiries. Egged on by the barrister Patrick Marrinan, with whom he was corresponding frequently, Frank decided to sue for libel. 'In some ways, it was to give me something to do, a focus while I was in jail,' he said. 'But I was also very upset about my name being dragged around like that, to make me look like I was informing on my best mates. Fortunately, they knew it was a load of old cobblers but it could have been very nasty if they hadn't.'

Unfortunately for Patrick Marrinan, his days as a barrister and pen pal to one of the most notorious prisoners in Britain were numbered. He found himself up before the Bar Council on disciplinary charges, after the Home Secretary handed over secret tapes of phone conversations with Billy Hill. It seemed that the Establishment had endured enough of the gangland boss and his cronies having friends in high places. Marrinan faced allegations that he had consorted with and given advice to people whom he knew were of disreputable character – Billy Hill, Albert Dimes and Bert Rossi – and assisted Billy Blythe and Bert Rossi in Dublin when they were facing arrest there over the Jack Spot stabbing. He was alleged to have tried to obstruct a police officer, telling Blythe and Rossi to 'make a run for it'.

Marrinan pleaded not to be disbarred, saying he had allowed himself to come under the influence of worthless individuals. His pleas were ignored and he was expelled from the Bar. He returned to Ireland and built up a successful career as a solicitor before his untimely death in a car crash several years later.

Billy Hill was none too pleased that Marrinan, whom he had considered a genuine friend, had disowned him so publicly. But he was soon distracted by some terrible news: his henchman and friend Billy Blythe, who was serving five years for his part in the Jack Spot stabbing, had died suddenly in jail. Blythe suffered a perforated ulcer and endured an agonising death at Liverpool Prison. Frank always felt that the authorities had ignored Blythe's complaints about his health in the weeks leading up to his death adding to his anger with the prison service. Billy Hill organised a huge send-off for Blythe, with a cortège of Rolls-Royces travelling to Kensal

Green cemetery and thousands of people lining the route on a bleak, February morning.

Frank was moved to Dartmoor, where he quickly became the leader of a protest about the appalling food served to the prisoners. Dartmoor's daily fare consisted of a breakfast of porridge, followed by a spoonful of inedible stew, a small piece of bread smeared with margarine, all washed down with tea. Lunch and the evening meal were the same and 'a hot, brown drink' – supposedly cocoa – was served for supper.

Frank realised that few prisoners would be able to last on a genuine hunger strike, so he hit on the idea of refusing lunch and their evening meal. 'The whole prison took part,' he said. 'I did feel quite proud of that because normally not everyone will join in, but the food was so bloody horrible, we all felt we had to do something. No one was asking for gourmet food. It was just inedible and don't forget men on the Moor were doing long sentences. It wasn't easy for family to get there for visits and bring things for them. We wanted things to improve.'

The ringleaders – including Frank – were moved to the punishment block after the food protest ended. 'The walls were literally running with water,' said Frank. 'It was probably the worst place to be in the whole prison system. Fortunately it didn't last long because I was moved to Lincoln and then on to Stafford.'

Although he started out well, under the leadership of Governor Bainton, whom he knew from his days in borstal, this calm spell was short-lived. When Bainton was transferred to another prison, Frank was almost immediately locked up and put in solitary confinement after another prisoner complained he had been involved in a fight. 'It wasn't true,' said Frank. 'But that didn't seem to matter.'

Part of Frank's problem was that his reputation preceded him and he felt the need to live up to it. The more he lived up to it, the harder life got and the more hard done by he felt. He had assaulted so many staff and prisoners by now that the authorities were bound to believe people who spoke out against him and in some way, the governor must have also been relieved to have an excuse to lock him up again, to prevent further attacks on the staff.

At this point, the prison authorities decided to turn up the heat. His letters to Eva and his family started going missing and, mysteriously, their letters to him did not get through either. For seven months, Frank was held in a strong cell down in the punishment block at every jail in which he was locked up. This meant he had no creature comforts, except for a hard, thin mattress, which was removed from the cell every morning after breakfast and not returned until lights-out.

At a time when he was being held in solitary confinement, in the harshest conditions, the impact of being cut off from his family amounted to psychological torture on a man who was already – according to the system at least – mentally unstable enough to warrant spells in the country's most secure psychiatric hospitals. 'When he was locked up in solitary on the punishment block he literally only had a pot to piss in,' said his son, David. 'The cell would be cold – you can bet the window would always be broken – the floor was damp and hard. His diet would often be just bread and water or something completely inedible, like a thin, watery soup with a bit of grey meat in it. The commissioners from the Home Office would come around and check the food and you can bet your life what he got was nothing like what was slopped up to the prisoners, especially in those days. Taking his letters away was just another cruelty, to try to put the pressure on him.'

Eva effectively acted as his second-in-command while he was in prison, overseeing his share in the business with Albert Dimes and ensuring that Frank's reputation as a gangster was unassailable. She fulfilled the role of spin-doctor for him on the streets of Walworth and with the Chaps in Soho. On receiving one of his many letters, she would convey Frank's thoughts to Albert and his other friends, so that they would be kept informed of his views. Although he was gone from gangland, business continued and he did not want to be forgotten. He urged her to find out when the libel action was going to take place, so that he could be present: 'I hope you don't mind Eve, but it is very important.'

In the midst of all this, in another letter he still found time to be a concerned father for his youngest son, Francis, though conspicuously, there is no mention of his other three children on whom he had completely turned his back. He wrote: 'I received a letter from Doreen today and she is very worried over the baby because he is very ill and his left leg is slightly bowed and it makes him limp a little. She is really worried over him.' Frank also made sure that Doreen was taken care of financially, telling Eva to see Albert about it because 'she has not got it to spare'. Albert Dimes found a way of getting money to Doreen to support her and little Francis in

Brighton. An Italian family in Soho owned a shop next door to his betting business and they had a relative in Brighton, known as the Italian Major, who would call on Doreen and hand over the cash.

His letters to Albert Dimes were closely monitored and one letter was withheld on the orders of the Home Office Commissioner for Prisons. Frank's tone became quite conciliatory because he knew that the prison authorities were reading every word. His experiences on the inside had taught him how to play the game and he knew how to work things to his best advantage. 'I also sent one to Albert but to make sure what my position was there I checked with the governor, and it was OK, as long as I kept to the seasonal greetings. I hope he received it all right,' he wrote to Eva.

As the months passed and he remained in solitary confinement, visits from his family became a lifeline, and when one was cancelled at the last minute, he was devastated. He wrote to Eva, in August 1958, from Liverpool:

Well, there's no need to let you know how things are for me, as after the experience concerning the visit, you could not have had a better view.

I was informed by the Governor on Monday that under the circumstances he was granting me a special double visit, which would be one hour and it was a very good gesture on his part, which I thanked him for but at the same time pointed out, that though our family is not exactly rich or poor, the amount of money it costs for one or more people to travel from London to Liverpool does not exactly grow on trees.

We could have enjoyed a much pleasanter visit if allowed in, in the first place.

Please help, as you can imagine what things are now.

Whether you can afford the money, also time, to come now I don't know but if you can or anyone of the family, I look forward to seeing you.

Your loving brother

Frank xxxxxx

As 1958 drew to a close, the *Empire News* offered Frank £50 to settle out of court, but he was minded to continue with his libel action. Eva was heavily pregnant with her son, Jamie, and Frank expressed concern for her running about doing his bidding: 'I know things must be getting awkward for you now, it is getting near time for your going into hospital. I hope it is a lovely boy, Eva.' He went on: 'For them to make an offer to me, a convicted criminal, a person with a bad record and no such thing as a good character in the eyes of the law means they know they are in the wrong. I will not accept those terms. My terms are all my legal costs and an apology with damages.'

There was one problem: the money for his libel action had run out. 'The brief wants more funds,' wrote Frank. He asked Eva to see if her husband Jimmy, or his brother Tom 'Thumb' Brindle or Albert Dimes would stump up the cash. They agreed to help fund the case for Frank and he was transferred to Pentonville, so that he could attend the libel hearing. Although the judge agreed that the newspaper had made an erroneous report and ordered the *Empire News* to pay Frank's legal costs, the damages he got were derisory. The judge awarded Frank just one penny, on the grounds that he had no good character to defame. It was a crushing defeat but Frank took it on the chin. 'I had my day in court,' he said. 'It was better than sitting in a cell all day.'

He was moved to Exeter after the libel action, where he was supposed to stay for a month before going to Dartmoor, but he got into trouble defending another 'face' who went on to become a gangland legend for all the wrong reasons, Jack 'The Hat' McVitie. Jack 'The Hat' earned his nickname because of the trilby he liked to wear to cover up his hair loss. It was a name used behind his back but never to his face, because he was sensitive about his thinning hair. He was at Exeter when Frank arrived and was spoiling for a fight with one of the prison officers. On exercise in the yard, the men were supposed to walk in pairs, with no talking. If anyone got too close to the pair in front, or guards heard them chatting, they would put their sticks down and halt everyone, sometimes handing out a cuff around the ear. One prison officer seemed to take great pleasure in doing this to Jack 'The Hat' and he was ready to swing for him. While Frank had perfected the prison murmur – talking in almost a whisper – which never left him, even on the outside, Jack 'The Hat' was more garrulous and so he was always being picked on by the staff for talking.

When McVitie made his move on the guard one morning, the other inmates were ready and crowded around to form a circle, to try to allow him to have a fair fight. McVitie knocked the guard out, but it wasn't long before other officers arrived, wielding batons. The chief officer was called and a stand-off ensued. Another prisoner said that McVitie would be handed over, as long as there were no reprisals, telling the chief 'or you'll get it'. 'Now that was very unfortunate,' said Frank. 'It was a sort of a challenge to the chief but we could also lose face if we did nothing about it. Of course, McVitie was paid in full down the punishment block. They threw him down the stairs and beat the living daylights out of him with their sticks and we got to hear about it. There was no choice. I had to do something.'

First, he made an official complaint to the governor over the way McVitie had been beaten up. Then, when he was sent back to the workshops to sew mailbags, Frank and the other prisoner seized their chance as the chief officer and the governor came past. 'We jumped up and attacked them,' he said. 'I knocked the governor out. I stood there, waiting for what was going to happen next. I knew it was coming, there was no point in trying to avoid it.'

Frank was beaten so badly that he urinated blood, his ribs were broken and he was taken for treatment to the Royal Devon and Exeter Hospital. 'That showed how badly I was beaten up. I'm not saying I didn't deserve some of it but it was way over the top. They really paid me that time. When I got out of hospital I had to see the visiting magistrates to find out what my punishment would be. I got awarded eighteen strokes of the birch, the other prisoner got fifteen and McVitie was down for twelve.'

Billy Hill, Albert Dimes and Eva started to pull strings to try to help Frank. Billy sent his MP friend, Captain Mark Hewitson, down to see Frank in the punishment block. The MP told Frank to take his shirt off so that he could see what had happened to him and was so shocked that he raised the matter in parliament, asking the Home Secretary to make a statement about why three prison officers had entered Frank's cell and beaten him up, as well as 'public disquiet at the number of incidents occurring in Her Majesty's prisons'. The Home Secretary replied that Frank had only been taken to hospital for an X-ray on an old shoulder injury.

In a written answer, recorded in Hansard, the Home Secretary said: 'I have no reason to believe that Fraser was, in fact, injured in the manner suggested. It was necessary to restrain him while he was resisting the officers escorting him after he had himself committed an assault and medical examination revealed only trivial abrasions.' To Frank's horror, the Home Secretary then intervened in his punishment for Exeter and he was denied the birching. 'It may seem strange but birching was preferable because the alternative was I lost 400 days remission,' he said. 'The other prisoner lost 300 and McVitie 200 and we all got bread and water and solitary.'

Still on the punishment regime, he was transferred to Birmingham. He heard a whisper that one of the prison officers could be bribed to bring things in and sent a coded letter to Eva, right under the nose of the authorities, who were still intercepting his mail, asking for 'Uncle Tom' to help out. This meant going to Billy Hill and asking him to organise for money to be sent to the prison officer. He wrote: 'Remember when I wrote you before I left the other place that it would be best for Tom to make himself busy again, such as going to Birmingham. Remember I have been in no trouble of any kind at all, yet for no reason I am deprived of privileges and locked up for over two months after my punishment is finished, punishment that also, remember, was imposed at another prison, which makes it more of a liberty.'

To make matters worse, Frank had developed a stomach problem which required an operation, but it kept being delayed. With the recent death of Billy Blythe from a perforated ulcer, Frank was getting more desperate by the day. Even though he kept being told by the governor that the operation would happen 'soon', Frank told Eva it was all part of the psychological pressure they were putting him under. 'In my opinion they are enjoying themselves by giving this impression,' he wrote. His requests to be removed from solitary confinement were also denied, something Frank thought was due to 'spitefulness and vindictiveness'.

It was during this long spell in solitary confinement that Frank first discovered his love of books. 'Even when I was on punishment, I could still have a book to read. They didn't take that away from me and so I started to read a lot. I chose Dickens because those were big, thick books and I had a lot of time to kill. To my amazement, I found I liked it. I loved *Oliver Twist* because it reminded me of my childhood in Waterloo, with all those characters. Dickens really knew how to capture people and even though I was reading it over a century later, I don't think people in my neck of the woods had changed that much.'

By early 1960, he was still in Birmingham, pushing to get taken out of solitary and to be transferred to Dartmoor, where – he reasoned – he might have a better chance of getting back some privileges, as after serving three years he would be allowed to associate with other prisoners and have a radio. In the prison system, with his every move tightly controlled, such privileges were like gold dust.

Spending so long in solitary confinement was beginning to get to Frank but it did not break him. He wrote: 'It is obvious, Eve, they don't want me to go there or else I would have gone ages ago and if you do upset them, it is worth taking that chance. I am the one who should know, I am the one who is suffering. If you had seen Tom before Xmas when I saw you and Mum we would have had none of this.'

Billy Hill managed to send money to a prisoner's family to give to the prison officer who then brought Frank a few little luxuries, such as chocolate and toothpaste and a toothbrush, to keep him going while in solitary. But he still had not undergone his stomach surgery and the fate of Billy Blythe loomed large in his imagination. He told Eva: 'You can bet they are getting something up for me, like where Bill died.' The prison officers used to goad him about his friend's death too, which made matters worse.

His letters were still going missing and so he told Eva to start sending a telegram to him in jail, telling him to expect some post and then send the letter by recorded delivery. Frank also wrote to Captain Mark Hewitson on a number of occasions about him being held in solitary for so long, even after his punishment had officially ended. In his letter to Eva, he went over the details of what he wrote to the MP, after five months in solitary confinement – three months after the official end of his punishment for his misdemeanours at Exeter.

Perhaps unsurprisingly, having been held in isolation for so long, his letters became more plaintive and repetitive. Despite the prison system's notion that he was 'mad', his thought processes in the letters were completely clear, revealing a man more determined than ever to win some small victory, even if it was just a prison move or a radio in his cell. He complained to the MP that since he had been in Birmingham he had been in no trouble, so it was not fair to be locked up. Frank, of course, didn't seem to appreciate that the reason he had been incarcerated in this way was because he assaulted the governor of Exeter in the first place. Knowing that his post was being read, he said: 'I did not talk about Exeter other than to say it was a complete frame-up. I thanked him for raising it in the house in November and December last year [1959] concerning brutal treatment etc.' He could not see the visiting magistrates to plead a case to get out because 'I am locked up all day long and do not get to see them.'

When he did finally go before the magistrates he complained that the 'staff, by that I mean the officers, have got it in for me.' The magistrates told him he was being held in this way for the security of the prison and Frank replied: 'Well, that stinks, to put it bluntly.'

Despite his own situation, he still found time in his letters to show concern for the health of his ageing father, James, who was now well into his eighties and not at all well.

Just when he was at his lowest ebb, Reggie Kray drove Eva over to see Frank in Birmingham. 'The Krays were good to Eva,' said Frank. 'I always respected them for that.' He added: 'They weren't working for Billy Hill but they were kind of doing him a favour by bringing Eva to see me because I was Bill's man. It was one gang helping out another, if you like, showing respect, which was important in our world.' Eva was grateful for the lift, but she remarked that the twins 'were always a bit strange. Nice looking boys and always polite – but strange.'

By May 1960, the Home Office Commissioner felt that Frank was showing sufficient contrition to be considered for a return to the prison system proper with a transfer to Dartmoor. He relayed details of this to Eva, again painting a portrait of himself as a model prisoner, knowing that the governor had his beady eye on the post. 'I must behave and keep out of trouble,' he wrote. 'The Commissioner asked me if I could do this and I reassured him that there was no question of any trouble.'

One can only imagine the trepidation that the governor of Dartmoor must have felt to have Prisoner Fraser back on the wing, but he was as good as his word and did behave himself, for once. He was devastated then to be 'shanghaied' out of Dartmoor only a few months later and sent to Durham, where he was locked up again in isolation. Once again, he appealed to Eva to pay off a prison guard – asking for news of 'Uncle Jack'. He wrote:

As you can see, by the above address, I am now in Durham. I don't need to tell you, I need all the help I can get as you can imagine the position I am in.

I arrived here late Saturday evening, after travelling very early from the Moor. I brought my radio and clockwork shaver and I have asked the Governor, may I have them and the answer is No. I explained I was on the fourth stage and had done the required time for them, in fact well over five years, and still he said No.

Since I arrived I have been locked up on what is known as Rule 3b.

The governor informed me it was on the commissioner's instructions and I will be on it a very long time. It seems more than extremely unfair, as I have just arrived in the prison. In fact, last time I was here, exactly the same thing occurred. I think it far better if I were transferred to another prison.

As well you know Eve, there are a lot more things I could tell you but space and other things do not permit this but I sincerely hope you will do your utmost for me. As I have said, you can imagine the position I am in. I don't know how Uncle Jack is, in fact, I only heard from him a couple of times after I saw you, but he was more than pleased with the news. The reason I mention Uncle was in case he phoned you since, which would go a long way to prove him genuine.

With Eva keeping him up to date with his business deals in London, he was upset to find one of the Chaps asking his family for some financial help. Frank was outraged as they were 'out and in a position to help themselves. He is the greatest Richard there is. When I am out I shall certainly make myself busy.'

Despite being in solitary, he also plotted a return to business when he got out. In one letter, he revealed that Albert Dimes and Billy Hill planned to set him up in the 'machines business' – operating one-armed bandits in Soho. By this point in his life, he was thirty-nine and had spent nearly twenty years behind bars.

Billy Hill, grateful for all Frank had done on his behalf, paid £5,000 into a bank account for him on his release in 1962. He also sent a pilot to collect Frank and fly him back down to London from Newcastle airport, on a private plane. 'I still had a little gift for the screws at Durham,' said Frank. 'I asked the pilot how low he could get over the prison yard and he said he could buzz pretty low over the exercise yard as it was only a small plane. I went to the toilet at the airport and did something in a plastic bag. As we came in over the prison, I slung it out of the window on to the screws below. Apparently I scored a direct hit. That was how I felt about my time at Durham. The screws there were worse than animals so it only seemed fair to give them back some of what they had given me in the months I was there.'

He was met at the airport in Elstree by Billy Hill and taken to a party at the Pigalle in Piccadilly, with Billy picking up the tab. The Kray twins also hosted a whip round for him at one of their East End clubs, netting Frank about £400 – a tidy sum. It was the done thing for big names in gangland to put their hands in their pockets when a face such as Frank came out of prison and, given the reputation the Krays were building at this time, it made perfect sense for them to help Frank in this way.

Billy then decided that Frank needed a proper holiday and whisked him off to the South of France. 'I needed a holiday and Billy knew how to do it in style but I also needed to get back to work,' he said. 'People think that villains have stacks of cash put by for when they came out but that was rarely the case. I had a few business interests but I had never been good at saving it, so I needed to put some plans into action.

I intended to work hard, be more legit and to stay out of prison.'

He added: 'Given that I was always going to be a bit of a villain, that last bit was never going to be easy.'

CHAPTER 14

MY GENERATION

Frank's son, David, grew up around the Mod scene in South London and when he wasn't breaking into shops, prided himself on his smart, tailored mohair suit, skinny tie and button-down shirt. Just as Frank had been one of the Chaps in the 1940s, David and his older brother Frank Jr entered the 1960s looking razor sharp. Patrick's mother bought him a smaller version of their suits for Christmas when he was just eleven, to emulate his brothers. But the boys were cut from a different cloth to their father, in that they did not live by the chiv or mete out violence. 'We were thieves but we really weren't out to hurt anybody,' said David. 'I suppose that is one of the main differences between us and our dad. We did have a gang of people we worked with, but it wasn't a street gang in the sense of the Elephant Boys and we weren't feared in the same way.'

That said, Frank, David and Patrick all carried knives and cut-throat razors and learned, from their early teens, to use them in street fights. The difference was that they did not relish the fight, as their father Frank had done. 'For us to be aggressive, someone else would have to be starting it with us,' said David. 'Of course, when you are a teenage boy, full of testosterone, it doesn't take much. I did stab another kid once, during a street fight. It was a case of him or me and he got hurt. I didn't like that feeling – sticking the knife into someone – but I was quick because of my boxing and I was good with the knife. I preferred the razor, like my dad, because you could cut someone if you had to, but it wasn't likely to be fatal.'

For Patrick, the first time he used a razor marked a rite of passage in his mother's eyes. He said: 'I was coming out of a cafe in Brixton when I was just into my teens and I got jumped on by three rockers who beat the shit out of me, quite literally. I was a mess. I went home to my mother and David offered to go up there and sort it out but I decided instead to go back and do it myself. So, I borrowed his cut-throat razor and I went up there the next day and slashed them all when they were coming out of the same cafe. They chased after me and I had to bang on someone's door to take shelter from them. Still, I was proud that I had done them. My mother said that moment was when I became a man.'

His stepfather, Salvador, also offered Patrick advice on how to cut someone during a fight. 'He told me to slash them on the arse,' said Patrick. 'That was because it hurt like hell but they wouldn't bleed to death. Well, the first time I tried it I got a bit carried away and I stuck the knife right in, almost up to the hilt. When I came to try and slice them, it wouldn't budge because it was in too deep.' David idolised his brother Frank Jr, who at seventeen was already 'on the pavement' – robbing banks and holding up Post Office vans, although he officially had a real job, as a fish porter. Frank Jr was the youngest bank robber of his generation and was known for sitting in the back of the getaway car reading a copy of the *Beano* before he went to work.

'He moved out of all the gang fighting stuff very early on,' said David. 'He became diplomatic and into making real money from the age of about sixteen. He was also quite religious. My brother Frank had been an altar boy as a kid and that never left him. Before he went out on a job he used to go to church and pray. When I asked him why, he used to say, "Well, it doesn't hurt to have an extra bit of help, does it?"'

David was still supposed to be going to school and Kate was increasingly desperate to keep him on the straight and narrow. He said: 'She did want all of us to go to school and I was good at history and art, so I can't say I hated it, but I did hop the wag a lot. My brother Frank obviously wasn't going anymore, so it was too late for him, but I used to pretend to go and sit in a cafe down the road. My mother used to come running along, with Patrick, who was just eight or nine and late for school himself, following after her, to find me, which was quite embarrassing in front of my mates.'

Patrick said: 'She'd be mumbling: "I know that little bastard ain't gone to school!" and then go in the cafe and shout at him. When he answered her back, she'd clasp her forehead and cry: "My eyes! My eyes! How can you talk to me like that?"'

David was fourteen when he first got into serious trouble with the police, for mucking about on the back of a scooter. 'I was taken to Carter Street police station and given a terrible belting,' he said. 'When you tell people these days how the cozzers were back then, it is hard to believe, but I had the Fraser name and as far as they were concerned, I deserved it. They were very heavy-handed and they looked on us as scum. By the same token, we hated them with a passion.'

David was also increasingly concerned about how his step-father, Salvador Manzi, was treating his mother. 'She would try to do everything for him but he would find fault with it and just hit her,' he said. 'I didn't like it and one day, when I was about fifteen, I had just about enough of it. He raised his hand to her and I stepped in front of him and said: "No, no more." I didn't have to shout or anything, I just said it quietly but he knew I meant it. We stood there, staring at each other. He looked down at the floor and stepped away. He knew it had to stop, from that moment.'

Patrick, meanwhile, was finding his feet as a cat burglar. He was probably the brightest of all three boys and could have passed his 11-plus exam but deliberately failed it – by two marks – because he 'didn't fancy going to the grammar school'. Instead, he went to the local comprehensive and played truant, going out to work with Salvador. 'He was a brilliant cat burglar and he taught me everything he knew,' said Patrick. 'He also used to hold the ladder for me when I went into places, so we were quite a family team for a time.'

One day when he was just twelve and not in school, he was caught stealing a pint of milk and sent to a remand centre for children for thirteen weeks. 'It was a heavy sentence for a first offence and I can remember my mum and her sister Jessie crying their eyes out as I was taken away from court in the van with the bars on the windows,' he said. 'I must admit, I didn't feel too clever myself.' Eva, too, was heartbroken. Patrick was her favourite nephew because he looked so much like her adored brother Frankie as a little boy. He had inherited Frank's dark hair and was frequently mistaken for an Italian, just as Frank had been. Patrick said: 'They needn't have worried because it was a doddle. It was more like a reform school and we were treated OK. My brother Frank used to throw me snout over the wall so I'd have something to trade with the other kids.'

Salvador also had an unconventional relationship with his ex-wife, Anna Mary Manzi. Although he used to lord it over Kate, he was a weak man who would sneak out of the back door when Anna Mary used to come round to have an argument with him. Kate would be left to have a cup of tea with Anna Mary at the kitchen table. Patrick said: 'My mum would be saying to Anna that she really shouldn't be coming around to have an argument with Dor, because she wasn't married to him now. It was a very strange set-up.'

Around this time, David also got back in touch with his father, Frank, by sheer coincidence, after bumping into him in Soho. With all respect for Salvador gone, David wanted to have his father in his life again and Soho was abuzz with the return of Frank. 'I was hanging around an arcade in Great Windmill Street with my cousin Jimmy Fraser and I saw someone I thought I recognised. My cousin said: "That's your dad." I felt really embarrassed because he was such a legend and I was just a boy. I hadn't seen him for so many years, I didn't know what to say or do. I knew he had split up badly with my mother, who didn't like the very mention of his name.

'He walked over and said, "Hello, David." I'm not sure what I was expecting but after everything that had happened between him and my mum and us not seeing him, I thought it could have been a bit better than that. That was just how it was. Just "Hello."'

Not long after that, Frank Jr drove David and his father Frank down to Brighton so that David could meet Doreen and their half-brother, Francis, for the first time. Frank Jr was already having some contact with his father, as they shared some of the same criminal colleagues. He even took the rap for Frank over possession of a firearm. Due to Frank Jr having a clean record, the charge was quietly dropped. The idea of introducing his two eldest sons to Doreen had been Frank's, but it wasn't the happy family get-together he might have hoped for. 'You could say it was an awkward meeting,' said David. 'Doreen was quite rude to me and my brother Frank. When we were kids, if you went round someone's house you would always be offered a cup of tea. She never offered us so much as a cup of water and looked at us with sheer devilment. Francis was just a little boy playing on the carpet, he didn't know who we were and Doreen never introduced us. We shrugged our shoulders and left.'

When David left school at fifteen, he got a job as an apprentice butcher in Brixton. It paid a pittance and he hated it, so it wasn't long before he graduated from shopbreaking to nicking things from the backs of lorries. This is known in the criminal world as 'the jump up', because it involved tailing lorries and then jumping up into the back and making off with the haul before the driver noticed. Frank had done the same thing back in his 1940s heyday, as an easy and quick way of making money, and now David followed suit. 'I was working and thieving, working and thieving all the time,' he said. 'I knew stealing was wrong but all my friends were at it.'

Handsome and slim, with his mother's piercing blue eyes, David was growing up in more ways than one. His first serious girlfriend was Tommy Steele's sister, Sandra, who has since died of cancer. David was a typical Mod teenager and enjoyed going out in Soho with his friends to a club called The Scene, where he had a chance meeting with another Brixton boy, David Jones: 'Our gangs of friends would meet up there and me and David Jones used to get the last bus back to Brixton. It was a regular thing – we chatted a lot about boxing because I was boxing at the time and he was very knowledgeable about the sport. He knew a lot about past champions, which impressed me. After about a year of going to the club, I never saw him much anymore.' Years later, David heard 'Space Oddity' while in the nick: 'Someone showed me a picture of this funny-looking bloke, the singer, and I thought how much David Bowie looked like David Jones from The Scene. I still didn't realise it was him until years after that, in about 1974, when I was in the Tramp nightclub in the West End. He was there with his missus, Angie, and he waved at me across the nightclub and mouthed "The Scene" and gave me a thumbs up.'

Although Frank Jr had a job as a fish porter, David knew he was busy robbing post offices and banks and was attracted by the prospect of easy money. 'I wasn't supposed to know and we didn't talk about it as a family but we did all know what was going on and that made it more acceptable, I suppose,' he said. 'Frank was very successful and it did make some people jealous. He kept his own counsel and was quite secretive. He would just tell us not to listen to arseholes talking rubbish. He was right.'

It wasn't long before David was in trouble with the police again, but this time he was wrongly accused of breaking into a shop in East Street, in Walworth. 'I'm not saying I hadn't done any shops down there, I just hadn't done that one,' he said. 'There were about eight of us walking past when we saw the police and, of course, we ran away. I got caught and when I told the cozzer my name, he said: "You'll do."'

'So, it was off to Carter Street nick for another belting. My mother got a solicitor and when it came to court it was clear that it was impossible for the cozzer who said he'd seen me do it to have seen anything from where he said he was standing. It didn't matter, if a cozzer said you'd done it, you'd done it.'

David got a five-shilling fine but the shopkeeper knew he was innocent and paid it for him.

He then got himself a job in a bed-making factory, earning a decent wage of £17 a week and when he tired of that, went to work on a demolition site in the City. One day, as he was smashing through the brickwork in the bowels of the building, he was amazed to see a little train chugging by on the mail rail. 'It never occurred to me that there could have been money in that mail,' said David. 'I could have had the Little Train Robbery right there. To my shame, I let that pass me by.'

His father, Frank, however, was about to be invited to take part in the Great Train Robbery. But there was just one problem: he was already a wanted man. In the months immediately after his release from his sentence for stabbing Jack Spot,

Frank had busied himself setting up a one-armed bandit business with Albert Dimes, but also settling old scores. He set about firebombing the houses of prison officers in revenge for the way he had been treated on the inside. He even had an accomplice who would later become famous as a victim of the Kray twins' violence. Small-time thief, drug dealer and gangster George Cornell, who was later shot dead in the Blind Beggar pub by Ron Kray, was a close friend of Frank's. Cornell, known as Georgie, had married a local Elephant girl, Olive Hudd, who was a friend of Eva's from her shoplifting days in the Forty Thieves. Olive was a good hoister who used to work on Eva's team and the pair stayed great friends even after Eva's stealing days had ended. Georgie only came along for one attack but Frank didn't mind that he had lost his bottle.

Many people found George Cornell overbearing – in fact, as a youngster he went to the same school as the Kray twins and had picked on them, which is where animosity between them may have started – but Frank never had any trouble with him. When he was drunk, Georgie was a foolish loudmouth, but Frank liked him and had known his family for a long time, so was quick to forgive any shortcomings. The Krays, of course, were less forgiving.

Frank said: 'The petrol bombs were a personal thing for me and I wasn't expecting anyone else to want to join in but it was nice when Georgie did, even if it was only that one time. I didn't feel bad about what I was doing. I was trying to get back at them for the way they had treated me and my family when I was in prison.' The matter came to the attention of the police who suspected Frank but didn't have enough evidence to charge him.

Living in Brighton with Doreen, he also did a few favours for a man called Harry Rogers, who had taken over from Sammy Bellson as the so-called 'governor' of Brighton. Rogers believed his wife was having an affair with a man in Lewes, so Frank beat him up. Rogers also then asked Frank to burn down a rival bingo hall in Eastbourne, which he did willingly. When Frank asked Rogers for some money to pay him for the arson attack, the relationship between the two men soured. Frank had already helped one of Rogers' cronies, Jack the Rat, get a job on his release from prison. As a warning to Rogers, Frank beat up Jack the Rat and dumped him outside Rogers' home. Both men then went to the police, sending Frank on the run.

He holed up in a caravan in Clacton but still managed to pop up to Soho to collect his weekly pension from Billy Hill and look in on his nascent slot machines business. The business was chiefly run by Albert Dimes and Frank, but they had another man, Joe Wilkins, nephew of businessman and former Billy Hill associate Bert Wilkins, as a partner. On one such visit, he was having a quiet drink in the Bon Soir Club in Gerrard Street with Georgie Cornell when he bumped into Tommy Wisbey, who – unbeknown to Frank – was planning one of the most notorious robberies of the twentieth century. The pair parted that evening, but not before Wisbey had found out how to get in touch with Frank. The crucial contact, as always, was Eva.

Frank would call a couple of times a week from a phonebox near the caravan site to get messages. One day, shortly after the meeting in the Bon Soir, Eva told Frank that Wisbey urgently wanted a meet and asked him to get to Liverpool Street Station. When Frank turned up, he was taken immediately to the farm – Leatherslade Farm in Buckinghamshire – where the team, headed by the 'brains' of the operation, Gordon Goody, was assembled for the crime of the century.

The gang that carried out the robbery consisted of fifteen criminals predominantly from South London, including Gordon Goody, Charlie Wilson, Buster Edwards, Bruce Reynolds, Roy James, John Daly (who was later acquitted), Roger Cordrey, Jimmy White, Bob Welch, Tommy Wisbey, Jim Hussey and, of course, Ronnie Biggs. There were three more men who have never been identified, who got away scot free to enjoy their share of the £2.6 million haul – which would be worth around £50 million today.

Frank freely admitted that he was at the farm for two days while the robbery was being planned but, after discussions with Goody, it was decided that he was too much of a risk because he was already on his toes. 'I respected that decision and they knew they could trust me not to say a word about it to anyone once I left,' he said. 'Billy Hill only found out about the robbery after it had happened. One thing is for sure, if he had known about it, he would have wanted in. If he had organised it, they would have all got away with it.'

In the early hours of Thursday 12 August 1963, the team from Leatherslade Farm put their plan into action and pulled off the most daring and lucrative robbery that Britain had ever seen. After tampering with the signals to hold up a Royal Mail train at Cheddington in Buckinghamshire, the robbers overpowered the driver and his second in command, forcing them to drive the train to a bridge about half a mile down the line, where a truck was waiting. The gang then attacked the 'High Value Packages' carriage containing large quantities of money and registered mail. They seized 120 sacks before making off with their loot in a van, sparking a nationwide manhunt.

Frank insisted he did not take part in the robbery, although the fact that he admitted being there at all certainly puts him in the frame. Tommy Wisbey was there to provide muscle and back-up if needed and Frank's reputation as a hardman, who would do whatever it took to make a job succeed, suggests he was being brought in to work in the same vein. Frank took his role as guardian of the secrets of the farm very seriously indeed and would not be drawn on it, even though nearly all of the Great Train Robbers are now dead. David Fraser said: 'He hated hearing about criminals confessing what they had got up to if it was something notorious, such as the Great Train. For him, if he was there, then that was a sign that he was trusted. He believed that those secrets should go to the grave.'

As the police stepped up their search for the robbers, it wasn't long before Frank's name came up on the list of people who might help with their inquiries. Frank always felt that the police had inside information, as around a hundred or so thieves could have been responsible for pulling off such a robbery at that time. It could have been a very tricky situation indeed for Frank, given his past record, had he not been aided and abetted by two tough scrap metal dealers from

Camberwell, who would come to cast a very long shadow over the Fraser family for years to come.

Eddie and Charlie Richardson offered their friendship and their police contacts – and Frank accepted.

CHAPTER 15

THE NEW GUV'NOR OF SOHO

Frank met Eddie and Charlie Richardson for the first time when he went to thank them for helping Eva's husband, Jimmy, after he suffered a beating. Jimmy, who always had one eye on staying 'legit' enough to keep his betting licence, had refused to be press-ganged into driving for a criminal colleague of Frank's, Jack Rosa. Jack Rosa had previously stayed with Jimmy Brindle and Eva when he came out of prison but that night, in drink, had become violent.

Jimmy was out for a drink in the bar of the Masons Arms in East Street, just off Walworth Road, when the row kicked off. Jack Rosa and a couple of accomplices took umbrage after Jimmy refused to be their driver and resolved to exact retribution. Jimmy decided to make a quick exit. After fleeing through the bar, he jumped into a waiting car to escape. The vehicle happened to belong to the Richardson brothers. Jack Rosa and his henchmen didn't realise this and pulled out both Jimmy and the driver, Reggie Jones, and gave them a thorough going over.

When the Richardsons found out what had happened, they were furious. The brothers, local scrap metal dealers, were already building a fearsome reputation and were very handy with their fists. At this point they were in their late twenties and not about to let the opportunity for a good fight pass them by. They gathered two carloads of henchmen and sped to the Reform Club on Walworth Road, where – they guessed, correctly – the culprits would be found propping up the bar. Charlie floored one with a head-butt while Eddie knocked out another. Soon half a dozen men were laid out on the floor of the bar, with the whole room wondering who on earth these pugnacious brothers were. Ronnie Richardson, Charlie's widow, said: 'Charlie was not by nature violent but he had a temper when riled and he was a very powerful man with his fists. He had done some professional boxing when he was younger and sometimes had to settle fights in the scrapyard with bare knuckles.

'He was not the tallest, but he packed a mighty punch. He once knocked out four blokes who were twice his size, who were spoiling for a fight. I can well believe that he went to help out Jimmy Brindle because it would have offended his sense of justice that Jimmy had been jumped on like that, for nothing.'

When he found out what had happened, Frank wanted to thank the Richardson brothers, so he called around to see them at their scrapyard. Testing the water further, he asked if they would mind contributing to help pay for the defence of Frank's friend and partner in crime, Jimmy Essex. In gangland, such an invite is a show of how willing you are to help a colleague in need. The Richardsons agreed and Frank knew then that he had found people with whom he could do business.

In the 1960s, London was a complex network of corruption, in which the police were hand-in-glove with the very mobsters they were supposed to be bringing to justice. Bribes and backhanders were a way of life, in return for the law turning a blind eye. When Frank's name was in the frame for the Great Train Robbery, Charlie Richardson found out through police sources and let Frank know that he could help get him off the hook, further proving their worth. In order to run the scrap metal business effectively, Charlie Richardson had been making regular payments to police officers. Stolen metal found its way into their yard and the Richardsons didn't want the law looking too closely.

So, when Eddie Richardson told Frank he had a copper straightened and they could make his name disappear from police inquiries, he was only too pleased to accept. 'It wasn't something I paid them for, the Richardsons did it for me out of respect,' he said. 'I knew then that they were people I could trust. The Richardsons got me dropped out of the Train inquiry.'

The landscape of Soho, where Frank earned his money, was also undergoing a seismic shift. The Betting and Gaming Act 1960 did away with many of the seedy spielers and gambling dens, ushering in a new era. Albert Dimes, who was Frank's best friend as well as his business partner, wanted to take a step away from the one-armed bandit business in order to concentrate on his legitimate betting shop empire. With Frank's notorious reputation, it looked better for him if they no longer worked together. Albert felt bad about it, but working openly with Frank meant that he ran the risk of losing his betting licences.

Frank took it on the chin but privately grieved that he was losing his mentor. Albert was great at problem solving and seemed to be able to ease his way through complex situations, without offending too many people. 'In Soho, he was like the United Nations, with all the different factions, from the Italians to the Cockneys and the Maltese, coming to see him with their gripes,' said Frank. 'He was quite brilliant at it.'

At that point, Joe Wilkins still had a half share in the business but the prospect of working without Albert seemed too much for Frank, although he kept his real feelings very close to his chest. David Fraser said: 'Frank really wasn't a businessman in the sense of understanding how business worked at that point. He had learned a lot from Albert but when he set up without him, he wasn't used to the day-to-day dealings. For instance, he didn't even know how to cash a cheque and had to take them to Billy Hill to ask him what to do. He had spent so long robbing that the legitimate side of things was a bit of a mystery to him.'

Billy Hill, meanwhile, wanted to retire from running clubs and protection rackets in the West End. Together with his girlfriend Gypsy, he had already developed an interest in card sharping, following many holidays on the Riviera. With the help of his friends in the Corsican Mafia, he had learned a method of marking cards known as the Big Edge, which involved bending them slightly in a special mangle to denote whether they were high or low value. Another ruse was to use specially marked cards that could only be read by wearing glasses with coloured lenses. The cards were then wrapped in cellophane and appeared to the punter to be brand new when the croupier – helpfully supplied by the Corsican Mafia – opened the pack at the table. Billy and Gyp had spent hours studying the methods and training a team of sharps to use the Big Edge in casinos, fleecing the aristocracy. It wasn't fool-proof but it was enough to tip the odds in Billy's favour and he, Gyp and their team made thousands.

The private gambling clubs of Mayfair were their targets and soon they found themselves rubbing shoulders with the aristocracy, including Lord 'Lucky' Lucan and the Duke of Devonshire at the gaming tables of the Clermont Club in Berkeley Square. The Clermont was owned by John Aspinall, a charming social climber born into a middle-class colonial family, who was desperate to belong to the upper echelons of society and had made his club the place to be and be seen. The standard bet was £1,000 – around £25,000 in today's terms – and Billy and Gyp reaped rich rewards.

There have been claims that Aspinall was in on the swindle but Frank always insisted that Billy Hill had told him Aspinall was kept in the dark about what was going on and never took a cut – a view echoed by Aspinall's family. When Aspinall eventually worked out what has happening – after watching some of the leading lights of London society lose a fortune at his card tables – his pride prevented him from admitting that Billy Hill, the lowlife thief and gangster, had trounced him. Billy simply moved on to the next casino and started working his magic there. Frank was even called on to play a hand or two at times but he wasn't a great gambler. 'Billy didn't mind,' said Frank. 'I was only there to make up the numbers and all I had to do was look smart and lose.'

By this time, Frank had hit forty and, having spent half of

his life behind bars, wanted to make a real go of the one-armed bandits game, which was the closest to going straight that he would ever get. But he wasn't keen on working with Joe Wilkins long-term and needed to find a replacement. Looking around him, he realised there was one young man who seemed to fit the bill as the perfect business partner: Eddie Richardson. Eddie was an astute businessman but still had the gung-ho attitude towards violence, which Frank understood and valued so highly. He was also thirteen years Frank's junior, which meant he would have no problem providing physical back-up when the situation called for it.

When Frank approached Eddie, he readily accepted. Frank had opened the door from scrap metal dealing and running a pound shop in South London to a potential gold mine in the West End and Eddie couldn't wait to walk through it. The pair hit on the idea of expanding the one-armed bandits business to reach as many pubs and clubs as possible. Patrick Fraser said: 'Frank liked Eddie, especially after he helped out Jimmy Brindle and then put money in to Jimmy Essex's defence. He realised Eddie was a tough young guy – just what he needed around the business but the truth of the matter is that Eddie Richardson was nobody in the West End before Frank invited him in. That is not to be disrespectful; it is just how it was.

'Eddie could not just walk into the West End and set up as the boss. He was very much the junior partner and his operation was south of the river. Frank was best friends with Billy Hill and Albert Dimes and knew everyone; he had done a lot of villainy over the years and was totally respected. Frank was giving him a leg-up. There has been a lot of rubbish written about Frank being the henchman and that is all – but it is not true. Frank was the main power and had the "in" with all the right people. Eddie joined him, not the other way around.'

The pair needed cash, a lot more cash, to achieve their dream of dominating the West End with their one-armed bandit machines. Frank already had some capital from his previous venture with Albert Dimes and Eddie had put in a few thousand but it was not nearly enough. So Frank went to see Billy Hill, taking his new young business partner along with him. In doing so, he was partly looking for Billy Hill to approve his choice. Eddie passed with flying colours and Billy made a mental note to call on Eddie for a few favours in the future if he needed to. Frank then put his proposal for expansion to Billy, who went over to his safe and produced a stack of cash – £5,000 in total. He placed his hand on Frank's shoulder as he handed it over, saying: 'You're the guv'nor now.'

It was the moment Frank had been waiting for all his life but now the power was his, he wasn't sure he wanted to go it alone. Frank said: 'Billy gifted me all his interests in night-clubs in the West End at that point, as a way of saying that his time running things was over. I had always been able to look after myself but for years my loyalty was to him, first and foremost. He repaid that loyalty in coin and now he wanted to give me the whole show. Part of me accepted it gratefully but I was also clever enough to know that being a leader out there on your own can make it harder to stay at the top. Look at what happened to Jack Spot, for a start. I still wanted to have a team around me.'

Frank enjoyed the camaraderie of being part of a team, one of the Chaps, and it was natural for him to want to share what Billy had given him with Eddie Richardson. There was also an element of him nurturing Eddie, to bring him on in the same way that Billy Hill had done for him. The age gap between Eddie and Frank was the same as between Frank and Billy Hill. Frank added: 'We got to put our machines in all the clubs he had dealings with and all I had to do was pay a fella he knew £100 a month, until I had given him £1,700. That was all Billy wanted in return, to settle an old debt.

'He was still very much in the background but he didn't want to do any more bird and was more interested in his card games and having a quieter life with Gyp. I was only too happy to accept and with Eddie Richardson by my side, I didn't see how we could fail. It was a legitimate business – if you had our machines in your club, you didn't get any trouble.'

And so Atlantic Machines was launched from its headquarters in Windmill Street, and one-armed bandits went into Soho clubs including The Stork, The Astor, The Log Cabin and The Pigalle; not forgetting The Modernaires and The Cabinet Club – still owned by Aggie Hill. Frank used his contacts with the MP Captain Mark Hewitson to get the dipsomaniac Labour Peer Sir Noel Dryden on the books as the company's respectable figurehead, in return for regular money for booze.

The West End was buzzing and clubs attracted quite a starry clientele as Swinging London found its feet. On nights out, Frank rubbed shoulders with A-list celebrities such as Shirley Bassey and home-grown London talent such as Diana Dors and Barbara Windsor. Through Albert Dimes, he met the actor Stanley Baker – later Sir Stanley Baker – who was best known for his role in the 1964 film *Zulu*, in which he played an officer at Rorke's Drift, alongside Michael Caine.

Stanley was often to be found sharing a drink at the Astor with Frank and Albert. It wasn't long before Stanley – who was Welsh – introduced them to his movie star pal Richard Burton and his glamorous wife Elizabeth Taylor. David Fraser can remember his brother Frank Jr rushing home to Brixton one night to breathlessly tell him: 'I've just met Elizabeth Taylor and she was fucking gorgeous!'

David wasn't overly impressed. He had not long returned from a Bank Holiday trip down to Margate with his fellow Mods and had unwittingly become a part of British social history by taking part in a pitched battle with a gang of Rockers. The Mods and Rockers warfare gripped seaside towns during the mid-1960s and David was there for inaugural battles at both Clacton and Margate. 'I remember the first fight breaking out very clearly,' he said. 'We were drinking in a little cafe and a friend of mine, Johnny Richardson, from Walworth, was having a row with his girlfriend, Sheila.

'Some rockers stepped in, trying to be gentlemen, and everyone ended up having a fight, which spilled out into the street. A load of motorcycles got pushed over. Suddenly there were hundreds of us joining in. It was the first time I really understood there was strength in numbers. I ran along the beach and picked up a lump of wood. God knows what I thought I was going to do with it. When the beach ran out I just dropped it.

'I was a young man and full of anger. It didn't take much

to get me going back then. There was the whole thing about the lower classes and particularly teenagers wanting to make their feelings known and, looking back, I had a lot of anger in me from my dad leaving when I was younger, I suppose. There came a point when I just wondered what it was all for. I started to prefer to shrug my shoulders and walk away, unless I was really pushed. After a couple more Bank Holiday trips down with the Mods I had enough of it and it just sort of fell away. I was too busy thieving and I was never into scooters. I had a Mini instead.'

Frank wasn't the sort of bloke who was bowled over by stardom either – quite the reverse, and that was part of his charm. He judged men on whether they were decent – in criminal terms – or not and with the fairer sex, he had a weakness for a pretty woman, particularly if she was blonde.

However, film star or not, Stanley Baker proved his mettle as one of the Chaps on more than one occasion and that stood him in good stead with Frank, who only revealed shortly before his death the full extent of what the actor had got up to on his behalf. Shockingly for a man who was later knighted, the more time Stanley Baker spent time with Frank, the more he was prepared to aid and abet his criminal pal.

Stanley enjoyed the frisson of hanging around with genuine crooks and even drew on his experiences with Frank and Albert for his role in the 1960 film, *The Criminal* – playing an anti-hero, an ex-convict who robs a racetrack and gets caught, leading to his return to prison. The film's violent portrayal of prison life led to it being banned in several countries, although it fell far short of anything Frank experienced on the inside and Stanley loved to hear Frank's stories about his time in the jail. But when the filming stopped and Stanley was in Soho, he found himself – willingly – drawn deeper into Frank's world.

The first time Stanley Baker blurred the boundaries between being a law-abiding citizen and one of the Chaps came in July 1965, after the Great Train Robber Ronnie Biggs escaped from Wandsworth. Frank had been out drinking in Soho with Stanley and the pair were making their way back to the offices of Atlantic Machines in Windmill Street when Frank spotted someone lying spreadeagled on Stanley's Bentley, wearing a convict's outfit. Frank was about to tell the man to hop it, thinking he was a drunk, when his friend Patsy Fleming – an ex-con and old mate from his school days, who was working at Atlantic as a mechanic – recognised the man on the car from prison.

Months earlier, Fleming had been on remand in Brixton with this bloke, Andy Anderson, who had told him he was planning to escape, as he was serving twelve years. Patsy had laughingly told him to come and find Frank at Atlantic Machines if he ever made it. Anderson had been in the exercise yard at Wandsworth one afternoon at three, when a rope ladder was thrown over the wall. He immediately climbed up it, making it to the top of the wall first. Ronnie Biggs and East Londoner Eric Flowers followed, as well as another man, Doyle, who also took his chance to escape. The plan had been only to help Biggs and Flowers but the rescue committee, who had parked by the prison wall in two vans, found it amusing that other prisoners had seized their chance to get away. Anderson and Doyle, who were wearing prison shirts and uniforms, were given a van, plus £2 each to aid their getaway.

They went their separate ways after their van broke down and Anderson – astonishingly – caught the Tube into town wearing his prison overalls, which were blue, with a bright yellow stripe down either side of his leg. Patrick Fraser said: 'Stanley Baker didn't hesitate when my dad asked him to help. They bundled Anderson into the offices of Atlantic Machines and found someone to swap clothes with him. They knew he was red hot and he couldn't stay in Soho, he needed somewhere to hide.

'Frank hit on the idea of taking Anderson to his mother's, Lady Margaret's, in the Borough but the question was how they were going to get him there when every cozzer was on the lookout for him because he had got away with Ronnie Biggs, the Great Train Robber. Stanley immediately volunteered to help by hiding Anderson in his car.'

Anderson was rushed outside and lay down on the back seat of Stanley Baker's car. He was covered with a blanket but was peeking out as Stanley looked over his shoulder and reversed out into the street, while Frank sat in the passenger seat. It was a nerve-wracking drive from Soho to South London, as the streets were crawling with policemen searching for the jail-breakers. But who would have suspected the actor Stanley Baker gliding along in his Bentley? No one, as it turned out.

Once he was safely delivered to Lady Margaret, who readily agreed to help out, Stanley and Frank resumed their night out. Anderson lay low in the flat for a few days while Lady Margaret made sure he had enough to eat. He passed his time watching the television and listening to radio reports about the manhunt. Anderson was moved on to stay with Eva for a few nights. Frank then organised for him to be spirited away to Scotland.

It didn't matter to Frank that he had never met Anderson before. The criminal fraternity was just that – a brotherhood of sorts. Frank looked on it as his duty to help a man on the run because he knew that the next time it could be him needing help. But Stanley Baker didn't stop there. Frank's criminal contacts in Glasgow had arranged to pick Anderson up at Waverley station in Edinburgh, so Stanley Baker loaned Frank his Bentley. An Atlantic Machines worker – most likely Patsy Fleming – dressed up as a chauffeur and drove Frank and Anderson up to Edinburgh with a flask of tea and sandwiches, helpfully provided by Lady Margaret. Anderson was on his toes for eight months before he was recaptured.

He never knew who the mystery man with the car was because Frank was careful not to mention Stanley's name to Anderson in order to protect the actor, whose career was about to peak with his role in *Zulu*. His cover was almost blown on film night at HMP Durham when Anderson and the other convicts were shown the famous film. Patrick said: 'When Stanley Baker came on screen, Anderson started looking rather quizzical and then halfway through the film, the penny dropped. He almost shouted out: "That's the bloke who helped me escape in Soho!" when one of the Great Train Robbers elbowed him the ribs and told him to shut up because the screws were taking quite an interest in what he was saying. It would have caused a furore at the time if it had come out.'

The second time the actor became one of the Chaps was when the police raided the offices of Atlantic Machines and found some thunder-flash grenades stored there. Frank hadn't known about it but one of his ex-con mechanics was keeping them for a robbery he had planned. Shotguns were also regularly stashed in the offices but on this occasion, luckily, there were none. However, it was still a criminal offence to keep thunder-flashes, which required a licence from the War Office. Billy Hill was called in to help via his police contacts and he persuaded Stanley Baker to come to the rescue again, preventing Frank and Eddie Richardson having to answer awkward questions. Stanley found a film producer who was willing to say he had only stored them at Atlantic Machines because he had missed a flight and was intending to take them overseas for a film he was working on. Fortunately for Frank, the ruse worked.

Business was booming and Atlantic Machines soon expanded from London to Manchester, Newcastle, Liverpool, Staffordshire, Scarborough and Wales. The machines were six old pennies a go and the profits were split 50–50 between the club and Atlantic Machines, with a one-armed bandit taking around £80 a week. Teams of up to a dozen mechanics – most of them Frank's old mates from prison – were paid in cash. George Cornell did a bit of work for them as a mechanic around this time. 'He could come and go and put in a few hours for us whenever he fancied,' said Frank. 'The only trouble I'd ever known from him was when he was drunk and got a bit loudmouthed but otherwise he was really very sensible and he could handle himself in the clubs so there was no worry there.'

Mechanics would have to be prepared to deal with local troublemakers who shoved buttons or duff coins into the machines to try to cheat them, causing hundreds of pounds worth of damage. Frank and Eddie deliberately paid their men well to avoid them stealing the profits. It was a wise move, given that they were employing thieves. Judged by criminal standards, Atlantic Machines was a straight business but Frank and Eddie were never going to be mugs. 'There were other rival operators and gangs who wanted in and we had to protect our interests,' said Frank. 'That was no different to running clubs, which I had known all about for years. We had a tough reputation and we were more than prepared to sort things out when required.'

But in terms of the club owners themselves, Frank and Eddie found they were more than happy to have Atlantic Machines offering their services. 'Our reputations preceded us on that,' he said. 'I would use my prison contacts in a particular area to find out who the local gangs were and then we would pay them a visit and make it clear that Atlantic Machines were going in and we didn't want any trouble. You never found a club owner who complained about that and they knew that once our machines were in, we could take care of any undesirable elements too. It was easy money for them and we made sure that the machines were always working.'

In Frank's world this did not amount to any kind of protection racket. It never crossed his mind that the club owners themselves might have known better than to refuse Atlantic Machines when they offered to install the one-armed bandits.

Perhaps, given Frank's reputation and the murky goings-on

in clubland, it was too much to expect that it was all going to be plain sailing. But Atlantic Machines was about to enter very choppy waters indeed and in many ways, Frank was already out of his depth.

CHAPTER 16

BRITAIN'S MOST WANTED

It was the year in which England won the World Cup, hemlines were short, hair was long and the clubbing scene in Swinging London reached its zenith.

For Frank Fraser, 1966 should have been a boom time. Instead, a fight in a nightclub – a chance fracas fuelled by drink – led to the downfall of not one, but two criminal empires. Much has been made of the end of the Kray twins' East End network of terror but without events involving Frank Fraser and Eddie Richardson at a little-known nightclub in Catford, their reign might have gone on for many years longer.

Frank was always very respectful to the legend that built up around the Kray twins in later years, not least because he became very close to them in prison. They were united by virtue of the fact that they were all social pariahs. But Frank was also a man who wanted to set the record straight and, privately, he would confess that back in their heyday, the Krays were 'little more than thieves ponces, just like their father'. He said: 'I'm proud to say I knew them because I liked them and they were good to my sister, Eva, but really, they were not people I would be seriously threatened by. They talked about being poor and how it made them tough. Seeing the Kray twins and the way they grew up made it look to me like their lives, even back then, were the lap of luxury compared to mine.'

It wasn't Frank's style to want to 'big up' his role in gangland – bearing the name Frank Fraser was enough – but he was always clear on one thing: he never saw the Kray twins as a threat. Frank was in a different league to the Krays. He knew it and they knew it. Eddie Richardson was a very dangerous man but if he had been on his own, they might have chanced having a pop at him. His close association with Frank, however, made him untouchable.

That didn't stop them wanting a slice of the action in the West End and tensions between the Krays and Frank and the Richardsons had been simmering for some time before they boiled over into fatal aggression. With Billy Hill taking a back seat, the Krays were coming into their own as nightclub bosses and enjoyed parties with a starry clientele, including Frank Sinatra, Shirley Bassey and Judy Garland. They also posed for photographer David Bailey, cementing their reputation as Sixties' icons. But they wanted more than just celebrity friends and public acclaim; they were jealous of the success of Atlantic Machines, particularly because of some nice little earners Frank and Eddie had picked up on the side. Once again, Frank's contacts with the criminal underworld had proved crucial.

This time the tip had come from old-time crook Jack 'Ruby' Sparks, who was one of Frank's all-time favourite thieves because he had not only pulled off a major jewellery heist and taken part in the Dartmoor Mutiny of 1932, but had also showed great kindness to Frank when he was doing his first prison sentence, by sneaking him food in solitary confinement.

Ruby got his nickname for a raid on a Maharajah's penthouse in Park Lane in the 1930s, in which he got away with £40,000 worth of rubies. He then sold them for pennies because he thought they were fakes. He had also famously once escaped from Dartmoor after copying a warder's key. He never got close enough to steal the key but memorised its shape and worked on a copy in his cell. Ever the enterprising thief, he got together his escape money by running a crooked dice game in the prison. Frank found a kindred spirit in Ruby. In turn, Ruby looked on Frank as a son and always gave him money when he came home from prison, to help him get back on his feet.

Ruby introduced Frank and Eddie Richardson to a man who was involved in a car parking scam at Heathrow – which was then called London Airport. The man wanted a greater share of the takings and was happy to give a cut to Frank and Eddie, in return for their muscle. The scheme was so successful that the man was worried that the Krays would hear of it and want in – so getting Frank and Eddie involved was insurance against Ron and Reg trying to take it over. The fiddle involved changing the time stamps on the tickets and creaming off a lot of the money that should have gone into the tills. Frank's way of getting into the scheme had all the hallmarks of his role as an enforcer. 'We waited for the two car park attendants to come off their shift and we kidnapped them,' he said. 'We took them back to Atlantic Machines and had a nice chat.'

There were no cups of tea involved, of course, and it wasn't nearly as cosy as Frank made out. The car park attendants, who had just endured a bumpy ride in the boot of Eddie's car all the way from the airport, were slung into the cellars of Atlantic Machines. Frank and Eddie then proceeded to put the frighteners on them. 'We had two rooms down there which were very handy because they looked like cells, with bars on the doors,' said Frank. 'I shoved them in and asked them which one they wanted to die in. I wasn't going to kill them, of course. It was just a case of showing them that we had the determination to do something. They gave in really quickly. I don't think I even gave anyone as much as a slap.'

The second sideline to Atlantic Machines was an involvement on the fringes of the porn industry. Jimmy Humphreys, the legendary 1960s porn boss, was running blue movies in seedy rooms all over Soho at that time, in league with Maltese crooks. Ticket touts would bring punters in and take a cut of the profits. Eddie and Frank asked Jimmy Humphreys if he would 'mind if they put their machines into the clubs'. Frank said that Humphreys readily agreed. The truth of the matter is that he had little choice. Frank's heavies from Atlantic Machines raided room after room, beat up the touts and took all the film equipment, only returning it on the understanding that they would be taking a large slice of the profits from now on.

Roughing up a few ticket touts amounted to small beer for Frank but that did not mean he had curbed his violent tendencies. If anything, he was becoming more brutal. Where he once used a razor – a chiv – he now carried an axe. One of those on the receiving end of it was a henchman of the Krays. This has led some commentators to conclude that there was all-out warfare between the Krays and the Richardsons at this stage, but that is merely some crime writers' convenient shorthand for a far more complex situation. There was rivalry but it was interspersed with a tangle of personal likes and dislikes, which cut a lot of ice with both Frank and the Krays.

Eric Mason, who had earlier beaten up Jimmy Brindle in Walworth with Jack Rosa, was on the receiving end of the most horrific axe attack from Frank. Mason's beating up of Eva's husband may have had something to do with Frank's retribution, but the comment that lit the blue touch paper was an inference that the twins were going to come down on Frank like a ton of bricks. Even at the age of ninety, shortly before his death, Frank could still recount what had happened in vivid detail, without a flicker of emotion or a shred of remorse in his eyes.

Frank had been drinking in the Astor nightclub with Eddie one night early in 1965 when a fight broke out. The police were called and Frank and Eddie were leaving by the back door when they met Eric Mason. 'He said something to the effect of the twins weren't going to stand for it. The fight had been nothing to do with us anyway but I wasn't going to have him talking to me, issuing veiled threats like that, on my manor,' said Frank.

'So, I kidnapped him and took him off in our car to Atlantic Machines offices. We were quite polite with him at first, down in the cellar. I told him to have a seat and then said we needed to have a chat. He was looking worried. I happened to have my chopper with me, inside my jacket, and I pulled it out as I turned and said: "The twins won't like what, Eric?" He held his hands up, as if to say "Sorry" and I went for him with it: "Take that back to fucking Vallance Road."

'I got him on the head first and then I went for his legs. He fell off the chair. There was blood everywhere. The amazing thing was, he kept getting back up. I couldn't believe it. I chopped at his arm a bit. He was screaming. I wanted to pay him for what he had said and I think I made myself clear. It sounds extreme but he had it coming. He shouldn't have gone around saying things like that to me.

'He had been a fairly decent guy up until then and I had known him in prison but he took a liberty and had to be paid for it. When I realised he wasn't going to die, I wrapped him up in a blanket and we drove him to hospital in White-chapel. We flung him out of the car. I think he was in hospital for quite a long time after that.'

No charges were ever brought against Frank because Eric Mason stuck to the criminal code and did not make any complaint to the police. When Mason got out of hospital he went to see the twins at their home in Vallance Road because he was on the Firm, one of their men, so he expected retribution for what Frank had done. His arm was twisted and he was dragging his leg where Frank had sliced at him with the axe. 'Look what Fraser did to me,' he said. The twins took one look at him, gave him £50 and sent him on his way. They were not about to take on Frank Fraser, that much was clear.

What they hoped, by keeping Frank sweet, was to have the chance to run some one-armed bandits in the porn clubs. They had already tried to curry favour by asking him for a drink over in The Grave Maurice, their favourite watering hole in Whitechapel. They let him know that one of their crooked police contacts had heard Frank was wanted over a wounding case – which came to nothing. A few months later they came to see Frank to ask him in person if he would mind if they got involved in the porn clubs and he told them, politely but firmly, 'No'. 'It was business and I had known them since they were little boys, so I didn't have a problem refusing them,' he said. 'I don't think they were delighted but they took the information on board. Ronnie particularly was not happy. Reg was OK about it. Ronnie then met George Cornell in the Stork club a few nights later and asked him again if he could try to find a way in for them. He said he couldn't and a big row between them kicked off.'

In fact, this was the row in which George Cornell is supposed to have called Ronnie a 'fat poof' – which effectively signed his own death warrant. Eva and her husband, Jimmy, were beside George in the club that night when the row took place. She later told her family that George had tried to make light of the situation and laugh off his gaffe with Ron, but had failed to appreciate how much offence he had caused.

Frank said: 'The row was over the twins coming in on Atlantic Machines but you have got to remember that George had been at school with the twins and had picked on them when they were little. There were long-standing resentments going on.'

Frank added: 'Ron was not open about being a poof – I

had only heard rumours about it back then – and he certainly didn't like comments being made about his weight so George was on dodgy ground there. He could be foolish in drink and turn very nasty. That was the George who mouthed off at Ronnie Kray that night, not the George who I worked with and knew and liked.'

In the background, as fate would have it, loomed the figure of Billy Hill. He had built Frank up and now, paradoxically, it was a request from Billy which would bring him down. Frank and Eddie were called to Billy's flat in Moscow Road, Bayswater, for a meet. They were asked to do a favour for some contacts of Billy's from Manchester and readily agreed.

The plan was to go and mind a club, Mr Smith's and the Witchdoctor, over in Catford, because the owners had been having some trouble with local tearaways. Frank said: 'We were hoping to put our machines in as well, in return for supplying the doormen. We had no idea of how things were going to turn out.'

The owners had promised to pay Frank and Eddie £100 a week – over £1,200 in today's terms. Frank and Eddie had looked over the club in the afternoon that particular Monday, 7 March, and then returned later in the evening. They took three of their men with them: Harry Rawlings, Ronnie Jeffreys and Billy Staynton.

When they got there, they found a group of men having a drink, some of whom were local 'faces'. They were Peter Hennessy, Billy Haward, Dickie Hart, Billy Gardiner and Henry Botton. Another friend, Jimmy Moody – a notorious hitman who later worked for the IRA – looked in on the club that night and joined Frank and Eddie for a drink. At one point, Henry Botton – who knew Frank from prison – said he was a bit hard up and Frank generously gave him £50.

What neither Frank nor Eddie had appreciated was that these local 'faces' thought the presence of Frank, Eddie and their men meant they were in for trouble. Billy Haward had been having an affair with the wife of one of the Atlantic Machine mechanics, and assuming retribution was going to be rained down on him, he sent out for guns. This was a game changer, as when the club was ready to close and Eddie Richardson tried – politely but firmly – to tell the men it was time to go home, a fight ensued and Haward and Hart started waving the guns around.

Rawlings leant over and tried to grab the shotgun from Haward, and Dickie Hart, who had a revolver, shot Rawlings in the arm. Hennessy chose this moment, as blood spurted out of Rawlings like a geyser, to have a full-on fist fight with Eddie Richardson on the dancefloor. He was a big man but no match for the powerful fists of Richardson, who pummelled him mercilessly on the ground, as guns went off left, right and centre.

Never one to hold back, Frank had jumped on Hart as soon as he saw the state of Harry Rawling's arm. The pair tussled their way into a back room, Hart still holding the revolver. Several others from both groups piled in after them. As Frank belted Hart one with his right hand, he grabbed Hart's wrist with his left, pushing the gun downwards. A shot was fired. A bullet ripped through Frank's thigh bone, shattering it. He went down, collapsing on the bloodstained floor.

Hart dropped the gun. Someone then picked up the

revolver, turned it on Dickie Hart and blasted him with it. Eddie was shot in the back of the leg as he fled the scene with Jimmy Moody, who had tied a tourniquet around Harry Rawling's arm, preventing him from bleeding to death.

Frank limped away from the scene carrying the murder weapon, his leg badly broken, and collapsed in a nearby garden. He was unable to flee much further and threw the revolver into a little alleyway over the garden wall, before crawling about fifty yards up the road and attempting to hide. But the police had by now turned up and, after finding Hart's body, were combing the area. It wasn't long before Frank was found.

He was taken to hospital in Catford, where his wounds were treated and he was put under police guard. He refused to say anything, hoping that everyone else there that night would do the same, as was the protocol. Eddie and Harry Rawlings were driven to hospital in Dulwich by Jimmy Moody and they soon came to the attention of the police because of their gunshot wounds, but they too refused to talk. However, Henry Botton – who Frank had loaned £50 – said he had seen Frank shoot Dickie Hart. That was enough for the police. Although Botton later retracted his evidence, at the time he told them: 'Two men went into that room with a gun – Dickie and Fraser – and only one man came out.' This still implicated Frank and it was enough for the police to charge him with murder.

In reality, there were a number of men in the room when Hart got shot. While it is true to say that Frank removed the murder weapon from the scene, he insisted that he did not actually shoot Hart. 'The cozzers would love to know who did it, even after all these years, but I am saying nothing,' he added.

When Frank's son David heard about the shooting and his dad being injured, he went to the hospital and found Frank lying there with his leg up, the bed surrounded by police officers. 'I asked him if he was OK and he told me to be lucky but not to come again because he was worried that the Old Bill would try to put me in the picture,' David said. 'As it happened, he was right. I hadn't been out of that hospital five minutes when I was arrested and taken to Catford police station for questioning. They wanted to know where I was on the night of the murder, all of that stuff. It was nothing to do with it but they were going to try to use me against my dad. They had to let me go.'

Years later, when David Fraser was in prison, on the special wing at Brixton, the prisoner next door to him was accused of murdering Henry Botton. Inmates are allowed their own court case papers and this prisoner shared that information with David. Leafing through the evidence, he was astonished to find police records dating back to that fateful night at Mr Smith's. David said: 'It turns out that Botton became a police informer that night. His withdrawing of his original evidence was a cover. He pointed the finger at Frank and that stuck. He did it to get himself off the hook on other stuff. The cozzers wanted my dad on a murder charge pretty badly. I always suspected it but in our game you can't call someone a rat unless you have evidence. I was there with the evidence in my hands, all those years later, and Botton was now dead, shot on his own doorstep. I can't say I shed a tear over that.'

Tommy Butler, the lead officer on the Great Train Robbery

inquiry, took over the Mr Smith's murder case. He had always felt that Frank had more to do with the Train Robbery than he could pin on him and saw his chance for justice to be done. Eddie Richardson was charged with affray, along with Jimmy Moody, Billy Haward, Ronnie Jeffreys, Harry Rawlings and Henry Botton. They were all remanded to Brixton prison while Frank was treated in the hospital wing, where the actor Stanley Baker came to visit him.

Two days after the fight at Mr Smith's, Ron Kray took matters into his own hands in the Blind Beggar and changed the landscape of gangland irrevocably. Pundits have postulated many theories about why Ronnie shot George Cornell. As well as the slight of Ron being called a 'fat poof', it was mooted that the Krays were annoyed with George for going south of the river with the Richardsons. This, as Frank pointed out, was nonsense. George had married Eva's friend, former Forty Thieves member Olive Hudd, in 1955, and was happily settled there with his children. Frank was clear about one thing, though had he not been laid up in hospital and facing a murder charge, with Eddie also in prison, Ron Kray would never have shot George Cornell. 'I would have made sure of that,' said Frank. 'It is a fact that he never would have dared do that to George if I had been around. It was only because I was laid up with the broken leg and facing a murder charge that Ron saw the way was clear to settle the score with George, who he had never liked anyway.'

Cornell and his friend Albie Woods had been over to see one of Frank's old pals, Jimmy Andrews, who was in hospital after an unrelated shooting. On the way back, the pair stopped in the Blind Beggar for a quick pint and seated themselves at the bar. At about 8.30 p.m., on 9 March, Ronnie Kray walked in.

A drunk sitting by the door said: 'Oh, hello, Ron.'

Cornell barely had time to turn around and say: 'Well, look what the cat's dragged in,' before Ronnie took out a 9mm Luger and shot him in the head. Ronnie then turned on his heels in the crowded pub and calmly walked out. The drunk, not realising what had just happened, then said: 'Oh, bye, Ron.'

As Cornell lay dying, Albie Woods carefully grabbed all the glasses he could from the bar, so that the police couldn't take fingerprints and start tracing people for questioning.

The police failed to find any witnesses to the Cornell murder, despite the pub being packed – no one was going to speak out about the Krays at that point – but the twins took up Billy Hill's invite to let the heat die down and travelled to Tangier in Morocco. Billy had opened a nightclub there with Gyp and was heavily involved in smuggling, including gun running. Gyp, meanwhile, found her calling as the glittering hostess of Churchill's – which became a magnet for everyone from local dignitaries to the Rolling Stones. Reg brought a girlfriend along with him and Ron chased after a lot of handsome local young men.

The holiday was cut short, however, when the head of the local police came to inform them that the twins had to leave, as they were deemed undesirable. Their notoriety preceded them and word of their murderous exploits in London had reached the ears of the powers that be. Billy Hill had the local police chief in his pay, of course, but the decision to eject them had been taken at national level and there was nothing he could do, so they returned, tanned, to England.

With hindsight, Frank said that the whole thing – Mr Smith's and the shooting of George Cornell – came down to stupidity in drink. 'A couple of drunken arguments and two empires came crashing down, just like that. We always knew there were people circling, who wanted us out, but once I was up on the murder charge things just started to unravel.'

He told the boys, David and Patrick, privately, that what happened with Ron blasting George Cornell in the face in a crowded pub was 'sheer stupidity'. In public he was more circumspect, out of respect for his erstwhile gangland rivals.

Frank's murder trial was the first of the Mr Smith's court cases to get underway. Tommy Butler, the head of the Flying Squad, could smell victory. He knew Frank had killed people before and got away with it. This time he was confident they were going to get their man. The trouble was, Frank did not murder Dickie Hart.

Frank had received word from Eddie Richardson and the others that they would not go into the witness box in their affray trial, so he should do the same on the murder charge, leaving it to his barrister to put his case instead. It was all going well for the prosecution until it emerged that the police, in their desperation to secure a conviction, had tampered with the evidence. It was not their finest hour. Frank said: 'A cozzer from Southwark had said he found the gun lying next to me in the garden where I was, with my leg broken. The only problem was, I had chucked it in a little alleyway about fifty yards away. They were done in by an honest policeman who had made a note of all the officers present that night. This patrolman from Southwark – who I honestly think was a put up by Tommy Butler to get me – wasn't even there.

'It broke their hearts but the case got chucked and rightly so. I was acquitted because I didn't actually murder Dickie Hart. That is not to say that in the heat of the moment it couldn't have been me but in this case it was not.'

Frank still had to face an affray charge and he got five years – a hefty sentence. 'It was probably made worse because I didn't go into the witness box to defend myself but I had agreed with Eddie and the others that was the way we were going on it and so I had to stick by that decision,' he said. 'Five years wasn't going to break me. I had done a seven for the Spot slashing.'

He returned to Wandsworth prison and awaited the outcome of the rest of the Mr Smith's trials. Atlantic Machines sank without trace – no one wanted to carry it on. The machines literally disappeared overnight. Few mourned Frank and Eddie leaving Soho – least of all porn baron Jimmy Humphreys and his Maltese cohorts, who had seen their own profits eroded.

David, then aged seventeen, was not there to support his dad in court because he was serving his first detention sentence in Aldington, Kent, for shopbreaking. 'They were wicked bastards,' he said. 'I got quite a few beltings and I was with another boy from Brixton, a black kid. Every time I got hit the screws called me a "bastard" and every time he got hit, he was called "black bastard". The racism was unbelievable. He told me he didn't mind the beatings so much as being called names.' His older brother Frank Jr was away on a three-year sentence in Maidstone for robbing Post Office vans and managed to lose six months' remission for taking part in a riot.

Two days before the 1966 World Cup Final, the jury in Eddie Richardson's affray trial failed to reach a verdict and a retrial was ordered. On the day of the big match, David Fraser and his fellow detention centre inmates lined up on chairs in the common room to listen to the match on a portable radio. 'We had to sit up straight, in silence. The miserable screws wouldn't let us cheer,' he said.

While England celebrated a thumping 4-2 victory against West Germany and Bobby Moore collected the gleaming Jules Rimet trophy, Frank and the Richardsons found little to celebrate. Eddie's younger brother Charlie was arrested in a dawn raid, along with seventeen alleged accomplices and the newspaper headlines screamed of torture, electric shocks and people nailed to the floor in the Richardsons' scrapyard, as gangland terror reached new heights.

Frank found himself given the most controversial soubriquet for supposedly pulling out a victim's teeth with pliers. It was another name that never left him: The Dentist.

CHAPTER 17

SHEER TORTURE

When it came, the fall of Frank and the Richardsons' criminal empire was like a house of cards tumbling down. The whole structure had become unstable after the Mr Smith's affair, but it was the dealings of Charlie Richardson that sealed their fate and led to its total collapse.

Society was outraged by the 'Wild West' style gunfight at Mr Smith's, followed so closely by the Krays' shooting of George Cornell in a crowded pub. It seemed, to Sixties London, as if the lawless were getting the upper hand. The police, politicians and the judiciary – fuelled by the headline writers, who had a field day – had had enough.

Right on cue, the shady business dealings of Charlie Richardson began to unravel. As well as the scrap metal yard in London and a series of fraudulent businesses, Charlie had invested in a perlite mine in South Africa. Mining was his one true passion but violence lurked just beneath the surface of his day-to-day dealings and it was to prove a weak link. A domestic dispute between Charlie's mining partner, Tom Waldeck, and one of their henchmen, Johnnie Bradbury, was the lynchpin in the whole saga.

Bradbury, who liked a drink and was a loudmouth with it, had been having an affair with Waldeck's wife, causing trouble for Charlie. Charlie sacked Bradbury, but that didn't stop Bradbury turning up on Waldeck's doorstep and shooting him in cold blood. He was arrested for murder, tried and found guilty and sentenced to hang in 1966 in Johannesburg – just as the Mr Smith's trials were getting underway in Britain. He then proceeded to sing like a canary to save himself from the noose. It was music to the ears of the British constabulary, who were desperate to have something to pin on Frank and the troublesome Richardson brothers. A couple of officers flew to South Africa to collect evidence in the warm sunshine.

And what evidence it was. Bradbury told tales of Richardson Gang torture techniques, with victims nailed to the floor and having their fingers and toes removed with bolt cutters. Some, allegedly, were stripped naked, dunked in a cold bath and had their genitals wired to a 'black box', which gave them electric shocks and burned their skin. Others were tied to a chair, beaten until they bled and then made to mop up their own blood with their underpants before being given a clean shirt and sent on errands – a practice known as 'taking a shirt from Charlie'. Those requiring 'special treatment' received a visit from Frankie Fraser, who tied them up before forcibly removing their teeth with pliers. Frank made no secret of his violent tendencies but even he was surprised – amazed, in fact – by the allegations he now faced and the things he was supposed to have done for Charlie.

Eddie had pulled out of working at the scrapyard with his brother Charlie and there were already signs of tensions and rivalry between the two, which would later turn into a major falling out. Frank was something of a go-between, a peace-maker in the relationship. Although Frank was in business with Eddie first and foremost, he genuinely liked both brothers and was happy to lend Charlie a hand – or rather, his fists – from time to time. This was seen as the norm in their business and they did not expect people to go squealing to the police about getting 'a clipping' for their transgressions, which usually involved quite large sums of cash. Frank said: 'I gave people quite a few clumps and there were occasions when I helped Charlie bring people in for a bit of a beating because they owed him money, but the idea that I pulled anyone's teeth out with pliers is just ridiculous.'

But the evidence against him was mounting. Back in London, the police set about finding more proof of the nefarious activities of the Torture Gang. They found it surprisingly easy. The Richardsons and Frank were all behind bars and there were a number of willing witnesses, some of whom were already facing charges for fraud or were serving time. Charlie had employed a number of these fraudsters in his 'long firms': the firms worked by Charlie and his frontmen placing lots of small orders with wholesalers and getting a good credit history before placing large orders with the same supplier. Once the goods arrived, Charlie and his men would promptly shut up shop and sell the goods elsewhere. It was a brilliant ruse for making some quick money. Once one firm closed, Charlie would get another frontman to open another business in a different part of London. Sometimes there would be a warehouse or shop fire, just to make the con look more convincing.

A lot of the fraudsters used aliases and were smooth-talking charmers who could lie their way in and out of anything. On occasion, they double-crossed Charlie as well, which is where Frank came in. These fraudsters, Frank would later say, were the lowest of the low, skilled operators who would say anything to the police to get off the hook. They were conmen, pure and simple. If there was honour among thieves, they had none.

These were the men used by the police as their main witnesses, in return for them being given reduced sentences, police protection and, in some cases, new identities. One of them – Christopher Glinski – had an even more colourful claim to fame, yet this didn't seem to make him any less attractive to the Metropolitan Police. Glinksi had been charged with perjury after the Spot–Dimes trial back in 1957, when he appeared as a witness for the Reverend Basil Andrews, the dodgy vicar who swore blind that Dimes had started the fight and then recanted his faith.

The police operation was headed up by Gerald McArthur, Assistant Chief Constable of the Regional Crime Squad, who appeared to have a link to one of the main witnesses, James Taggart, whose girlfriend had given evidence in an earlier trial. Taggart approached him – or, perhaps as is more likely, Taggart was already on his books as an informer – and alleged he had been chased and beaten up by Frank Fraser, who he claimed was wielding a pole at the time. 'It was nonsense. If he had said it was an axe, we might have believed him,' said David Fraser. Years later it emerged that throughout the trial in the spring and summer of 1967, Taggart had been running a long firm just around the corner from the

Old Bailey, right under the noses of the police. It was a nice touch.

In all, the charge sheet contained dozens of charges against the Richardsons, Frank and seventeen accomplices. The committal proceedings in the magistrates' court almost descended into farce when all of the accused had to cram into the dock together. Frank and the others kept changing places to delay things further, leading the magistrate to call for two policemen to stand in the dock with them and keep order, making for an even more ludicrous scene. 'We practically had to sit on each other's knees,' Frank said.

The men tried to disrupt proceedings further by catcalling as the evidence against them was read out. At one point Frank shouted that the case against him 'was like reading a James Bond book'. But the charges they faced were no laughing matter and made headlines around the world. In those days, committal proceedings were not subject to any reporting restrictions, so the prosecution were free to outline in the fullest detail all the horrific claims and evidence in the case, which were taken down by eager hacks and splurged all over the front page. Eddie Richardson still faced a retrial on the Mr Smith's affray case and felt – quite rightly – that he could not now get a fair hearing on that, in the light of the 'Torture Trial' allegations. In the early seventies, the rules changed to prevent such prejudicial reporting, but back then it was open season and Fleet Street went into a feeding frenzy.

During this time, Patrick found that bearing the Fraser name brought him close scrutiny in decent society. He had left school for good and got himself a job as a bellhop at the Berkeley Hotel in Knightsbridge. 'I loved it but the head of security would eyeball me every day and scratch his chin, muttering, "Fraser, Fraser," as if he was trying to work out whether I was related to Frankie Fraser. The Torture Trial was coming up and the papers had been full of what my dad was supposed to have done. He was right though, I made myself really busy nicking out of the rooms – cash, jewellery, the lot. But he never caught me.

'Once I got to meet Ava Gardner, the actress, who was staying at the hotel. I had to deliver the most massive bunch of flowers to her room. When I went in, there was a fella strumming a guitar, serenading her, and she was reclining on the sofa. I will never forget, she said to me: "Come over here, honey, you look sweeter than those flowers."

'It was every schoolboy's dream come true. I learned my manners in that job, how to eat properly, how to sip from a wine glass. I watched all the posh people doing it and copied what they did. It was an education.'

When the Torture Trial started in April 1967, Frank faced three main charges of demanding money with menaces from three men: Christopher Glinski, James Taggart and Bennie Coulston. As well as whacking Taggart with a wooden pole, he was supposed to have yanked the teeth out of Bennie Coulston's mouth with a pair of pliers after stripping him naked and punching him.

The background to the allegation was as follows: Bennie Coulston had conned the younger brother of Atlantic Machine worker Harry Rawlings (whose arm was injured in the Mr Smith's fight) using an age-old trick involving a case full of cigarettes. Coulston, from Lambeth, had sold the cigarettes for £650 but when the young man unpacked the carton, underneath the top layer was just sawdust. Frank and Charlie Richardson were furious and tracked Coulston down to make him repay the money. They took him to Charlie's scrapyard and gave him a belting. 'There was no torture, I just punched him, called him a rat and told him to give the money back. I drove him home to his place in Lambeth afterwards. He said he would give us the money but he just went to ground after that,' said Frank. Coulston's version involved being dunked in a cold bath, punched, wrapped in a sheet tied down with weights, burned with cigarettes and then having his teeth pulled out with pliers by Frank. He also pointed the finger at Frank's nephew, Jimmy Fraser, who hadn't been anywhere near him. Jimmy Fraser was later acquitted.

When the case came to trial at the Old Bailey, the press and public gallery of the sombre oak-panelled courtroom were stuffed to the gunnels as the trial of the decade got underway. In all, it lasted ten weeks. Each day the accused were transferred from Brixton prison to court in a fleet of Black Marias, sirens blaring, with police outriders and dummy vans, to foil any escape attempts.

Frank and the others had hoped that their contacts on the outside – Albert Dimes, Billy Hill and even the Krays – would get busy trying to nobble jurors, as was the norm in the past. But the judge had thought of that. Every juror was offered police protection and provided with a phone hotline to the police in case they were approached. Frank's heart sank as that avenue was closed off. But that was not all. As the trial progressed, police persuaded some of the accused to give evidence against the Richardsons and Frank, in return for reduced sentences or charges being dropped altogether. They included Jimmy Kensit, father of actress Patsy Kensit. Frank could never hear his name mentioned after that without muttering: 'Grass'.

By today's standards, the Fraser family feel there were massive flaws in the evidence used to convict Frank and the others. But, by the same token, Frank and Charlie did not tell the truth about the beatings they handed out. Their version was that they did not happen at all. As Frank later admitted, that was a lie – there were punishment beatings, some quite severe, and people were held for hours (on one occasion Charlie even sent out for fish and chips so they had the strength to carry on).

Their version of denying everything may have made matters worse, because the jurors – who in all likelihood had read the press coverage at the committal hearing stage – were easily persuaded that these men were capable of violence. It was a short step from there to believe that Frank and the Richardsons had hammered nails into hands and chopped off toes with bolt cutters. Yet there was no physical evidence of this presented to the court.

Where were the maimed hands and feet of the victims? In the case of Bennie Coulston, where were the dental records showing what had happened to his teeth? Mysteriously, his hospital records disappeared and there was no attempt to get an expert witness to peer into his mouth in court. Coulston had eight convictions for dishonesty before the Torture Trial and was in custody when he was called as a witness. The one attempt that Frank's solicitor did make to discredit the 'black box' of torture, which was used to inflict shocks on naked victims' nether regions, was swept aside. An independent scientific expert was produced to reveal that such a box would only be capable of producing a very minor shock. Frank insisted he never used the black box or even saw it, but in his memoirs, *The Last Word*, Eddie Richardson revealed that he did once see his brother Charlie using it on someone who owed him money. 'The pain was not that great, but the humiliation of being stripped and wired up was worse,' he wrote.

Another twist in the case involved Frank's old enemy, Governor Lawton, of Wandsworth Prison. The judge who presided over this trial was Mr Justice Frederick Lawton, his son. Frank felt the odds of a fair hearing were stacked against him, particularly as he had once attempted to hang the judge's father from a tree on Wandsworth Common and killed the family dog at the same time. He had actually met the judge before, about two years prior to the fight at Mr Smith's, at Victoria station, as he waited for a train back to Brighton. Frank recognised the judge as the son of the hated governor and went over to berate him, before Doreen dragged him away, fearing he would get himself arrested.

Frank's lawyers raised this in court at the Old Bailey, saying that Fraser wanted the judge to stand down. At first, Lawton claimed not to remember the incident at Victoria but the next day addressed the court, saying he did recall being approached by a drunken oaf, but it would not affect his ability to give a fair trial.

When the jury returned their verdicts, the courtroom sat in stunned silence. Frank was handed a ten-year sentence for demanding money with menaces. Eddie Richardson got ten years plus two years to run concurrently and Charlie

Richardson got twenty-five years. As he sentenced them, Mr Justice Lawton said: 'One is ashamed to live in a society with men like you.'

Mr Justice Lawton had been a committed fascist during the 1930s, who had wholeheartedly supported Oswald Mosley's Blackshirts and even stood as an electoral candidate for the British Union of Fascists. The Establishment saw this as no bar to the advancement of his legal career.

Frank knew what to expect as he was transferred to prison. He was already serving five years for Mr Smith's and now faced a further ten years on top of that for the Torture Trial. But the severity of the sentence handed down to Charlie Richardson shocked him. 'I actually apologised to Charlie for it,' said Frank. 'When it first came to court, I was number one on the indictment, Eddie was number two and Charlie was number three. Suddenly he ends up being the Richardson Gang boss and getting twenty-five years.

'There was no Richardson Gang. It doesn't make such a good headline, does it? But that is the truth. It was me and Eddie in business together and me doing a few favours for Charlie.'

When Charlie was sent to join him in Durham jail, the truth about Charlie's mysterious dealings in South Africa began to emerge. What he told Frank sounded like something from the plot of that spy novel he had joked about back in the magistrates' court. The trouble was, it was true. Ronnie Richardson, Charlie's widow, said: 'Charlie had a lot of mining interests in South Africa back in the Sixties and had met this beautiful girlfriend, Jean La Grange, whose uncle was head of BOSS, the secret security service. Charlie had a forged a letter of support from Harold Wilson and so BOSS thought he could bug the prime minister's phone for them. Charlie was not in a position to refuse. He agreed to do it because it was made clear that if he didn't, his mining interests would come to nothing. He loved mining, lived for it. He was an extremely clever man but found himself in an impossible situation.'

BOSS were convinced that Wilson was a Soviet spy and also wanted to know more about the prime minister's dealings with Ian Smith in Rhodesia (now Zimbabwe). The late 1960s were a turbulent time politically, as Ian Smith had tried to hold back black rule in Zimbabwe by declaring independence from Britain in 1965. Talks were held between Ian Smith and Harold Wilson on HMS *Tiger* in 1966, amid fears that his office was being bugged. Ronnie explained: 'Charlie knew someone who ran the cleaning firm at No. 10 and managed to get a bug planted on Harold Wilson's phone. But he also went further than that. He persuaded someone to steal some cabinet papers to do with Ian Smith and Rhodesia. He got them out of England and to South Africa on a plane. He always felt that the sentence he had reflected his helping Jean La Grange and BOSS.'

It was, perhaps, no coincidence that officers from Special Branch were present in court every day of the Torture Trial. Frank said: 'Both Eddie and I felt that the long sentences we all got were in some way due to the government getting even with Charlie. That is not to blame Charlie because I never did, but the whole thing looked like a fit-up for him and we got extra punishment by association. I had used violence but nothing like what I was supposed to have done. It was normal in our business to give people a beating now and then. A ten-year tariff for a few clumps seemed extreme.'

While Eddie and Charlie struggled with the years behind bars stretching ahead of them, Frank knew he could do his bird. What he hadn't bargained for was that his beloved sister Eva would be caught up in a web spun by conman Bennie Coulston as well and this almost broke him. Beverley explained: 'My mum would do anything for Frank and she was devastated about the whole Torture Trial, so she was very pleased to hear one day, through a relative of Coulston's, that he wanted to change his evidence.'

When Coulston finished his ten-month sentence for fraud, Eva met up with him. Albie Woods – who had been by George Cornell's side when he was shot in the Blind Beggar – drove Eva and Benny Coulston to a solicitor to make a statement about his evidence in the Torture Trial being false. Coulston then went to the police and said Eva was trying to get him to change his story. She and Albie Woods, who seemed to have the perfect knack of being in the wrong place at the wrong time, were then arrested for perverting the course of justice. Beverley said: 'The police turned up mob-handed in the early hours of the morning and arrested her. They took her off to a police station and held her for two days before we found out where she was.'

Coulston claimed Eva had paid him £1,000 – even though no money had actually changed hands. The judge who presided over the trial was none other than Lord Justice Lawton. Eva and Albie both got two years in prison. This was no breezy shoplifters' sentence. Eva was now a mother to an eight-year-old, Jamie, and a doting grandmother to Beverley's daughter, Evelyn, born in 1965. Her other daughter, Shirley, had a young son, Tony, and gave birth to a baby while Eva was in prison. Beverley said: 'It upset her terribly to be parted from the family. I remember she used to save half her lunch on visits so she had something to give Jamie when he came up to see her. It was the injustice of it that hurt her too. Coulston's family had approached her, not the other way around. It just looked like a case of spite against the Fraser family.'

The whole experience started a deep mistrust of authority in Eva, who now felt the system was out to get her. The only good thing that came of it, she would later say, was that she took the chance to attack the child killer Myra Hindley in Holloway Jail. Beverley said: 'She jumped on her and gave her quite a belting, which she was proud of. It was the least she could do, even though she got into trouble for it. She wasn't going to let that chance pass her by.'

Frank didn't care about what happened to him – he knew he was hard enough to make trouble in jail and take whatever punishment came his way – but the fact that Eva, the woman he valued above all others, was behind bars made him almost senseless with anger. He determined to make everyone working for the Prison Service pay, even if it took every day of his fifteen-year sentence.

CHAPTER 18

LIKE FATHER, LIKE SON

As her boys reached adulthood and carved criminal careers of their own, Kate began to fret that she would lose all three to Her Majesty's Prison Service. Frank's long sentence shocked her, even though they were estranged. She determined to keep at least one son at a time out of jail and came up with a set of rules for the boys to follow. David was allowed to work with Frank, Frank was allowed to work with Patrick and David and Patrick could work together – but never all three on the same job. That way, she reasoned, she might avoid having them all banged up at once.

Not that she wanted them to go straight, far from it. David recalled: 'I was a typical teenager, getting up to no good in the bedroom with a girlfriend, sleeping in late, that sort of thing. One day she shouted upstairs: "David, have you got a girl up there?" I did and I had to tell her to hide, naked, in the wardrobe, just as my mum stormed in and said: "For God's sake, David, will you either get yourself a proper job or get out of that bed and rob a bank!"'

On the whole, they did stick to their promise, apart from one memorable job up in the West End, when all three broke into a shop. 'We had heard there was a big safe with a lot of money in it,' said Patrick. 'The safe was behind a cage and David and my brother Frank spent ages trying to squeeze me through the bars, but I had a big head, so that didn't work. Then we realised the cage door wasn't locked. We got into the safe and found £32 and a huge box of chocolates. It wasn't a great prize for all that effort. We split the cash and Frank took the chocolates and that, we thought, was that.'

David said: 'The next thing, about a week later, I was round at my mum's and she was telling me off for forgetting her birthday. She picked up a huge box of chocolates from the sideboard and said: "Your brother Frank got me this lovely present. What are you getting me?" I struggled to keep a straight face. He'd only gone and given her the chocolates from the safe. It was just his sense of humour to do that, knowing he'd get me into trouble. I didn't have the heart to tell her they were nicked.'

Frank Jr was also famed for his shrewd business sense. When he and David went out on a job, Frank handed him a tube of gold sovereigns and told his brother he would get them later, as he was rushing out on a date. 'As we were counting out the money, he was getting suited and booted,' said David. 'I met him in a nightclub later. I handed over the sovereigns but a couple had got stuck in my trouser pocket. He realised it straight away and patted me down to find them. You couldn't get anything past my Frank.'

Patrick had already done ten months in borstal for stealing a car and came out fitter than your average athlete. 'We had to do speed laps carrying a medicine ball, then two medicine balls. I came out so fit, it was unbelievable. It made me into a very speedy burglar, all that training. It was good for running away,' he said.

He got a job in a steel yard in Walworth and while on holiday at his mum's caravan in Bognor Regis he met Susan, a girl from Swiss Cottage, and they fell in love. 'But her parents didn't like me at all and so we had to have our romance in secret,' said Patrick. 'Then, one day, when we were back in London, she climbed out of her bedroom window, shinned down the drainpipe and ran away from home to be with me. We got married soon after and managed to get a council flat at the Elephant. The whole building was due for demolition six months after that and so we got moved to a little estate in Walworth.'

His brother Frank and his mother bought him a car for his twenty-first birthday, in the hope that he would go straight as a minicab driver, but before long he did a job in Soho. 'It was a screwer, a break-in, and the fella I did it with was quite impressed with me so we started going out as a team,' he said. 'It was quite exciting. I treated it like a proper job, working five days a week. I got arrested and got a suspended sentence, got arrested again but the copper was sweet so I got the silver back.

'Then I got arrested in Hampstead breaking into a shop to get at thousands of cigarettes. It was a big prize, maybe forty grand's worth in today's terms. The thing was, it used to be an old bank and the walls were about half a metre thick so the neighbours heard us drilling and called the police. When the Old Bill came in at first, they didn't see the massive hole in the wall. We tried to say we were just looking for some lead. Then they saw the hole and tumbled what was going on. I got three-and-a-half years and was sent to Wormwood Scrubs.' Patrick was the 'star prisoner' – the name for a first-timer in jail. After there was a sit-down protest over the conditions in the Scrubs he was ghosted out to Wandsworth, the prison so hated by his father. 'They took me and about four or five others who had been involved in the protest,' he said. 'They hated my dad in there, he had lost about twelve months for a riot in the security shops, and it was a bit of a nightmare at the start. I was put in a single cell and then they took me to see the governor. You had to carry your greys – which were like overalls – and look neat and tidy. As I walked in the screw knocked the greys out of my hand and flung them in the corner. The governor came up and said: "I am fucking telling you, you start in here and we will break your fucking arms and legs." I wasn't planning to cause any trouble because it is not in my nature but they certainly hated me because I had the same name as my father.'

On a positive note, Patrick relished being with other crooks. 'I learned a lot from them, which set me up for when I came out,' he said. 'And bird used to fly in Wandsworth because I started reading and really got into books. I read everything I could get my hands on, starting with Harold Robbins novels.'

David, meanwhile, served four months of a six-month sentence, after a stolen radio was found in his mother's house. 'It was a fit-up,' he said. 'Someone had robbed a rent office in Bermondsey and got away with about £20,000, which was a lot of money. I was put on an identity parade and I wasn't picked out. So the law came around my mother's

Frank with Stanley Baker (centre) and Eddie Richardson (right).
Frank invited Eddie to join him in his one-armed bandit machine business.

Frank arriving in court in 1970, charged with incitement to murder
and grievous bodily harm after a prison riot at Parkhurst.

Sir Stanley Baker attending Albert Dimes' funeral in 1972.

Lady Margaret's funeral in 1982.

Frank with all his sons.
Left to right: Frank, Francis, David, Frank Jr and Patrick.

**FRANK FRASER
BENIFIT NIGHT**

to be held at GRAY'S CLUB

14, FULWOOD PLACE, LONDON W.C.1

(NEAR CHANCERY LANE)

ON WEDNESDAY, 12th JUNE, 1985

from 8.00 pm. until 2.00 am

TICKETS — £50.00

Strictly no Admission without Tickets

N° 220

Frank Jr and Frank's nephew Jimmy Fraser organised
a benefit for him in one of their bars in 1985.

After so many years in prison Frank was longing for a soul mate when he met
Marilyn Wisbey, daughter of Great Train Robber Tommy Wisbey.

Frank and Marilyn with Charlie Kray. Frank testified in court on behalf of Charlie, who was accused of drug smuggling.

David's passport photo at the time he was living on the Costa del Crime.

Above Frank standing next to Reggie Kray at Ronnie Kray's funeral in 1995.

Left Patrick with his mother, Kate.

Opposite page, top Frank with Eddie Richardson in 2012.

Opposite page, bottom Frank and David in 2012.

In his eighties Frank loved to take trips on the River Thames,
past the places he used to play as a boy.

Patrick, Beverley Brindle and David today.

house and found a car radio they said was stolen and I got nicked for it.' Several months later there was another attempted robbery at the same rent office in Bermondsey. This time David was arrested for it, with his best friend and partner in crime, Roy Hilder. 'I got picked out on an identity parade and Roy was nicked close by with a gun,' he said. 'The story was that during the robbery I had hit one of the staff with an iron bar. They tackled Roy and tackled me and I got away. It was nonsense.'

The case was heard at the Old Bailey at the same time as Ron and Reg Kray were finally brought to book. Leonard 'Nipper' Read of Scotland Yard had been after the twins for years but it took time for him to break through the East End's wall of silence about the villains, and gather enough evidence to charge them. The twins faced a thirty-nine-day murder trial for the killings of George Cornell, Jack 'The Hat' McVitie and convict Frank Mitchell, whom they had sprung from Dartmoor Prison. Ron Kray had served time with Mitchell in Wandsworth and wanted to help him out but once he was holed up in a flat in East Ham, the twins found his mental disorder too hard to cope with and had him killed in December 1966. His body was never found.

Jack 'The Hat' McVitie had met a grisly end on 29 October 1967 after double crossing the Krays over some hit money. He had been paid £1,500 to kill an associate, Leslie Payne, but failed to carry out the hit and kept the cash. McVitie was lured to a basement flat in Stoke Newington on the pretence of a party but the Krays had spent the evening getting rid of the other guests. When he arrived, Reg tried and failed to shoot him, so Ron grabbed him in a bear hug.

Reg then proceeded to stab McVitie repeatedly until he was dead. His body was never found.

David met the Krays in the holding area beneath the courts and was introduced by Freddie Foreman, who was also facing a charge of killing Frank Mitchell. David knew Freddie because he had been a regular at his pub in the Borough for a number of years. His stepfather, Salvador, also had a son, Tony, from his first marriage, who had been best friends with Freddie Foreman's son, so there were already close family links. It was to be the start of a lifelong friendship between David and the Krays, particularly with Reg, with whom he went on to serve time. 'They were having a smoke during a legal break,' he said. 'There is an area where you can sit down underneath the courts, where the screws sometimes sit and have a fag.

'Fred said to Ron and Reg, "This is David, Frankie Fraser's boy." They shook my hand when I was introduced to them, they were saying how lovely my dad was, because he had just been up giving evidence on their behalf. Reg had a lot of life in his eyes but Ron had a vacant look about him, even then. He really was mentally ill at that point.'

In his evidence, Frank did his best to dispel any notion of Reg and Ron being crime lords or that they had been involved in a war with the Richardson Gang. David recalled: 'He told the court that there was no Kray firm and there was no Richardson gang, they were all just respectable business-men who knew each other and were friends. It was a long shot, really, but he did his bit.

'He did like Jack the Hat. In fact, a few years earlier when McVitie was in Brixton doing a bit of bird, my dad had sent him a box of McVitie's biscuits as a joke between them. He used to say McVitie was a game bastard but he could be saucy in booze and when the twins done him, it was just one of them things and my dad was now trying to help the living, to help the twins, which he felt was the right thing to do.'

David was found guilty of the armed robbery and given a seven-year sentence. It was the longest he had yet to serve. 'I was twenty-one and I was gutted but I took it on the chin because that's how we did things,' he said. 'As the judge was sentencing me I was busy working out how long I would actually be inside.' David expected to serve four years and eight months but that he'd probably lose at least three months' remission – 'because everybody did back then, even for minor things – so I would be twenty-six when I came out. It didn't seem too bad, looking at it that way.'

Meanwhile, the twins and Freddie Foreman were acquitted of the killing of Frank Mitchell. But Ron and Reg were found guilty of the murders of McVitie and Cornell, and given thirty years each with no chance of parole. Chris and Tony Lambrianou, members of the Krays' 'firm', who helped get rid of the body, received fifteen years each. It was the end of an era in gangland as they were driven off to prison to join Frank, the Richardsons and the Great Train Robbers behind bars.

David found himself in Wandsworth Prison in the cell next door to Tony Lambrianou, who was on bread and water after a row with a prison officer. David tried to help him, by arranging to leave a jam sandwich for him in the lavatory block. David said: 'We'd communicated with each other that

I would bang on the wall when it was there and he would then bang for the screw to let him go to the toilet and get it.

'The only problem was that Tony, God bless him, heard me coming back to the cell and shouted out: "Is it there yet?" which tipped the bloody screws off. They went and found the jam sarnie. I had the good sense to hide the jam under the bed because I knew it wouldn't be long before the screws came to look in my cell. Tony later said he was so hungry he had forgotten what the plan was. It sounds daft, but in prison, little things like people giving you bits of food made all the difference when you were on punishment diets.'

During this sentence, David got to know Charlie Richardson and all the Great Train Robbers, who became firm friends. In a letter to Frank, Reg expressed his thanks for him coming to support them. He wrote:

Dear Frank,

I would like to say thanks for giving evidence on our behalf.

There is many people outside that could have come forward to tell the truth as you did but have been warned off. The fact that you have enough problems of your own and yet still came forward is something that I shall never forget.

Please give my best regards to Eva and the rest of your family.

Here's a little proverb I picked out to add to my thanks:

True friends visit us in prosperity only when invited but in adversity they come without invitation.

I'll come to a close now, Frank, take it easy and look
after yourself.
God Bless You,
Reg

Frank hadn't expected that giving evidence on behalf of
the twins was going to do much good – his own character
was so notorious – but he felt strongly that doing so showed
support for a fellow criminal in need. It also upset the
authorities to have to allow him out to court, which was
another bonus.

He had already caused as much trouble as possible wherever he was jailed, ranging from going on hunger strike and
refusing to wear 'patches' – clothes for high-escape risk prisoners – to joining forces with Great Train Robber Tommy
Wisbey to chuck a bucket of filthy water over the governor.
'That was brilliant because Tommy is a tall bloke, so he got
the bucket right on top of the governor's head and rammed it
down,' said Frank.

Frank was transferred to the maximum-security wing in
Brixton, just as Tommy Butler from the Flying Squad arrived
with James Earl Ray, the man who shot Martin Luther King.
He had been arrested at Heathrow Airport, travelling under a
false name, having flown in from Canada. Frank was one of
the few prisoners who managed to speak to Ray during his
brief time in Brixton before he was extradited to the United
States for trial. 'He was totally unrepentant about what he
had done,' said Frank. 'He just wanted to justify himself.
There was a lot of concern that he might be assassinated
before Butler could get him on a plane out of the country.'

While other long-term prisoners, including Eddie Richardson, made sure their lives were as comfortable as they could be, given the length of time they had to serve behind bars, Frank was still waging a one-man war against the system. He wasn't interested in feathering his nest with luxuries by running betting rings or securing a cushy job as a cleaner or a gym orderly. Throughout his time in prison, Frank and Eddie Richardson both received around £100 a week cash from a casino they had invested in. Frank made sure that the majority of that money found its way to his wife Doreen in Brighton to look after their son, Francis. His family – principally Eva – made sure that he had cash to buy things he needed but he spent so long down on the punishment block on bread and water for all his misdemeanours that he went without, more often than not. 'It is true to say that I have done more bread and water than any other prisoner in the British penal system,' he said. 'The hunger was hard but you got used to it.'

One of the chief reasons Frank was placed in 'chokey' down on the punishment block was for assaulting the prison governor – something he made quite a habit of. His attacks made him even more popular with high-risk prisoners, in particular the IRA, with whom he built up such a camaraderie that Frank would claim he had been made an 'honorary member'. One attack in particular passed into prison legend because Frank was restrained in a body-belt at the time. Frank had been transferred to Leicester and went to see the governor to ask for more relaxed prison visits because the prison officers were overbearing. The application was dismissed and so Frank decided to seek retribution. The next day, when the governor was down in the workshop, Frank swung at him with a huge punch and spat in his face. He was beaten up by the prison officers, who later spat in his food and when he slung his tray back at them, he found himself before the governor again, this time restrained in a body-belt – with his hands pinned to his sides.

David later heard the story from Paul Sykes, a six-foot-four-inch tall Yorkshireman, who was due to see the governor after Frank that day. 'The governor wasn't taking any chances with Frank so the screws had got him in the body-belt and the governor was sitting behind a really long table at the other end of the room,' David said. 'As the charge against him was being read out, Frank flung himself bodily down the table and skidded along, his hands by his sides, and managed to head-butt the governor on the nose. He was taken out and given a proper beating for that but he didn't regret it at all. Paul had to go in to see the governor as Frank was dragged out and he couldn't believe it when the governor was sitting there with his nose bleeding.'

It was this attack that led to him being sent to another prison. Rather than sit quietly in his cell, Frank then became a ringleader in a major disturbance. Its name is still synonymous with some of the worst violence in the history of the British penal system: Parkhurst.

CHAPTER 19

RIOT

Parkhurst Prison on the Isle of Wight first opened as a jail in 1862 and gained a reputation for the harsh treatment of its inmates, who were often clamped in leg-irons. By the time Frank arrived there in 1969, the shackles were long gone but anyone sent to 'The Island' knew they would be serving a long sentence in harsh conditions, with little contact with their families.

Some prison staff took to their duties with extra enthusiasm and made the most of the prison's isolation, leading to complaints of segregation and brutality, including a 'round robin' petition sent out by prisoners, which made it on to the front page of the *People* newspaper.

It wasn't long before Frank had organised a protest to improve the regime for prisoners. He was the ringleader but eight other inmates – including Andy Anderson, who had escaped from Wandsworth with Ronnie Biggs earlier in the 1960s, and Frank's old friend Jimmy Robson, from Walworth – played key roles in sending word around the prison. The plan was to stage a sit-down protest after evening association – the hour in which prisoners were allowed out of their cell to play cards and chat. The men would then call on the governor to come and listen to their grievances before returning to their cells.

But a number of prisoners had informed the authorities of the plan in advance and, without Frank or the others knowing, some 200 extra prison officers had been drafted in from Winchester and Portsmouth prisons on the mainland. The governor had made ready for a war, bringing in warders with riot sticks.

Barney Ross, a prisoner who took part in the riot, later documented his experiences and gave them to Frank in the aftermath. In his account, which Frank presented to the court case which followed the riot, Barney wrote: 'The first I knew anything was going to happen was when I went to work in the afternoon, where it was the only topic of conversation. I myself was in a particularly vulnerable situation as I had convictions for violence in prison and I did not have too long left to serve. It would have been very dangerous for me to have anything to do with a violent demonstration.

'I was satisfied it would be peaceful, a barricade would be made and then they'd ask an official to come and listen to the grievances and look into them. That night, about 7 p.m., the prisoners started making the barricade at the end of the passage, using all the furniture, the billiard table, anything available. I took part in moving this furniture about. There was a lot of confusion as there were so many people trying to move things in a small space, so I went into one of the television rooms and was talking to people there.'

The demonstration did not remain peaceful for long. 'The minute those barricades went up, they were on us, dozens of them,' said Frank. 'We had a pitched battle. They were armed with sticks and we grabbed whatever we could. At one point a prisoner was smashing a warder in the face with a billiard ball. We fought like animals but they treated us like animals. I got into a fight with a big lump of a screw and took a chunk out of his ear. I spat it down the drain and moved on to the next one.'

Prisoners took two prison officers hostage but Frank gave strict instructions that they were not to be harmed at all – although he felt it was fair to dish it out to a screw in a fight, it went against his sense of honour to hurt them if they were hostages. The hostages were also there to be used as a bargaining chip with the prison authorities and so Jimmy Robson ensured they were safe. However, after two hours' fighting, the riot was put down and prisoners crowded into the television rooms to decide what to do next.

In his account, Barney Ross wrote: 'I heard someone shout, "They're coming in!" A warder appeared at the door, carrying a stick. It seemed he was drunk. He was shouting: "Where's Fraser? We're going to kill him." I saw Frank Fraser standing in the room. He already had a cut on his forehead and blood on his face. This warder must have called to the others because a bunch of them came into the room and immediately started attacking Frank. They beat him unmercifully with riot sticks. He was not fighting back or resisting. He was beaten until he collapsed.

'In my life I have seen quite a lot of violence but I have never seen such a murderous attack made on any man. When I saw him lying on the ground I thought he must be dead. No man could survive that. In that same room I saw other attacks made on prisoners. The warders were like animals, lusting for blood. It was a terrifying scene which I will never forget.'

Frank and half a dozen others were beaten unconscious and laid out on the floor of the association room. But worse was yet to come. When they came around, the prisoners were made to run the gauntlet of a 'guard of honour' of prison officers, who lined up either side of the stairs down from the association room. An officer called out the names of the prisoners as they were sent down and a hail of riot sticks descended on them. Frank said: 'When it got to my turn, he shouted out "Fraser!" and I had to go about a hundred yards to the punishment cells with them all beating me, whacking me on the head, legs, body, all over. One of them had an iron bar, not a riot stick. I kept going but by the end of it I could barely walk because they had fractured my leg.'

Frank was thrown into a punishment cell and left bleeding profusely. When a doctor came around to see him, he was immediately taken to hospital, where he spent the next six weeks.

The riot made headlines and Frank was charged with incitement to murder and grievous bodily harm, along with nine others. A trial was convened on the Isle of Wight, with the presiding judge to be none other than the Honourable Mr Justice Lawton. However, he was swiftly dropped out when the *Observer* newspaper started to make inquiries about his fascist past.

In a letter Frank sent to Eva – who had by now been released from her sentence for perverting the course of justice – he once again appealed to her in code to try to pay off a prison warder to bring him a few luxuries. He wrote: 'I expect Doreen brought you right up to date and this is where Uncle Tom really could do us a very good turn, like he did years ago. Somehow Eve can you get hold of Uncle Tom and can he do the trick? You can imagine how I feel.'

As Frank was laid up in the hospital and contact with other prisoners was virtually impossible, he hit on an ingenious idea to get messages to and from his co-accused. Jimmy Robson, his old pal from Walworth, was by now a red-band – meaning he was able to work as a cleaner and move around the prison. Frank would slip him notes that would be left for collection in the font at the prison chapel. But so many prisoners appeared to have found God over those weeks preceding the trial that the governor became suspicious and the ruse was outed. One note found in the font recommended a particular barrister because he was 'shit hot'. When this was raised at the trial, the barrister assured the judge, 'My Lord, I regret to inform you, I am not.'

In a letter to Eva, sent close to Christmas, Frank seemed in high spirits despite the charges he faced. He fretted about sending cards to all his friends, including Billy Hill and Gyp, Albert Dimes and family. 'I could go on and on, but I would need to virtually save up for ages,' he wrote. 'If Uncle Tom can keep the good work up that will be good.'

Eva's granddaughter, Evelyn Margaret Wolff – known by the family as Bub – remembered spending weeks in a caravan on the Isle of Wight in the summer of 1970 with her family. Every day, Eva would disappear and come back late at night. 'We didn't know it then but she was visiting Frank and

attending the court case into the Parkhurst riot. We thought
we were just having a nice holiday.

'When I was very little, I knew my uncle Frank was in
prison but it was not spoken about openly and I wondered
what he had done and what he was like because he always
sent me the most beautiful birthday cards every year. Eventually, when I was about ten, we were allowed to go and visit
him and he was a charming, softly spoken man who was
really kind to me. He got me a wooden jewellery box in the
shape of a book, engraved "Lady Evelyn Margaret, the most
beautiful girl in the world". Later, I found out it had been
specially made for me by Reggie Kray.'

The jury acquitted Frank of the incitement to murder
charge but he was found guilty of GBH on the prison officers
and sentenced to a further five years. In his summing-up, the
judge said that the injuries suffered by the prisoners could
only be explained by the excessive use of riot sticks. Frank
said: 'The fact that the judge recognised this and made this
point meant a lot to all of us who took part in the riot.
The five I got for my trouble was on top of the fifteen I was
already serving. I would not admit guilt on Mr Smith's or the
Torture Trial, so I wouldn't qualify for parole. The way
things were going I knew I was going to lose all my remission, so I was in for a very long stretch.'

Frank and some of the other prisoners then decided to sue
the Home Office for their injuries. Despite the Home Office's
initial arguments that Frank had not suffered any serious
injuries, he was awarded an out of court settlement of £750.
David said: 'I later heard from people who were there at the
riot that the screws had said to let Fraser come out last

because they were saving the best until last. They were really riled up by the time it was his turn. They broke his leg in three places and he was in a wheelchair for months after that.'

Frank's lawyers had relied on the evidence of a report into the dispersal stages of the riot, by the Assistant Director of the Prison Service, which said that while there was no evidence of concerted or organised violence by the prison staff 'it would be naive to try to escape the reality, that there were probably isolated opportunities taken by certain staff, particularly those who are that way inclined of whom Parkhurst has its fair share, to retaliate or pay off old scores, in the form of the odd blow, kick or push beyond that which was strictly necessary.'

Frank considered £750 a good result and gave the money to his youngest son, Francis. His son David, meanwhile, was halfway through his sentence for armed robbery, as a Category A prisoner – requiring maximum security – when he was moved to Albany Jail, on the Isle of Wight. 'I wasn't there long before I had a row with two screws and I was taken to the punishment block,' he said. 'It all kicked off because my dad's old mate, Andy Anderson, had heard I was coming to the jail and he was on the landing when I arrived and the screws started mouthing off. He just wanted to say hello to me but they were not having any of it. He started rowing with them and I joined in; it was me saying something like "Who the fuck do you think you are talking to like that?" That was enough to get you down the punishment block. I wasn't looking for trouble and I wasn't violent like my father but I did have quite a few tussles and fights with the screws over the years. When you are in the nick, it is like a pressure cooker and things can kick off any moment. It was particularly like that back then. It wasn't long after Parkhurst and prisoners were up for a fight.

'Anyway, a Scottish screw told me there were a few down there who didn't want me because of my father and the Parkhurst riot. They had been there with him. I went to the governor and told him that I wanted to be transferred, but in the death, nothing came of it and I never got any hassle because of my dad. It was a sweet nick.'

On the way back from the governor's office, he was taken past a door with a name he recognised: 'Brady'. 'It was Ian Brady's cell, the Moors murderer,' he said. 'The screw confirmed it and there was a glass viewing panel in the wall, looking down on to the cell. I had a look and couldn't believe my eyes. He had everything in there – a typewriter and a record player and a great big radio. Well, I had to do it. I kicked the door and shouted, "Oi, you nonce!" He must have heard it so many times – but he just blanked me. I wanted him to look around.'

A year later, Albany was also the scene of a prison riot, in which David found himself caught up. In the day before the riot, word had spread around the prison that trouble was coming and, as a security measure, the warders had removed all prisoners they deemed 'high risk' of escape or troublemaking and transferred them to the security wing. David was moved from his cell and placed on the security wing, next door to Andy Anderson – by now a veteran of these protests – who was smashing up his cell. David remembered: 'Everyone was shouting: "We're coming to get you, Brady!" The screws had to move him out pretty quickly. I hate to say it but when people are angry, God knows what could have happened. There's a few guys would have ripped him to bits. The riot wasn't about him, it was about the conditions we were living in but if they could have got a nonce like Brady at the same time and done him in, then they would have done.'

After the riot, David and the other inmates were all beaten. 'We all got clumped,' he said. 'It was pointless to resist. The screws just came in mob-handed and thumped you. It was part and parcel of the way things were, getting a belting.'

A few months after the Albany riot, David was transferred back to Wandsworth punishment block. 'I was still finishing some bird for the riot. After a few days down the block, the door opened and a screw said: "You're going upstairs." I went up to the cell up there on the wing in the morning and in the afternoon the door opened. A couple of screws and the chief prison officer were standing there and said I was wanted downstairs, meaning back downstairs on the block. Now, I didn't ask why. That is part of the whole thing when you are in the nick. You don't give them the satisfaction of thinking you are worried but I was wondering what on earth I had done wrong. They were talking out of the side of their mouths to each other, as prison officers do. So, they take me back down the block to the very same cell I was in before and I notice the name on the door in chalk: "Fraser". I am now thinking "Oh, shit". The door opens and one of them says "There's someone to see you, Frank." And it is my dad sitting there. He recognised me straight away and says "David!" I just said "Hello, Dad" and the screws shut the door and let us have a visit.

'I told him all about the riot in Albany and then they let us out on exercise together. When we get out in the yard, all the other prisoners can see us walking around together and they start chanting "Frank! Frank! Frank!" It was a rebellious time and my dad was seen as a rebel leader in them days.

'I can't pretend the conversations were easy. I had a lot of feelings about him walking out on us but I was a man now and I had to swallow that. We got to know each other bit-by-bit. I didn't expect too much of him and he didn't ask anything of me. We preferred just talking to each other about people we knew and what was going on in the prisons and that is how our relationship with each other was re-established.'

After a couple of months, Frank was moved on again to another prison away from David. The bad blood caused by the Parkhurst riot followed Frank throughout the system. He was 'ghosted' around – moved with no notice – from prison to prison and even his closest family were targeted by rogue elements in the service who were hell-bent on revenge. After a transferral to Wakefield, a prison officer took it upon himself to try to drive 'Mad' Frank insane as retribution for what had happened in Parkhurst. First, the few personal items he owned started going missing from his cell, so he took to carrying his belongings around in a pillowcase. Then, when he had been out of his cell, he noticed the letters of his sister's name spelled out in the dirt on the window, so that it read EVA.

The final straw came when Eva received hate mail – a Christmas card with a pornographic message inside. Eva complained to the Post Office about the offensive mail and they set up an investigation into what was going on, tracing the mail to the prison. The police were informed and the prison guard, who by now was under suspicion for tormenting Frank, confessed he had sent the card when a handwriting expert was brought in. He was prosecuted and received a suspended sentence. If anything, it made Frank more determined to pit himself against the prison service.

On one occasion, in Liverpool, a prisoner who Frank was close to clambered on to the roof in a protest. The governor came to see Frank and asked him if he would talk to the prisoner, to persuade him to come down. David said: 'He told the governor that he would like to help, so he was taken out into the prison yard and the chief and all the prison officers were lined up there, looking hopeful, thinking Frank was going to bring it all to a successful end. Frank then yelled out: "Whatever you do, don't come down! They're going to give you a right belting!"'

Eva, too, had her revenge. When a prison governor and his secretary were taken hostage in a protest by a convict who she knew from Brixton, the authorities rang and asked her if she could talk him into releasing them. Patrick said: 'She listened and then made them repeat who had been taken hostage before saying: "Fuck 'em" and putting the phone down. I don't think it was quite the response they were expecting.'

Frank's prison records, obtained from the Home Office, revealed another of his favourite protests: throwing his chamber pot over the staff. One report said: 'Following completion of the punishment awarded him in March for disobedience, attempted assault and using abusive language,

Fraser refused to leave the segregation unit and was placed on Rule 43 by the governor. After a certain amount of threatening behaviour he emptied the contents of his chamber pot over the officer who unlocked him to slop out last Friday evening.'

David said: 'He must have thrown his chamber pot over thirty times. His thinking was that they were treating him like shit, so they could have some back.' His determination to protest by any means possible became more entrenched. Often, this was achieved using violence and abusive behaviour to the staff. The Home Office was very concerned that he should not ever be allowed to gather a groundswell of support in any prison. His prison records stated: 'The regime at Hull had prevented Fraser from influencing large numbers of prisoners and thus denied him the support which had previously enabled him to become a disruptive influence at other establishments.'

At times his protests were petty but to Frank they remained important, because it annoyed the prison authorities. Once he had been put into the punishment cells and completed his time there, he would then refuse to come out, just to be difficult.

During the early 1970s, when he was in the punishment block at Hull prison, his shoes were taken away and he was only allowed to wear prison slippers. After he returned to the wing, the warders tried to get him to put his shoes back on and he refused. He kept that up for the remainder of his twenty-year sentence. 'I decided that I wouldn't do what they wanted me to just because it was convenient for them,' said Frank. 'In the end, they begged me to put my shoes back on.

They even offered to have some shoes made for me. They offered me trainers.

'I wore slippers in the sun, the rain, the ice and snow. It was worst in the northern prisons, such as Durham, where it was bloody freezing in the winter and you can bet the guards made sure I went out when the yard hadn't been cleared of snow and ice. Slosh, slosh, slosh, I went through it all, with a smile on my face, just to show them I wasn't beaten. I always had my full hour exercising. It's a wonder I never got frostbite.'

If he hated Her Majesty's Prison Service, the feeling was mutual. One missive from the Home Office to Norwich Prison, informing them it was their turn to have Frank from November until January, signed off knowingly: 'And a very Happy Christmas to the Governor!'

CHAPTER 20

COPS AND ROBBERS

With prison sentences under their belts and empty wallets in their pockets, David and Patrick entered their heyday as robbers in the mid-1970s. David was settling into married life in East Dulwich with his first wife, Stephanie – known as Stevie. He had met Stevie – who was small and dark-haired, with a vibrant personality – in his cousin Jimmy Fraser's pub shortly after his release from his seven-year sentence for robbery, in 1974. The pair quickly fell in love and moved in together.

Patrick and Susan had started a family in their little council house in Walworth, with the arrival of son Paul, in 1973, while Patrick was still in Wandsworth. When he came out of prison in 1974, rather than being reformed by his experiences inside, a twenty-three-year-old Patrick was ready to rob banks. 'I knew I could handle a bit of bird and not be a grass or a danger to anyone,' he added. 'It wasn't that we were expected to be criminals, it was just what we knew and to be honest, at times, it was a great life,' said Patrick. 'Some people like to paint, some like to garden; I liked to steal. It was that simple.'

They started off breaking into luxury goods shops all over

London but rather than the smash and grab, this time the operation had become more sophisticated. 'There was a good deal of planning went into things because we didn't want to get caught. We had people in our little gang who had keys so they could switch off alarms,' said Patrick. 'Other shops had glass doors with a lock at the top and the bottom and we had a way of doing those locks so you could just get in.' On one occasion, they brought along their dad's old friend, Jimmy Robson, who kept a nightwatchman occupied with a bottle of Scotch while they went through a wall to get at the goods they wanted.

Sometimes their older brother Frank would put in an appearance, although he was very busy with criminal links he had forged while in prison during the late 1960s.

Frank Jr and David sometimes worked with an associate known as The Bosh – 'bosh, and we were in,' said David. 'The Bosh was brilliant with keys. He could look at a key, memorise it and file a replica on the spot. Other times one of us would make an excuse to get into the back of the shop and grab a key, take an imprint in some putty and give it to The Bosh to make a copy.'

Another method was to get into the shop and take out the locks during the day while a gang member created a diversion. Part of the lock mechanism was removed before the locks were put back into place. Patrick said: 'When they came to lock up, they would think the place was secure, but any key would fit. It was a lovely trick.' Sub-post offices were another target, as they would close for lunch and once the locks had been fiddled, Patrick would arrive in a van with his team as the staff were on a break, and go in and rob it. David was skilled at breaking through door locks using a filed down piece of celluloid: "We called it a 'loid' and it was a bit like what you see on the films today, when they are using the credit card to get in.'

Planning a job could take several weeks – watching a shop or a bank, scoping out escape routes and finding out as much information about a business as possible. 'We had someone who used to like to walk the routes to work it out,' said David. 'He would walk for miles, find cut-throughs and walkways and report back. Most of our meets back then were done in Kennington Park so that we couldn't be bugged.'

The landscape of the underworld had changed dramatically from the days of their dad Frank and his boss Billy Hill. Patrick said: 'There was no Mr Big, no Billy Hill any more. There were different firms of people – maybe five or six in London – who had their teams but who all knew each other and might work together when they fancied it.'

The teams of people they worked with changed from job to job, depending on what skills they required. 'Some were good at safes, others were good at keys, some were good as getaway drivers,' said David. 'We had a network of about forty people across London who we could call on at any one time, as well as dozens of other people in other cities. There were a lot of people at it because the money was good but the risks were high, so you had to build a reputation. There were also contacts abroad, in France, Spain, Italy and America. Like-minded people will always find ways of getting in touch.' In addition to this, the Frasers had dozens of cars, fitted with false number plates, parked at various locations all over London. David said: 'We would do a job, change cars and drive off. Once someone found three grand in used notes stuffed in a glove compartment. Someone had dumped their share in the car and just forgotten to go and pick it up.'

Patrick also kept himself busy robbing apartments in the West End of London and was once chased out of a block near Harrods. 'Many of these blocks were minded by porters but once you had managed to get through the entry phone, it was a case of brute force on the front door. If someone tumbled what was going on and chased you, you ran like hell. The thing is, some of those flats were lovely and I got a lot of ideas about interior decoration from going around them. The way these people lived and they had done up their places was something that I liked to see. In fact, I got into collecting onyx at that point and it got me into trouble with the police.'

Police raided Patrick's house in South London and confiscated a large collection of onyx and antiques, which he had bought legitimately. The police also took several oil paintings, believing them to be masterpieces stolen from country houses in a series of raids. They had actually been painted by his brother, David, in HMP Chelmsford when he took up art during his last sentence. One painting, based on a picture of Leonardo da Vinci as an old man – repainted and named 'Fred' by David – had won a Koestler Trust Art Award. Another was in the style of Picasso, while others were based on historical paintings of Vikings. 'I had tried to make them look old by using boot polish and varnish,' said David. 'I think that is why the copper thought they were Old Masters.'

Patrick's first wife, Susan, had taken quite a shine to David's paintings. She had hung them proudly all over the house. 'They were painted on hardboard, because in the prison we couldn't get hold of canvas. I'd even signed them "D. Fraser". It was nice to know the law thought my paintings were so good but the fact is the frames they were in were worth more than the pictures,' said David. Patrick added: 'The cozzer wasn't having any of it. He said we could have just painted David's name on the front of real antiques and took them all away.'

A couple of weeks after the raid, David and Patrick were watching the television when a haul of valuable items recovered after burglaries was showcased on *Police 5* – a forerunner of the TV show *Crimewatch* – presented by Shaw Taylor. 'My paintings took pride of place next to Patrick's collection of onyx. It was a quite a moment,' said David. 'Shaw Taylor was busy appealing for the owners of these priceless items to come forward and claim them and we were falling off the sofa laughing because they were genuinely ours.'

Although stealing was a serious business, David and Patrick had plenty of fun doing it. 'We devised ways of tricking people into giving us what we wanted, without having to hurt anyone,' said David. 'There were some very funny moments. Of course, we now realise, with hindsight, that what we did was wrong. At the time, it was all we knew and we felt like we were just earning a living.'

One of their favourite ruses was for David to dress up as a policeman and 'arrest' Patrick for selling stolen goods to a jewellery shop. Patrick would go into the chosen business over a period of a few days and bring watches, rings and necklaces for the jeweller and sell them to him. He would then arrange to be in the shop at the precise moment that the 'police' turned up to break the news that the goods were stolen and would have to be confiscated. 'It was basically a confidence trick,' said David. 'We even had cars done up as police cars. There wasn't the traffic back then like there is now. You could be up in the West End and away in no time.

'We'd have the owner open the safe and say we'd have to take stuff to the police station and they'd get it back, that sort of thing. They would hand over everything to us and we would just walk out of the shop.'

The police uniforms dated from the Second World War and had been picked up at the Army Surplus Stores, with the collars turned up and altered. Their caps were actually chauffeurs' caps and the distinctive tartan check of the policeman's hat had been pinched from a child's play set.

Part of their approach when stealing was to avoid hurting people. 'It was partly to do with the fact that if you hurt someone, you face a longer prison sentence and partly because it just wasn't in our nature to want to be violent,' said David. 'With that in mind, we worked out ways of tricking people into giving us what we wanted, with the minimum violence involved.' However, during one robbery, the shop owner had the keys to the safe back at his house and so David and Patrick and their team had to come out of the shop and drive him to get them. Unfortunately, a genuine police raid was happening across the street at the precise moment they emerged from the shop. David said: 'I had to make it look real, so I gave Patrick a clip around the ear as we were getting into the car. I was then trying not to laugh as his ear was bright red and he looked really pissed off as we were driving away.'

When they moved on to robbing banks, the fakery didn't stop there. Although the guns they used were real – American Colt .45 semi-automatic pistols dating from the First World War – the bullets were dummies. The gang would take a shotgun cartridge and remove the lead shot, replacing it with dry rice. The cartridge was then sealed with beeswax before being loaded into the gun. David said: 'When the gun went off, it made a big explosion and flames would shoot out. It was a loud noise. It was enough to scare people but obviously not to hurt them. It was all about the mind-set.' Patrick added: 'I loved my .45s, I had a pair of them. It wasn't about being aggressive – all you had to do was pull the gun out and show people you were serious. Bank robbery was in its heyday then. There were so many people at it.'

He kept the guns in a holdall under his floorboards or in his shed, to ensure that no one could go on a job without him. The police later referred to this weapon stash as Patrick's 'happy bag'. 'Because, I suppose, it did made me very happy,' added Patrick.

To confuse people during robberies they would use fake accents – Irish or Scottish – and keep moving around. 'If people don't have time to concentrate on what you look like, because you are fogging them with information by moving around, talking and so on, it can make it harder to identify you later on,' said David. 'We used to do that. If there were six of you doing it, all moving around a lot, it could make it really difficult for people to focus.

'Overall, we would just be as pleasant as we could. "Give us the money, you will get it all back on insurance, no one will get hurt," that sort of thing. Another reason to keep everyone calm was to make it easier for the person who had to open the safe. If they were shaking, thinking they were about to get shot, they wouldn't be able to do it.'

On one occasion, after pulling off a heist and abandoning the getaway car, David returned to the scene of the crime to do a spot of shopping and parked his own vehicle nearby. 'I just strolled along as if nothing had happened,' he said. 'The cozzers hadn't even traced the getaway car. It sounds cocky but that is how you got away with it.'

On another job, at a time when the IRA were very active in London, the gang decided to talk in Irish accents. David said: 'During the robbery, one of the people we were robbing asked us why we were doing it. One of the lads said: "It's for the cause." So, the person we are robbing asks: "What cause?" One of the gang then blew it by saying in a Cockney accent: "It's 'cause we're skint. Now, open the safe."'

Sometimes, things did not go to plan and the ease of travelling around central London by car played to the advantage of the police, who could get to the scene of the crime quickly. Many of them were armed. There were chases across London involving smashing into parked cars, driving along pavements and even hijacking vehicles to get away. David said: 'We did have to drag people out of cars at times to get away. We didn't want to hurt people but we didn't want to get caught either.' Patrick said: 'I had one moment during a getaway when the car door hadn't closed properly and as we screeched around the corner, I almost fell out. I had a bag of money in my hand and it was dragging along the road. I was holding on to that for dear life.'

'The high when it all went right was just amazing,' said

David. 'We would go out clubbing afterwards in the West End, wear designer clothes, buy drinks for people and treat our families to nice things. The adrenaline rush was huge. It took days to come down.'

At one point the Fraser boys pulled off three jobs in one week. 'It wasn't meant to be like that but it just worked out that there were three heavy bits of work which all had to be done one after another,' he said. 'I think we took a holiday after that.' David went to Spain to see his mate Johnny Fleming – who was later acquitted of the Brink's-Mat bullion robbery. Fleming was serving time in Bilbao for being caught with forged currency. The trip was David's first taste of the Costa del Crime, travelling by boat to Bilbao before making his way to a village near Laredo, in the Basque region, which was a target for action by the armed Basque separatist group ETA. Spain in 1974 was still under the rule of General Franco and when David and his wife and their friends pulled up in the town in their VW van, they were surprised to see armoured cars and soldiers with rifles in the streets. David said: 'We got out of our van, all long hair, flares and platform shoes, in the middle of this little village – where Johnny was going to meet us – to be greeted by soldiers in uniforms, wearing helmets and looking a bit scary. It was as if we had come from another planet.

'We went into the only cafe we could find and tried to order some teas – we were gasping – but that didn't go very well because none of us spoke a word of Spanish. We ended up having a drink instead and buying one for all the locals and the soldiers. They were pointing at us and saying "Georgie Best" and "Bobby Charlton". We all ended up getting hammered on the local wine and teaching them to sing "Knees Up, Mother Brown". It was a very surreal experience.'

Frank Jr had already bought a plot of land in Spain, near Marbella, on which he wanted to build a house. He also bought a caravan in Bognor Regis for his mother, Kate, who loved it and spent as much time there as possible. 'It was like posh hopping,' said Patrick. 'She used to take all the grandkids down there for holidays. Salvador used to drive her down and he must have made that journey God knows how many times but he always got lost. She made friends down there with some hoisters who were nicking stuff from M&S. She'd buy it off them cheap and then take it back to the shop and get the full price. It was a nice little fiddle.'

The family had quite a menagerie – two dogs and a monkey – and, knowing how much Kate loved animals, Patrick asked his mum to look after a Doberman for a friend, who was on his toes. Kate readily agreed. 'It was the most beautiful dog,' said Pat. 'It was like a puppy with my mum but with anyone else, it bared its teeth.' One summer Kate went down to the caravan early and the dog came along with Salvador later. But it took a dislike to all the travelling, and started to growl at him every time he turned left or right. By the time he pulled up at the caravan in his Mini, the dog had its muzzle next to Salvador's face and was snarling and baring its teeth. David said: 'My mum could see Dor in the car outside and put the kettle on for a cup of tea. He was in the car a good hour before she went outside to see what the matter was. He didn't dare move for fear that the dog was going to have his hand off. The minute my mum opened the car door, it jumped out, licked her and bounced around like a little puppy. She certainly had a way with animals.'

Their father Frank, meanwhile, was eventually downgraded to a Category B prisoner during 1974, because he was seen as less of a security risk. However, what the Home Office referred to, ruefully, in secret memos, as 'the Fraser saga' rumbled on. He was, according to prison reports, 'suspicious, taciturn and constantly saying that staff are very much against him'.

Little glimmers of hope – signs of good behaviour and compliance, which meant that Frank had finally stopped being a menace to the running of the prison – were quickly snuffed out. One governor wrote: 'The "happy mood" which I had hoped might last for a reasonable period into the New Year did not, in the event, endure beyond the third Sunday in Advent, when Fraser abused and assaulted an officer after refusing to go to his cell.'

One memo, dated 1975, revealed that despite being into his fifties, Frank had lost none of his strength: 'On 7 June, Fraser assaulted an officer by punching him in the chest and kicking his legs and on 8 June he punched another officer in the face, bruising his cheek and causing a cut in his mouth. Fraser was charged with these assaults and remanded to the Board of Visitors [visiting magistrates] but stated he would say nothing in reply because he intended that the matters should be heard in an outside court. Someone acting for him issued a writ claiming a declaration that he was entitled to be legally represented.'

The case was dismissed and so Frank's lawyers took it to

the Court of Appeal where it was again thrown out – but not before it had been reported in national newspapers, to the acute embarrassment of the Home Office. The exasperation of the Prison Service is almost palpable in his prison records: 'Since then, he has daily abused staff, made frequent threats of violence and been further charged with gross personal violence to an officer. Since last Friday, Fraser has been involved, with four Irish prisoners, in a hunger strike.'

Frank felt an affinity with the plight of IRA prisoners, because as well as being Catholic, he saw himself as suffering persecution by the system in the same way that they did. These IRA contacts also helped Eva, who was now so disillusioned with the Establishment that she was too scared to go into hospital when she needed a minor operation. Her daughter Beverley explained: 'She felt that people were out to get her over here and if she went into hospital, she might not come out. The IRA paid for her to go to Ireland to have surgery. Everything that happened to her over the Torture Trial and then Frank being treated the way he was made her very suspicious.'

Frank's notoriety also brought his family some very famous visitors. Ol' Blue Eyes himself, the great Frank Sinatra, paid a house call on Eva and Jimmy Brindle in 1975, when he was over playing dates at the Albert Hall. The visit was shrouded in secrecy. Patrick said: 'He came round to the house and Eva had a cup of tea with him. He wanted to pass on his best to Frank in prison but couldn't be seen going there, so came to Eva's instead. Frank knew Sinatra through Albert Dimes and the Italian mafia connections. David explained: 'Dad had travelled to America on false passports with Albert Dimes and Billy Hill back in the early 1960s and met the Italian mobsters over there and Sinatra. They liked each other. It was a mark of how highly respected my dad was that Sinatra came calling.'

The boxing legend Muhammad Ali came to visit Frank when he was in Strangeways Prison. Frank had contacts in the boxing world through his own interest in the sport and through his friend and colleague, Albert Dimes. Albert knew Angelo Dundee, Ali's trainer, who asked Ali to go and visit Frank to cheer him up, as he was serving a long sentence. Unsurprisingly, the governor made sure he sat in on the visit. When Ali asked Frank: 'How are they treating you in here?' Frank replied with a grin: 'Well, I'm all right, Muhammad, but you should see what they do to the black kids.' The governor shrank visibly under Ali's trademark fierce glare. He put his hands up to protest and started to say that Frank was lying. But Frank was having none of it. Patrick said: 'He actually told the governor to leave it out, because it was his visit and he could say what he liked. That meant he got another belting later on but it was worth it.'

In virtually every prison he went to, Frank was held under Rule 43 – meaning he was segregated, with limited opportunity for work, education or association. In short, he spent most of the time banged up on his own. Another document, detailing a protest in HMP Wandsworth, was redacted by the Home Office censor before being released, but one name still loomed large as the ringleader – 536648 Fraser. The document went on: 'This morning, seventy-one prisoners began a sit down demonstration in the special shop. It is understood that the prisoners are demonstrating against a decision that more stitches should be worked to the inch when sewing mailbags.'

Frank was moved every two to three months, with no notice given to him or his relatives, staying in eight local prisons: Bedford, Leicester, Durham, Manchester, Canterbury, Norwich, Bristol and Exeter. In the end, Eva instructed solicitors to force the prison authorities to inform her when Frank had moved because she and Doreen were travelling to jails on visits and would find him gone.

No governor wanted him in their jail, but as the decision had been made to keep moving him around, all of them had to have him at some point, whether they liked it or not – usually not. Frank begged to be sent to Lewes Prison to be nearer Doreen and his son Francis in Brighton but Lewes did not want him and feared he would cause too much trouble for their regime.

That said, many governors found him reasonable and articulate – especially when he was asking for something he wanted. They clearly relished relaying Frank's thoughts and feelings to the Home Office. In HMP Leicester, he had a long meeting with the governor requesting a transfer. The governor warned the Home Office that Frank 'is not yet the burnt-out case that many might like us to believe' before being moved to almost poetic heights about the impending threat of further Fraser violence: 'It is crystal clear that he has no intention of remaining at Leicester for any further length of time without characteristically kicking over the traces in what he sees as a confined harness of an existence at this establishment.'

The governor, who appeared to have some grudging respect for Frank's intellect, reported: 'With tongue in cheek, he made reference to a transfer to HM Prison Ford, which indicates he still has a sense of humour, albeit only when he is making the joke.'

The game of pass the parcel – with Frank as the parcel no one wanted – sparked fury from the governor of Durham Prison, who returned from a nice summer holiday to find Fraser lurking in his cells. 'This prisoner was received by the Deputy Governor during my leave period,' the memo began. 'The decision to place Fraser in ordinary location [i.e. on the wing with other inmates] was correct and one with which I am in full agreement – or was, until I read his history over the past few years. It seems to me that various governors have placed this man in ordinary location and then praised their staffs for patience and forbearance in the face of abusive truculence from this vicious, evil psychopath; this invariably preceded an explosion of violent misconduct.' He thundered on: 'I do not intend to deal with such creatures using this method. He will conform to normal routines like any other prisoner.'

When Frank refused to be parted from his slippers and put on prison shoes, the governor of Durham saw red and put him on Rule 43, but to no avail. Weeks passed and the governor complained to the Home Office that Frank 'continues to be intractable, and abusive on occasions, and endeavours to subvert the good order and discipline of the prison by inciting other disaffected prisoners'.

By October 1977, the governor of Durham had been all but broken by Frank. Efforts to get the 'creature' to conform to Durham's rules appeared to have failed spectacularly. The governor now found himself forced to take a different tack –

wheedling to try to get the Home Office to remove this most troublesome inmate: 'He is now in his fourth month at Durham and from past experience the staff are aware that the "pot is likely to boil over" at any time. Fraser dislikes this prison, possibly because of previous experience and he is continually on edge. His stay at Durham has not been uneventful and a favourable consideration to his re-location would offer some welcome relief on the segregation landing.'

By the time he reached Canterbury Prison, the governor reported that Frank was refusing to associate with other prisoners. His reputation as a hard man and troublemaker had effectively created a prison within the prison for Frank. The governor reported: 'He is not willing to stop being a semi-recluse because he knows he is the potential centre of any inmate discontent and also the potential centre of staff attention.'

Ever watchful, the prison officers reported back to the chief, with Frank being likened to a volcano about to spew forth lava. 'There are signs of tension building up and he may erupt at any moment,' one memo to the Home Office said. Another reported: 'He appears to be playing it cool with a hope of coming off Rule 43, which is a forlorn hope while he is in my establishment.'

So far, so good, then. Except, the governor couldn't help adding, forlornly: 'Could I be given his next port of call and date of sailing please?'

David and Patrick were powerless to help their father do his bird in the quietest way possible. 'The old man was a law unto himself on that,' said Patrick. 'There was no point us telling him to do it differently. In fact, it would probably have only made things worse.' All the Fraser boys visited their father regularly but they couldn't tell him what they were really up to in their criminal careers, in case the screws overheard. They would tell him that work was going well and he would grin at them and say: 'I'm very happy to hear that.' David added: 'I did write to him quite a few times but he preferred talking face to face rather than writing letters because by then he had been in the nick a long time and he was getting bored with writing the same old stuff. It wasn't as if he had much news to tell, being banged up in there.' Besides, both David and Patrick had their hands full keeping the police off their backs. Both found themselves under surveillance – although one incident was so bungling that it could have come from an episode of the TV show *Minder*.

David had a friend who ran a garage and had borrowed a car on long loan. The friend was in the Masons and eventually sold some cars – including David's Morris Minor – to police officers who worked in CID. So, when David saw his old car parked outside a pub in Mayfair one night, with two men sitting inside it, he guessed – correctly – that CID were on his tail. 'I went into the pub and told the others I was meeting that the cozzers were outside and the next thing, they came bursting in and arrested me and my friend, trying to pin all sorts of burglaries on us,' he said.

'When we got down to the police station, I told the detective I had recognised his car and his face fell. It solved a bit of a mystery for him, though – he couldn't understand why every villain in London had been beeping and waving at him as he was driving around, supposedly undercover. 'It was because they thought it was me,' said David.

Relations with the law were not always so cordial. At one point, detectives looking for David burst into his home in the middle of the night, with guns drawn, and when they couldn't find him, took away his wife Stevie and his eighteen-month-old daughter. Stevie and the baby were held in a police station for three days, before finally being released without any charge. 'To keep a baby in the cells like that for that long seems inhumane but that is what they did,' said David.

David also found himself fitted up on a charge of grievous bodily harm, after witnessing a fight between a rugby player and a journalist at a Mayfair nightclub in 1977 – but the Brindle family came to his rescue. 'I was just having a few drinks and a fight broke out between these two blokes. Rod Stewart was leaving the club at the time and he was wearing a white suit and I remember thinking to myself that if he didn't get out quick, he would get covered in blood because these two fellas were smashing the hell out of each other,' said David. 'Then, one of them came towards me and I ended up with blood on my back. Two policemen arrived and I got arrested. They just took me because of the Fraser name.

'Later that night I happened to bump into Bobby Brindle, one of my uncle Jimmy Brindle's other brothers, and he pointed out that as I had blood on my back, rather than my front, I couldn't have been involved in the fight. I decided to call him as a witness for me, which turned out very handy, as it happened.'

As Bobby Brindle was giving evidence at the trial several weeks later, the prosecuting barrister made a comment about a livid scar running down Bobby's cheek. Bobby then regaled the court with his full military history, including service in the Commandos during the Second World War and many acts of bravery. The scar, he said, had been gained in hand-to-hand fighting with the Germans on the beaches during D-Day. The judge listened intently and later warmly praised Bobby as a witness of good character.

'I was acquitted and we were all celebrating down at my cousin Jimmy's pub when Bobby Brindle came in,' said David. 'I went up to him and told him it was amazing how brave he was getting that scar like that. He had fought in the Commandos in the war, that was true, but as he ran his finger down his cheek, he smiled and said: "I knew it would come in handy one day. I got this fighting one of the Carter brothers back in the 1950s."'

Frank Jr was in the frame for one of the biggest bank heists of the 1970s after the Bank of America in Mayfair was relieved of £8 million from ninety-four safety deposit boxes. He was arrested but the charges were dropped at the magistrates' court. Seven others were not so fortunate and received jail sentences totalling nearly a hundred years. The heist is still feted in criminal circles as one of the most successful in living memory, as of all the money taken, only £500,000 was ever recovered.

Frank Jr and his associate George Copley were then jailed for two years for robbing a jewellery shop in the East End and were later charged with a £520,000 raid on the Williams & Glynn bank in the City of London in 1976. The charges on the bank robbery were then dropped at the magistrates' court but the pair were re-arrested on the evidence of the supergrass 'Fearless Fred' Simfield. However, Copley had the foresight to make a secret tape recording of his police interview, after hiding the recorder among his deposition papers as he sat at a desk with detectives from Thames Valley Police. Corrupt officers were recorded falsifying his statement – a process known as 'verballing'. Copley had answered 'no comment' to everything put to him but the police then revealed they were going to invent a tissue of lies. They bragged about having the judge in their pocket and how they were going to 'fit up' Copley and Frank Jr – all of which was eventually revealed in the court. As a result, the whole case was thrown out and Operation Countryman was launched to look into police corruption.

Frank Jr and Copley – who had been unable to communicate with each other for months, as they were held in separate jails – sat grinning in the dock as the detectives realised that they had failed to nail their prime suspects. However, by now the police had recovered some diamonds and platinum from a tiara found at premises owned by Frank Jr. The police case was that these had come from the Bank of America raid and when it came to trial, a jury supported their claim. Frank Jr pleaded not guilty but he got a five-year sentence for receiving stolen goods. However, like the other Fraser boys, he saw it as a hazard of the profession, took it on the chin and got on with doing his bird.

Patrick, meanwhile, teamed up with Harry the Rat, an associate of both George Copley and his older brother Frank Jr. The Rat got his nickname after a senior police officer was overheard telling drinkers in an East End pub: 'I'll get that Harry Wright, the little rat.' Copley had a flat he used as a hideout with Harry the Rat in Pimlico – known as Bunker One – and Frank Jr shared another flat with Tony White, later acquitted of the Brink's-Mat robbery. Their place was known as Bunker Two.

Pat went out on a bank job in the Elephant and Castle with the Harry the Rat but got caught red-handed, with £20,000 worth of stolen bank notes. The problem was that Pat had not realised he was under surveillance. He was already on bail for possession of a machine he and associates were using to make amphetamine pills. The machine had been stolen from a sweet factory and could stamp out 5,000 pills per hour. Patrick said: 'We ground up calcium tablets and cut the speed with that, because it was chalky and neutral, and then pressed up our pills. It was a nice little sideline, making drugs to sell in nightclubs. But to be honest, drugs weren't really our scene. I would have rather been robbing banks at that point.

'When I got arrested for the pill machine, the detective from the Drug Squad was the silliest sod ever. He made a big show of banging his hand on the table and asking me if I knew who sold it. I didn't know what he was talking about. He meant smack. I hadn't even seen a cannabis joint at that point, let alone smoked one, so I certainly didn't know the slang name for heroin. I was only making pills to make a bit of cash.'

The night before any robbery, Pat always stayed away from home, with relatives or in a hotel, to avoid being followed by the police. 'But they had been on me for weeks without me knowing,' he said. 'The job itself went off well. We got the cash off the van just as it was about to be taken into the bank. It sounds simple, because back then it really was that easy.

'The security guards were under orders to drop the bags. It wasn't a case of me being nervous really because I knew it was going to be easy. We would show them the tool – the gun – and say: "Drop it!" and they would let the bags go.

'You knew what each company would take across the pavement from the van into the bank – Security Express was twenty-five grand, Group Four fifteen grand and Securicor only about ten grand, which meant there was less for us to steal, the greedy bastards.'

He added: 'That day, after the robbery, I didn't fancy the look of the car we were supposed to be switching to after leaving our getaway vehicle, so we drove back to my house. Patrick and Harry the Rat were dividing their loot upstairs when the Flying Squad burst in downstairs. 'It was like something from *The Sweeney* when they came in through the door,' said Patrick. 'There was twenty grand in used notes lying all over the bed and they found my tools – two .38 revolvers and two shotguns, plus another one under the floorboards – along with some fake arrest warrant cards.

'I ran into the back garden and there were more armed police there waiting. One of them shouted: "Don't move, Frank, or we'll blow your head off!" I remember thinking: "Great, I'm going to get topped and they can't even get my name right." In the end, it didn't matter because I was well and truly nicked.

'They even pulled my old woman in, which was out of order because she had nothing to do with it. They found four and a half grand in the bathroom and tried to pin it on her, for handling the money. She got a suspended sentence in the end but the whole thing was a nightmare because they had me in Greenwich police station for ten days before they charged me and they took her away too. My mother had to look after the kids. It was all pressure on me to go crooked but I wasn't interested in helping the Old Bill.'

When Patrick appeared at the Old Bailey, he faced several other charges of bank robbery but he was acquitted of these. 'My version was that I was the fall guy and I had never seen those guns before in my life,' he added. 'I was lucky because I could have been looking at a twenty.' His accomplice, Harry the Rat, was also charged with robbery but pleaded not guilty. He got a ten-year sentence. As Patrick was found guilty of the Elephant and Castle bank job, his father Frank was still fighting the system. But at least Frank would now have some company. The judge sentenced Patrick to serve eleven years.

CHAPTER 21

A MODEL INMATE

From: The Governor, HM Prison Manchester.
To: Home Office Prison Department.

December 1st 1978
FRASER, Frank.

I have to say, since being at Manchester, he
has been a model inmate. There has not been the
slightest outburst, physical or verbal, from
him and he has conformed in every respect. He
has been cheerful and co-operative with all
members of staff.

He has opted out of work, remaining in his
own single cell, which must be the most clean
and tidy cell in the prison. He enjoys exercise
with the other inmates and has not tended to
mix with a particular group or individual. He
has received his regular monthly visit without
any of the fuss which has occurred in other
establishments.

At no time have we seen the slightest aggression from him. He has been smart in appearance and respectful and polite with the members of staff, even the most junior officer with whom he has come into contact.

I personally feel, having had him on two occasions now, that there has been a genuine change of heart and he is no longer the vicious character we knew of days gone by.

It certainly didn't sound like Frank. But for the first time in twelve years, he settled down to prison life and found a sympathetic ear in a governor who, it appeared, sincerely believed he had reformed his wicked ways. Frank declined to work, telling the governor that in a large local prison, such as Manchester, there were many 'idiots' who would want to use him and his reputation. He had kept out of trouble for over a year. For Frank, this was no mean feat. Frank knew he only had five years to complete his sentence and was on his best behaviour in the hope of a transfer to Lewes Prison, near to his wife Doreen and son Francis. What the governor described as the 'travelling circus' of moving Frank from prison to prison had weighed heavily on Doreen and his sister, Eva. Without Frank knowing, Eva had borrowed money from his ex-wife Kate at times, in order to pay the train and bus fares to get to see her beloved brother.

He was offered a place at another prison, Coldingley, in Surrey, where he would be expected to work to show he was ready to return to society, but he refused, making an impassioned two-page plea to the Home Office. In his characteristic neat, copperplate handwriting, Frank wrote: 'I explained to the governor that I was not at all keen to be transferred there as I did not believe I would be suited to Coldingley Prison system and that I would not last a long time there before being moved out, either for not adapting to their system or losing more remission etc.'

He assured the Home Office, with almost childish logic, he was 'not anticipating any trouble or looking for it' but if he didn't fit and he was moved out 'it would be pointed out to me that I had blotted my copybook and that is why I was back in local prisons'. He went on: 'The prison I would like is Lewes Prison. I have been in custody now over twelve and a half years and I think it is quite reasonable for one to ask for such a move, if not for my benefit, on my wife and son's behalf, who live in Hove.'

But what started as a reasonable request, deteriorated into a rant against the authorities, as years of pent-up rage spilled out: 'I am always reading and listening to the media about how it is the authorities' main task to help keep families together while a person is serving a sentence. Well, I should think my wife thoroughly deserves such a thought from the authorities, as in over twelve and a half years in custody she has never missed a visit.

'I would like to point out we are not rich or wealthy in any way but my wife does not get any such reasonable acknowledgement for her efforts from the authorities. Despite the rubbish the authorities give out to the media about their main aim is helping to keep families together, they have never ever in any way helped my wife and if anything have done their hardest to try to disrupt it.'

The Home Office response was, perhaps predictably, not favourable: 'It would be quite wrong to allow Fraser to dictate where he would like to serve the remainder of his sentence and in any case the training element of Lewes is now drastically reduced.'

Frank was reported to have received the news rationally and without any outburst but within months the old Frank, the scourge of the prison system, had returned with a vengeance. The governor of Manchester reported: 'He is becoming aggressive in his attitude and his verbal expression to staff. It is quite obvious that this is because he has been in Manchester for nearly seven months and cannot obtain a decision from headquarters about a move to the South region. Fraser has threatened to take the law into his own hands and therefore I have placed him on Rule 43 for good order and discipline.'

It was the start of a downward spiral and in 1979, at the age of fifty-five, Frank had his most violent year in prison. In HMP Bedford in June, it was reported to have taken three prison officers to get him out of the cell in front of the deputy governor, who asked him to stand. He replied: 'Fuck off, bastard,' and spat at him. The governor said: 'It would be superfluous to use any further adjectives to describe this man; however, it does appear that he has outstayed his welcome at this establishment, which is in line with his previous history.'

He was sent to Wandsworth, the prison he hated most, in July 1979 and began a spate of violent attacks on staff. The governor wrote: 'It is obvious he has set his face against Wandsworth. From the date of his arrival to date – a mere twenty-one days – he has been the subject of ten reports of indiscipline and is currently awaiting adjudication for a further offence of abusive, insolent and improper language to an officer. He has lost 188 days' remission.' The governor of Exeter thought he would do better than the others but even he couldn't wait to get rid of Frank. He wrote: 'I regret to report my efforts to assist FRASER have failed', before requesting that Frank be removed from his jail as soon as possible.

By the end of 1979, Frank's prison records charted no fewer than thirty counts of assault, resisting and disobedience involving staff, all of which amounted to loss of more than four and a half years' remission. His expected date of release kept being put back – from 1980, to 1981, then 1982 and 1983.

In March 1980, Frank at last got his wish, and was transferred to Lewes. What transpired there during his three-week stay is contained in another memo to the Home Office. The governor wrote:

His behaviour was extremely difficult and provocative but at my insistence staff persevered and tolerated a great deal of abuse and aggression. The situation on the Wing became progressively more intolerable both for staff and other inmates and finally Fraser was placed on report for using abusive language.

From then on he had to be physically restrained and controlled. He became almost insane in his aggression and violence and after

```
several days of not eating and spitting and
throwing urine at the Governor and anyone else
who attempted to speak to him he was removed to
Dorchester.
   Fraser seemed to take his failure at Lewes in
a particularly personal way and I am sure that
any suggestion of return to Lewes would bring a
violent reaction from him. It would be out of
the question to have him on normal location in
C wing and if he came into our Segregation
Unit, I am sure his behaviour would oblige us
to transfer him again within a few days. I am
sorry not to be able to help in this case.
```

David explained: 'He was only in Lewes a few weeks but got into a row with some screws and ended up throwing a bucket of shit over the governor. It was no wonder they didn't want him back.'

Patrick has always wondered whether this bout of violence was triggered by heartache over Doreen, his second wife. 'He wanted to be there in Lewes to make it easier for visits but I have always thought that reality could have started to hit home and the cracks had started to appear in their relationship. He had spent so long in jail away from her, maybe she didn't come to visit him as much as he had hoped she would. We had started hearing rumours that she was involved with someone else by this point.'

Things were no better after his return to Wandsworth in 1981. 'Fraser is refusing work and refusing to wear prison shoes. He displays a sullen and uncommunicative attitude.

He is seen daily by the governor or myself. He refuses to engage in any conversation and declines to reply to any questions, fixing the questioner with a blank stare. He has lost a total of thirteen days remission so far on this latest visit to Wandsworth.

'It is readily apparent that we are on the familiar roundabout with Fraser and your instructions regarding transfer to another establishment at the end of his current two-month period with us will be welcomed.'

Patrick, who never courted trouble in jail, was in regular contact with his father and saw him on visits every three months in the early part of his eleven-year sentence for armed robbery. Allowing such visits between jailed family members was normal practice within the Prison Service at the time, but the governors had their own agenda, as Patrick discovered. 'Every time I went on a visit, the chief prison officer would come up to me and take me to one side and say: "Do you think you could ask your dad to put on these lovely shoes?" Or: "We have got a great job in the library, could you ask him?" I would have to say, politely, fuck off and leave me out of it. I knew whoever could control him got kudos throughout the whole prison service and didn't want to be part of that.'

But although they enjoyed each other's company, Patrick was under no illusions about the huge gaps in their past relationship, which did cause tension at times. 'It was nice to see him and we discovered we had a very similar sense of humour but he would talk about Doreen and I would talk about Dor – just to piss him off. He didn't like it but I wouldn't back down. I would say: "You are my real dad but

Dor raised me. He was a father to me and I ain't going to forget it.'"

When Patrick was in Wandsworth, he saw Frank three times a week, as Frank was held in solitary confinement on the block, for misbehaviour. Patrick was a calming influence on him. They would exercise together, walking around the yard for an hour, chatting about family news and any snippets of gossip from around the prison. Patrick noticed that because of all the time Frank had spent on the block – in solitary – listening to Radio Four, his pronunciation and accent had changed and become more refined. Frank had also educated himself, reading widely, and encouraged Pat to do the same, starting with the works of Dickens. 'He enjoyed all the political stuff on Radio Four and was an avid reader of newspapers,' said Patrick. 'People may have had an image of what prisoners are but Frank was actually a very educated man in the end.'

Back on the pavement, David was about to become involved in one of his most daring robberies – a raid on the home of an Iranian businessman in Prince's Gate, overlooking Hyde Park, using fake Diplomatic Protection Group cars and fake police uniforms. David and his friends, Bobby Davey and Chris McCormack and another man, who was never caught but has since died, had been tipped off weeks earlier that a safe at the house contained about £2.5 million, including £800,000 in loose trade diamonds. It was a hefty prize.

It was a dark October night in 1983 when they put their plan into action. The team had found out the make of the Diplomatic Protection Group cars and fitted the red vehicles

with false number plates, before dressing up in fake uniforms, in the hope of fooling the businessman into letting
them through the door. 'Bobby and Chris were supposed to
pull up in the car and get through the door first and me and
this other friend of mine were going to walk up, to provide
back-up, after parking our car around the corner,' said David.
'It was all part of the ruse. We were coming from the direction of the Albert Hall, a few hundred yards along the road,
but the area was really busy because Siouxsie and the Ban-
shees were playing a concert that night.

'There were all these goth kids done up in black, with spiky
hair and eyeliner. I was walking along, doing my best to
look like a cozzer, when I noticed a few funny looking heads
– I mean, blokes who were not goths, hanging around near
Princes Gate. I got a bad feeling about it. I said to my mate:
"It's a ready eye." But we kept on walking towards the house
and just as we get near, all these cop cars come screeching
around the corner, sirens blaring. It is too late for Bobby and
Chris because they are already inside the house now and the
cops are on them. I leg it back towards the Albert Hall, dart-
ing into and out of the crowd of goth kids. I look over my
shoulder and there is a car parallel with me and the barrels
of two handguns are pointing at me – one from the front
passenger side and one from the back of this cop car.

'The goths think we're making a film and start jostling
next to me and laughing and I am telling them to fuck off
out of it because I know the weapons are real and the police
are not exactly known for their great marksmanship.'

Realising one of the goths could get shot, David decided to
run across the road, away from the crowd, but he quickly

found himself facing a line of policemen, kneeling in the road, guns drawn. In the confusion, the Iranian businessman's family had pressed the panic button, believing they were about to be caught up in a siege – it was only three years since the Iranian Embassy next door was taken over, bringing yet more police to the scene.

'That was it, they were on me, I was nicked,' said David. 'They dragged me into the police car and this copper then starts smashing me in the bollocks with his truncheon. Meanwhile, my mate has fallen over and managed to throw himself over a wall and has hidden himself in a pile of leaves under a hedge. They never caught him. He stayed under that hedge for eight hours and he could hear the cozzers on the walkietalkies trying to find him. We had a good laugh about that later.'

By the time the robbers reached the police station, tensions were running high. David and his friends were wearing police uniforms and the arresting officers were in plain clothes: 'Bobby Davey was handcuffed to one of the detectives who was in plain clothes. These were the same detectives who went on to nick everyone in Brink's-Mat. As we came in, the desk sergeant looked up and thought the detective was the prisoner. He said to Bob: "Put him in there," and the detective said: "I'm the copper, he's the robber!" And Bob said: "Oh, leave it out, take no notice of him, lock him up."

Everyone burst out laughing but one policeman – who had earlier acquainted his truncheon with David's undercarriage – didn't see the funny side and hit David with his gun. David said: 'I made to punch him but missed, hitting him with my shoulder. The gun flew out of his hand and he made to grab it but another cozzer kicked it away, or who knows what would have happened? We were wrestling on the floor. He gave me a few more clumps. I wanted them so I could show the jury what they had done to me in custody by that point.'

David said: 'I pleaded not guilty, of course, and I would do the same again tomorrow. Our argument was that this was clearly an insurance swindle and the Iranian was in on it. We had needed guns and uniforms and cars to make it look good. It came out in court that there had been an informer who tipped the police about it. If we had acted more quickly and done it a few weeks earlier, it might have been a different story.'

When the case came to trial, the accused had to put on their police uniforms to show the court. David said: 'We all had lost so much weight on remand we looked like the Keystone Cops. Bobby Davey had the hat pulled down over his head.' Bobby Davey then brought the courtroom to a standstill when he went into the witness box. 'He stepped up, tucked his thumbs into his jacket and bent at the knees, saying: "Evenin' all!" just like Dixon of Dock Green. Everyone was laughing, even the jury.

'If that wasn't bad enough, when the prosecution got going, he turned to the judge, and said: "If I may refer to my notebook, My Lord?" My mother, who was in the public gallery, actually wet herself, it was so funny.'

The sentences, though, were no laughing matter. David, then aged thirty-six, got fourteen years, reduced to eleven on appeal, for his part in the armed robbery. Kate now had all three sons locked up in different prisons. Patrick said: 'It was the one thing she always wanted to avoid. It broke her heart.'

David was a Category A prisoner, meaning he required maximum security and was always 'on the book' – with two prison officers escorting him, signing him in and out of any particular area of the prison. He was first sent to Brixton Prison, where he received a visit from his dad, Frank, who was by now nearing the end of his sentence. In a bizarre twist of fate, David found himself imprisoned in the very cell in Brixton which had been occupied by James Earl Ray, the killer of Martin Luther King, all those years before. His dad, Frank, told him this when he was transferred from another jail for a visit. 'We were sitting in the cell having our dinner – which had been brought up by my mum, Kate, for us – because you could do that then,' said David. 'My dad suddenly came out with this fact about James Earl Ray being held in this cell and he had spoken to him here,' said David. 'It was strange to think about all those years passing and here we both were, father and son, having dinner together in prison, where one of the most notorious killers had sat. My dad definitely got direct access to people in jails, in the way that straight people never did. It was like living history.'

In Durham prison, David found that memories of his father loomed large when he was transferred there on a lay-down – a month-long stay – which was a feature of the early years of his sentence. He was in one of the cells in the special wing, which the prisoners called 'the fridges' because they were so cold, when a prison officer approaching retirement came in to tell him that the cell had also been home to his father. 'He then pulled out a yellowing local newspaper cutting from his top pocket and showed it to me,' said David. 'It was a story about my dad flying over the prison after his release in 1962 and chucking a shit bomb into the yard. The funny thing was, I always thought that story might have been made up or a bit exaggerated, but it was true. And funnier still, the screw had even kept the cutting all those years.'

As a Cat A man, David mixed with many other notorious criminals, including Mafioso Art Rachel and his accomplice Joey Scolise – known as Jerry – from Chicago, who, armed with a handgun and a grenade, had pulled off a £1.5 million diamond robbery in under a minute at Graff in Sloane Street in 1980. He first met Art and Jerry in the special wing on remand in Brixton and their trials ran side by side at the Old Bailey. Art was with David in Wandsworth Prison after they were sentenced and the American told him: 'I have been in Sing Sing, San Quentin and Alcatraz and believe me, this is the worst prison in the world.'

The pair bonded as they were both on the book, both Catholic and David admired Art's daring. He said: 'We had considered doing a bit of work at Graff but we had a problem getting away so hadn't bothered with it. They had a lot of front going in as they did.' When David was moved to Liverpool, he met up with Jerry Scolise in the church. David said: 'All the prisoners were looking at me as the new guy coming in and checking out this American fella and when we greeted each other, we gave each other a hug and you could see them all thinking: "Jesus, it's the Godfather." I didn't get any trouble in that nick.'

At Frankland Prison, in Durham, David was marched in and proudly shown the new, modern-look cells, complete with their own latrine. David said: 'Before this, slopping out was still the norm. If you were any sort of man you never crapped in your cell unless you were desperate.' Patrick added: 'The stench was shocking. Rather than go in the pot, some people used to crap in plastic bags and chuck it out of the window. That was the worst job in the nick, picking up the shit parcels.'

David was suitably impressed with the new facilities but asked the prison officer escorting him, why, when there were toilets in the cells, was the prison yard still full of little plastic bag parcels? David said: 'He looked at me, sucked in a breath and said, "Well, David, we still have our traditionalists." I knew then that he had a good sense of humour, which was a rare thing in a screw.' David went on: 'When I got to see Art Rachel, on exercise, I asked him if he had been shown the new toilets and he told me he had put the governor in his place: "Gee, we had them in Alcatraz, seventy years ago."' Art was better than David at understanding the Geordie accents of the prison officers and acted as a translator for him.

David was also incarcerated with a couple of Libyans who had been arrested doing some dirty work for Colonel Gadd-afi. David had a way of getting money brought into the jail for him and so was quite flush with cash and the Libyans were desperate for him to help them get some money for themselves. They kept pestering him until he agreed that some money could be sent to his mother Kate's house in Brixton and he would then find a way to get it brought into the prison for them. The only trouble was, the cash – £1,000 in total – was hand-delivered by a driver in a car with diplo-matic number plates, which caused a bit of a stir in Kate's neighbourhood.

A plan was hatched to bring it in, little by little. David had a prison friend whose visitor had worked out a way to smuggle in cash in 20p pieces stacked inside a plastic tube. The tube was inserted somewhere about his person that the guards would not easily find it. He brought in £20 at a time. 'I am not sure how he got it all up there, but he did,' said David. 'It was quite a money transfer.'

Just as Frank worked the system by refusing to change his jumper or put on prison shoes, David now got involved in his own footwear protest, of sorts. He suffered from pain in his feet and so was referred to the hospital wing to have a fitting for some orthopaedic shoes. Somewhere along the line, David decided it was quite a good way to spend time out of his cell and so, over the course of several fittings, always managed to find fault. Each time, the podiatrist – an officious little man – would sigh, put his hands on his hips and take the shoes away for further alteration. One day, as David was escorted into the room for yet another appointment, he noticed that the two medical prison officers, who were there to keep an eye on him, were unable to look at him. 'One was bent over the sink, shaking, and the other one was sort of half collapsed on a little examination sofa,' said David.

'Then I saw them, like exhibit A, in the middle of the table. These shoes would not have looked out of place on Franken-stein. They were like massive boots, with lumps and bumps all over them where I had complained that this bit was too tight, or that bit was too sore. The podiatrist was standing there, hands on hips, as usual. The hospital screw was crying with laughter as I put them on.

'Suddenly, I was four inches taller. I giggled so hard I

collapsed on top of him and he was hanging on to me.' The pair made so much noise that two prison officers came rushing in, believing that there was a fight going on. 'We were helpless with laughter,' said David. 'And I will never forget the look on the face of that poor little fella who had made them, when I said I wasn't going to wear them for love nor money.'

But the saga didn't end there. Whenever David was transferred around the prison system, the medical shoes went with him, in his personal belongings. He was due to leave Albany Prison on the Isle of Wight, when he surreptitiously swapped the orthopaedic shoes for a pair of black brogues and when he got to Wandsworth Prison, he then produced a medical note saying they had been specially made for him on medical grounds, so he couldn't wear regulation prison shoes. 'I then had the medical shoes sent home,' said David. 'God knows where they are now. Hopefully making someone laugh.'

As David and Patrick got on with their bird, Frank was finally released from prison on 17 May 1985, after serving every day of his twenty-year sentence, with all remission lost. His youngest son, Francis, came to collect him from Wormwood Scrubs in a Rolls-Royce. David clearly remembered the day of his dad's release because the pop song 'Frankie' was at number one and it was also his mother's birthday. The prison governor also paid him a visit, peering around the cell door to grumble: 'I don't suppose you will be going home in a Rolls-Royce.'

Frank's other son, Frank Jr, brought his belongings home in a transit van. His most valuable possessions – a gold watch gifted to him by Stanley Baker, engraved 'To Frank, from

Stan', a gold chain and gold pens – had all gone missing, stolen, Frank believed, by someone within the Prison Service, as the most valuable items were always kept in the chief prison officer's safe.

But freedom did not provide the happy homecoming he had hoped for. Returning to Hove to see Doreen, he didn't even make it over the threshold. In the final years of his sentence, she had quietly set up home with another man. Frank had paid for the house, using the monthly wage from a business he had owned with Eddie Richardson, throughout his time on the inside.

Patrick said: 'He knocked on the door and she answered. She told him it was over. She didn't want him. We had all known about it for years. Everyone in the family knew about it by then but didn't dare to say anything because we all feared he would start trouble again in the prison and he would never get out.'

Heartbroken and with his pride in tatters, Frank turned quietly on his heel and came home to London, to the woman who understood him the most and loved him best: Eva. Once there, he finally gave vent to his anger over Doreen cheating on him.

He would never speak publicly about it or blame her in any way. To the outside world, she remained the staunch, loyal wife, who had stood by him through thick and thin. Privately, in a rage, he went upstairs and punched a hole in the bedroom wall.

CHAPTER 22

THE TIN PAN ALLEY YEARS

Frank's famous prison slippers and the tattered prison jumper he had refused to take off on many of his protests took pride of place on the wall at his nephew Jimmy Fraser's bar, The Tin Pan Alley, in London's Denmark Street. The club was hugely popular with celebrities, including the actor Ray Winstone, the dancer Wayne Sleep, models and footballers, who used to like popping in for a drink and chat before they went out clubbing.

It was the beginning of a new era for Frank, who found the world had moved on enormously since his incarceration. The Swinging Sixties were long gone, along with pounds, shillings and pence, and he had bypassed the Seventies, with its strikes, three-day weeks, swirly wallpaper, brown flares and bad haircuts.

Frank emerged from prison to find himself slap bang in the middle of the Eighties, in a London full of Yuppies yelling into brick-sized mobile phones, with women out for a good time, wearing big hair and bigger shoulder pads. He insisted that he didn't find it difficult to adjust to life on the outside: 'I hadn't had a phased re-entry into society or anything like that,' he said. 'No one even offered me home leave. One minute I was banged up, the next minute I was out. But it never bothered me. I just took up where I left off. I wasn't going to bear grudges against people who might have wronged me. I was interested in enjoying life and seeing what came my way.'

But his family believe it was harder than he admitted. His friend and business associate Albert Dimes had fallen victim to cancer at his home in Islington in 1972 and his old mentor, Billy Hill, had died on New Year's Day 1984. David said: 'He was a bit lost because the world he came from was gone and the way criminals operated had changed so much. Suddenly, he didn't have to fight the screws or the system on a daily basis. He had to work out what to do with the rest of his life.'

With David and Patrick still in prison, it fell to his oldest son Frank Jr and his nephew Jimmy Fraser to look after him. The pair organised a benefit for him at one of their bars in Charing Cross Road, which netted around £50,000. Eddie Richardson, his old business partner, also had a benefit which raised a further £50,000 and individual 'faces' who had known Frank back in the Sixties also donated £10,000 or £20,000 each. Frank immediately counted out £50,000 and gave it to Doreen in Hove.

Money seemed to run through Frank's fingers like water – he was overly generous, giving money to people, sinking cash into ill-advised schemes. He also quietly made several large donations to various charities before setting up a second-hand car dealership with Charlie Richardson down in New Cross. He had no home to call his own and moved from one friend's sofa to another, spending time at Eva's before he eventually moved in with Charlie and his second wife, Ronnie, for a few months at their home in Kent.

It was there, in the offices above the garage, that Charlie and Frank made a prank phone call to the judge who had put them away all those years before. David said: 'Charlie Richardson had somehow got hold of the home phone number for Mr Justice Lawton, who was by now long retired, and the pair of them, giggling like naughty school-boys, rang him up for a chat.'

Frank put on his best BBC radio announcer's voice – perfected over many years tuning in, in solitary confinement. 'I'd like to tell you about Mr Charles Richardson,' he began, as Charlie laughed his head off in the background. 'He is simply the most mah-vellous chap and Mr Francis Fraser, well, I think you have heard of him. He's another top fellow.' When the judge asked who was calling, Frank continued: 'Oh, I think you know who it is. I was well acquainted with your father, Governor Lawton. What a wonderful man he was. He really used to love making sure the prisoners in Wandsworth got a proper belting. What a kindly gentleman, simply mah-vellous.'

The judge hung up.

Only two weeks after his release, Frank travelled with Eva to Maidstone Prison to see Patrick, who was completing his sentence there. Frank found himself treated like something of a celebrity by the prison officers and the other prisoners. 'There had been quite a lot of publicity about his release,' said Pat. 'It was a bit like being visited by a pop star. People were nudging each other, trying to get a look at him. I think it was his first inkling that he might be able to use his fame, or notoriety, in some way.' David added: 'He said to me, quite clearly, that he was too old to rob banks or go thieving. He didn't want to get into the drugs game. He needed to find something else he could do and he definitely didn't want to go back to prison. He knew all about the old days and that was something people were interested in, so that set up the germ of an idea.'

Frank also had a nightclub with Charlie in East London but that closed after a raid by the police found a small amount of cannabis on the premises. He volunteered to do favours for Charlie but ended up getting himself into more trouble than it was worth. On a trip to Spain, to pick up some cash from a property deal, he was arrested carrying £18,000 in cash and slung in jail, on suspicion of money laundering. After a couple of days sampling Spanish prison food – 'not bad' – he was released without charge. It was months before he managed to get the cash back from the Spanish courts.

When Pat came out in 1986, he didn't get the homecoming whip round from his dad Frank for which he was hoping. Instead, Charlie Richardson and Frank gave him a case load of porn movies that were so bad they were unwatchable and, unfortunately, unsaleable. Pat quickly realised that there was a sure-fire way to make money that didn't involve robbing banks: cocaine. 'There was cocaine everywhere you looked,' he said. 'We had a lot of people coming into the Tin Pan who liked a line. Alex Higgins, the snooker player, was a terrible cocaine ponce.'

Frank, meanwhile, was then caught with some antique

coins, which later turned out to be stolen. He had been holding them on behalf of a friend of a friend, who he refused to name to the police. But the arrest itself was organised by Interpol, who were intending to catch his son Frank Fraser Jr, after he was named as part of a drug smuggling gang by someone in Belgium, who had been caught with a large amount of cannabis. Jimmy Fraser had also been captured in the smuggling operation and got five years in prison. His co-accused then blamed everything on Frank Jr in order to try to get off the hook. David said: 'It was one of those situations when the uniformed police pull you over because they are on orders from a higher authority.

'They realised, when they asked Frank his age and he replied that he was in his sixties, that they had the wrong Frank Fraser but they had to do something and so they arrested him anyway. The cozzers have a history of getting us all mixed up. Many years ago they thought I was my brother Frank and put me on an identity parade in Brighton and, of course, I wasn't recognised because I was nowhere near the bit of work.'

Frank was charged with receiving stolen goods. Even though he could have named names and got himself off the hook, he didn't. The old criminal loyalty in him stood firm. Before he knew it, he was back in Wandsworth Prison, with David. 'He had the right hump over the whole thing but he only got a two-year sentence and served a year of it,' David said. 'The screws gave him his own cell and let him do pretty much what he liked. They didn't want him there. He didn't want to be there. If it was a bad dream for Frank, it was a nightmare for them. They just tried to stay out of each other's way.'

By now David was three years into his sentence for armed robbery and was being moved every three months, from prison to prison, as a Cat A man. The one benefit of being in Wandsworth at the time was that there were so many of the Frasers and Brindles and their cousins, second cousins and South London friends, they were quite a force to be reckoned with. 'The screws hated it,' said David. 'There were so many of us in there, we had the run of the place. They couldn't wait to get rid of us.

'One day I was chatting to my dad on the landings – we had already been on exercise and were coming back in to go back into our cells – and a screw said: "Oi, come on, move along!" and my dad turned and said: "When I'm finished talking." I went into one and told the screw to fuck off and the next thing there was about ten of us, Frasers and Brindles and Walls, all surrounding the screw, who was squaring up to everyone. In the end the senior prison officer came along and told the screw to calm down and just let us disperse. There were just too many of us for them to confront us, without it becoming a major incident. The old man said, "See you later!" and we all went back to our cells.'

While David was inside and Frank Jr was busy running his two bars, Patrick had started dealing in large quantities of cocaine but he was using it a lot too, which made him less cautious than he would normally have been. His marriage to Susan, his first wife, was in trouble after his years away in prison, and he turned to drugs as an escape from his problems. 'I was out partying,' he recalls, 'having too much to drink and lines of coke. My marriage was all over the place and I was on the gear all the time because it was available to me. I don't think I done myself any favours at the end of the day because the problems were still there in the morning when you woke up.

'I was coming down Farringdon Road one day to deliver the drugs,' he said. 'I was nicked with half a kilo of coke. It was only a matter of time before I was going to get caught because I was all over the place, really. I soon straightened myself out when I got in the nick because there wasn't the drugs and the booze available on tap. It wasn't a case of going cold turkey because it was just coke. I just stopped and that was that.'

He was arrested with a friend, Jim, and both were remanded in custody to Pentonville. After a few weeks he was taken to Southwark Crown Court, with no legal representation, and charged with smuggling 168 kilos of cocaine. This was news to Patrick. He was named as the lieutenant in a major drug-smuggling operation and his friend, Jim, was named as Mr Big. Police had traced the cocaine to a lock-up in Surrey, where a team of Peruvians had been busy cooking it up and cutting it. 'Basically, they had half of Peru in there, 168 kilos of cocaine, 400 grand in cash and enough chemicals to blow up Guildford,' said Patrick.

'These Peruvians running it were quite middle class – a racing driver and a show jumper – but it was in their culture to inform and they did. I had never seen them before in my life but my mate, Jim, knew them. They turned supergrasses and it turned out they had information on drug-related crimes in Germany, America, all over the place. It was just our luck to get caught up in it.'

His friend, Johnny Bindon, the sometime actor, former lover of Princess Margaret and purveyor of underworld muscle when required, tried to help out by securing Patrick the services of a psychiatrist. The psychiatrist told the court that Patrick was completely addicted to cocaine, taking five grams a day, and his family had all-but disowned him. 'I was convinced I was going to get a suspended sentence but I got eight years, reduced to six on appeal,' said Patrick. 'I'd only been out less than two years since my last conviction and here I was, back in jail again. When I got to Wandsworth, the regime had totally changed. They were killing us with kindness by this point. I got a job straight off, which enabled me to move all around the prison. It was unheard of.'

He spent time in jail with Tommy Wisbey, the Great Train Robber, who was by now a close friend of the family. 'I'd only served three years of the sentence by the time I was going home at weekends, before I even went up on appeal. They even let me out for Christmas.' Pat was discharged into the care of a seminary but on Christmas Day, after attending church, he persuaded the priests to let him sneak off to the Tin Pan Alley club to meet up with his family for a drink, before returning to jail. Patrick's home leave was nothing compared to that of a former inmate friend of David's in Parkhurst, who was let out on leave, flew home to Australia, robbed a bank, and then returned to jail, right under the noses of the authorities.

There were funny moments too such as when David's cousin, the armed robber Brian Wall, who was also in jail with him, celebrated his birthday in Long Lartin in Worcestershire. The IRA were experts at brewing up hooch and so they provided the alcohol and somehow someone got hold of some disco lights and snacks. David said: 'I don't know what the IRA did to make their liquor but it was very good. It was a bit like having a Scotch when you put it with lemonade.' A transvestite murderer, known as 'Wendy', who hailed from the North-East of England, then made a guest appearance, as a 'Kissapoof', wearing a flower in her hair, a short skirt, stockings, suspenders and high heels. 'It's hard to describe how funny it was when Wendy peered around the cell door,' said David. 'When she turned up in drag like that, the whole place just collapsed laughing. It was a brilliant party. In fact, one of the IRA guys said that the drink was so good, even Wendy was looking quite tasty.'

David was also in HMP Lewes with Reg Kray, who became a close confidante. They would exercise and socialise together every day. David said: 'Reg always had a lot of younger blokes hanging around in his cell, because he was such a legend. I used to ask him how he could stand it, because they were such silly sods half the time, but he quite liked to be treated with respect. Wendy the transvestite was also transferred to Lewes and again put on a show for the other prisoners, including Reg, during another party. Reg Kray said: 'Wendy, I have seen some sights in my life, but I think you have just beaten them all.'

By the time David was released in 1990, his marriage to Stevie was virtually over. 'I have the greatest respect for her and she brought our daughter up beautifully but it just wasn't working,' he said. 'It isn't that hard to adjust to life on the outside when you have got a home to go to. I was gutted the marriage was over but I had to move on.' He met his next wife, Jane, working in a general dealer's shop in Forest Hill, and friendship blossomed into romance. 'We just took it day-by-day and found we got on really well. I took great comfort in that after my marriage break-up.'

Despite being back on civvy street with several long prison sentences behind him, David had no intention of finding himself a respectable job. 'I knew I had to earn money but I never gave going straight a second thought at that point,' said David. 'It was just a case of making money the only way I knew, but me and Patrick decided the world had moved on. It would have been like Butch Cassidy and the Sundance Kid robbing banks on horses and the cozzers coming after them in cars. I knew nine people who got shot by the police on jobs. I wanted to get out of it alive and Patrick felt the same way. Drugs was an easier game and there was money in it.'

Patrick said: 'When the cages went up in banks and the alarms were fitted and all the money went into the safe, we went after the vans. Then the vans got better security, there were cameras everywhere, so it just became too difficult and people were getting shot. Brink's-Mat was the end of it, really. There was bundles of money in drugs and relatively speaking, it was safer than robbing banks. Any bird you got was just a hazard of the profession.'

David made up for lost time, socialising as much as he could. Once he met up with his brother Frank Jr and their friend, armed robber Bobby Dixey, in the nightclub Tramp in the West End. That night, when David walked in, Bobby was deep in conversation with none other than George Harrison.

The pair were chatting away, trying to work out how they knew each other. David said: 'In the end, Bobby, who had done a fair amount of coke by that point in the evening, leaned over and said: "Here, we weren't in Parkhurst together, were we?"

'George looked a bit bemused and shook his head. I said to Bobby: "It's George Harrison, you idiot." And Bobby then turned to George and said: "Oh, that's right! You are one of the Harrisons, from out of the Elephant!"

George was speechless.

David said: 'I don't think George Harrison had ever been confused with a member of a family of thieves before.'

Pat was released in 1991 and, with his first marriage over, walked into a bar in Rotherhithe and met the love of his life, Lisa. Her uncle, Johnny Virtue, had done a seven-year sentence for armed robbery – which he did not commit – and was a firm friend of Pat's. 'When I walked in and saw her, Johnny made the point of saying that Lisa was his niece,' said Pat. Lisa sometimes worked behind the bar to help her uncle out and was often around. Patrick needed a base to use as his office but also found himself drawn to blonde and calm Lisa, who seemed wise beyond her years. 'I was forty but we grew really close over a couple of months and that was that. In fact, I fell in love and bought half the bar, just so I could be near her. I always like to joke that it was a very costly court-ship.'

Lisa said: 'It was an immediate attraction, we just con-nected. There was a seventeen-year age gap but it didn't seem it. Pat is a very funny and charming man and we just clicked.' Lisa then had to meet the rest of the family, in particular,

Pat's favourite aunt, Eva. Lisa said: 'I was terrified of Eva because she adored Patrick and I don't think she thought anyone was good enough. When we went to see her, she was standing there, with this long black hair, like a squaw, looking really striking.

'Pat's aunt Kathleen was over visiting and Patrick just disappeared under these two women. They were kissing him and pinching his cheeks because he looked so like his dad, Frank.' As Lisa shyly stepped forward Patrick introduced her to Eva, saying: 'This is Lisa.' Lisa said: 'Eva took one look at me and said: "Would you like a cup of tea, Linda?" She called me every other name beginning with "L" that day. I thought she was scarier than his dad!'

Lisa, who had lost both her parents in an accident in 1987 when she was just seventeen, bonded with Patrick's mother, Kate, who had also lost her father, Danny, at the same age. But even she had some words of warning: 'She would just speak her mind; there was something ageless about Kate. She said never to marry Patrick because the minute she had married Frank, he treated her like dirt. She was still bitter about that, all those years later. Fortunately, Patrick is nothing like Frank.'

Later that year, David was arrested for possession of fifty-eight kilos of cannabis and a firearm after being caught in a flat in Streatham, with another man, a friend and business associate, Kevin Cressey. They were both given bail. The law on evidence had recently changed and David and his solicitor determined they would go for full disclosure – meaning they could see everything that the police and prosecution had on him. This included the police logs – evidence of when and how they had tailed him and who they had received their information from.

Sources had told David that Cressey had turned informer and tipped off the police. He had no proof of this, so arranged a meet with Cressey, at the Imperial War Museum, to talk things over. 'I made it clear I was going for the logs and his face fell. He knew then it would reveal he had put it on me,' said David. 'The two people he had been working with had informed on him about three weeks before, when they were arrested and he then brought the police observation on to me, which is when we got nicked. It was a waiting game but I knew it would all come out in the wash.'

With court appearances forming part of the normal fabric of life for the Frasers, business carried on as best it could under the circumstances. It wasn't long before Cupid came calling for Frank. He spotted a woman singing 'Crazy' in a bar one night and, thinking she was making fun of him for being 'Mad' Frank, went over to have a friendly word in her ear.

As they chatted, he realised that she was the daughter of his friend, the Great Train Robber Tommy Wisbey. Marilyn was twenty-six years his junior, blonde and styled herself as a 'gangster's moll'. It was love at first sight and Frank fell head over heels. After all the years in prison, he now longed to have a soulmate to share the rest of his life with. Their first date, fittingly, was a trip to Parkhurst Prison to visit her father, Tommy. David said: 'Frank was besotted with her. In some ways, it was good because he really couldn't do anything for himself. He didn't know how to keep a house after all those years in prison. But she also took him out drinking and nightclubbing a lot and that wasn't great for him.'

Several months after they got together, there was an attempt on Frank's life during a night out in Clerkenwell with Marilyn. A young man with a gun rushed up to him as he was leaving Turnmills nightclub and tried to shoot him. 'It was nothing like the papers described; there was no bullet in his head or his face. He didn't have half his mouth shot away – utter nonsense,' David said. A friend of the family, who was at the club and carrying a gun at the time, chased after the culprit, who got away. Police inquiries drew a blank and Frank refused to cooperate. David said: 'The hitman shot at point blank range and missed. My dad was drunk and chased after him and tripped. He cut his hand. He had blood on his face because of that, not because of the shot. Lots of different people started saying they knew who it was; they had their own reasons. When something like this happens, people can start wanting to get you involved in things.'

Frank's view of the attempt on his life was sanguine: 'He was a bloody idiot because there I was, an old fella with a bit too much to drink in him and he had me at close range, took a shot and still screwed it up. The worst thing was the hangover I had the next morning. I didn't take it that seriously. If someone wanted me dead, they could have done a better job of it.'

The attention that the incident brought for the Fraser family – David, Pat, Frank Jr and cousin Jimmy, who were making themselves quite busy – was most unwelcome. Pat said: 'We heard the cozzers were expecting a gang war to erupt. It didn't but it was a pain because we got followed everywhere and couldn't go to work. We'd been doing quite good business up to that point. It was a total pain in the arse.' David added: 'We had been making ourselves busy and living quite a good life on it until that point. After that, it all came on top.'

They had already been tipped off that some of the restaurants and bars they were using had been bugged. They found bugs in the Tin Pan Alley on the bar counter, in the lavatories and in the back room, where business deals were done. 'We left the bugs there and used to go on meets somewhere else,' said David. 'We didn't want the cozzers to know we were on to them but we were.' A favourite restaurant, near Tower Bridge, was also bugged. A waiter quietly took them outside and warned them off. They left the restaurant, never to return. The police, though, were rather cack-handed in some of their observation attempts. At one point Patrick was driving home, with a friend following behind, who realised that half of the Met Police appeared to be tailing him across London on motorbikes.

David's court case, meanwhile, was becoming more intriguing by the day. Unsurprisingly, the police logs were not forthcoming. In the end, the magistrates lost patience and told the Crown Prosecution Service that without full disclosure the case would be thrown out. David said: 'It was 17 December when I walked out of the court. I went to Langan's Brasserie, where the family were having our annual get together and walked in, with everyone cheering and clapping. I knew I was on borrowed time, that I would be rearrested and charged again, so from that point, I never went home. I took Jane with me and we left the country and travelled to Spain.'

Patrick stayed in South London and ran the bar, The Office, which was a great success, despite him not being pub landlord material. Lisa said: 'Pat would get irate if people were drunk. I used to have to remind him we were selling alcohol and that was part of it.' But the police were never far away and during one raid, a gun was found. Several days later, a large white van parked opposite Patrick's flat aroused his suspicions when he noticed someone taking teas and coffees into it. 'I was under obo – observation – and I had had enough,' said Pat. 'It was time to head to sunnier climes and get the law off my back for a while.'

Lisa had just given birth to their daughter, Amy, but was seriously ill after suffering life-threatening complications. Six weeks later, when both she and the baby were well enough to fly, Lisa and Pat packed up their bags, ready to join David and Frank Jr.

Spain beckoned. It was a land of sun, sangria and a distinct lack of police surveillance – the Costa Del Crime.

CHAPTER 23

THE COSTA DEL CRIME

The yachts bobbing in the harbour at Marbella were a lovely sight for the tourists, but for David Fraser the view was more than picture postcard prettiness; the high seas were to provide a good source of income throughout his time in Spain. As he sipped a coffee down at his favourite cafe, watching the sunlight glint on the water, David had one thing on his mind: smuggling.

Shortly after arriving in Spain, he had found a way of getting a good income, using his entrepreneurial spirit and the services of a caretaker of a set of time-share apartments. While the flats were empty, David let them out cheaply to golfers he met through local bars. In the end, the scam became quite large, with about twenty flats being used and people handing out flyers to golfers arriving at the airports along the Costas. 'We only took good clients – golfers who were not going to trash anything. We had cleaners and the whole thing was run really professionally. It was a good living, considering I didn't actually own anything,' he said.

David's family expanded after Jane gave birth to his daughter, Charlotte, in Spain.

David knew, through his contacts, that there was more money to be made importing goods from Morocco, which lay just ten miles off the Spanish coast. Through friends, he secured the services of a couple of willing young men to go and pick up the consignment, while he and an associate provided back-up. Another mate loaned him a Sunseeker motorboat and the young blokes used David's rigid inflatable – called a RIB – fitted with a powerful outboard motor: they were in business. But things didn't always go to plan.

On one occasion, the young smugglers had set out for Morocco on the RIB but had lost phone contact. David and his friend Jim set out to find them in the Sunseeker, as they had the GPS co-ordinates the RIB was sailing to. 'I'm no sailor but Jim was, so I had a lot of respect for that,' said David. 'We set out and it was baking hot, then the sea started to get choppy. We weren't seeing motorboats and yachts any more, but fishing boats, then tankers and cruise ships.

'We had a lot of petrol on board so Jim said we would be OK. Then we saw another little boat, it looked like a RIB, and the guys on board were wearing wetsuits, like our blokes. We didn't want to panic them and make them throw whatever they were carrying overboard, so we approached slowly, and waved at them. They were looking sheepish. 'I shouted: "Are you all right, fellas?" One of them popped his head up, his face all sunburnt, and said: "Hello, Dave! It's Bob! We were in Long Lartin together, remember?"'

David said: 'I couldn't believe it. It was my old mate Bob who I had done time with – we called him Colombian Bob, because that is how he made his living. There we were, in the middle of the ocean, bumping into each other. We were both up to the same thing, obviously.'

Bob told David that because no one had paid the customs officials at Morocco to turn a blind eye, all the boats had been delayed going ashore. David and Jim headed back to Marbella, eventually catching up with the RIB. They transferred the goods to the Sunseeker and told their young associates to sail the motorboat – loaded with its cargo – into the harbour at a port further along the coast, where it was registered and where they kept a van waiting. The plan was for David and Jim to sail to Marbella in the RIB and get a taxi down later to unload the gear. But when they turned up at the other port, several hours later, the Sunseeker was docked, the hold was empty and the van was gone. 'Jim turned to me and said he thought they had gone and done a runner with all the stuff,' said David. 'I said they might well be up at the villa, but I couldn't see how they had shifted the gear from the boat in broad daylight.'

The men went to their villa and found the young smugglers, exhausted and with badly sunburnt faces, still wearing their wetsuits, sipping a well-earned cup of tea. David said: 'When I asked what had happened they said that there weren't many people around – apart from a load of holidaymakers – so they just took the stuff off the boat and loaded it on to the van, in the middle of the afternoon, with a crowd around them watching.

'My jaw hit the floor. We couldn't believe they had got away with it but they did. Sometimes life is like that and if things happen right under people's noses, they are either too shocked or too disbelieving to know what was going on. We were all cloak and dagger and they just brazened it out.'

Another fiddle was importing clothing by big name brands in the back of his Jeep, from Morocco to Spain, to sell on to the willing golfers and their friends. Sometimes, people he was in business with tried to take advantage of him but learned the hard way not to cross the Frasers. One deal ended up with David more than £500,000 out of pocket. 'I took their villa, the boat, the contents of the safe and their car and that just about settled it,' said David. 'I was a very shrewd businessman. I do have a long fuse but once I'm crossed like that, I won't forget it.'

For Patrick and Lisa, living abroad was a dream come true. They bought a one-bedroomed flat opposite Puerto Banus and David had an apartment villa around the corner. Frank Jr had a villa a short drive away. All three of the Fraser boys were living the life they wanted. Lisa remembers: 'It was idyllic, the lifestyle was totally different and brilliant if you had a young baby. You could go out walking with the pram to get them to sleep in the evening and it was warm and no one would bat an eyelid. They had restaurants and bars with a plaza. We loved it.' But reality was to come crashing in.

One day, while Pat was watching his favourite police TV show he realised that the bar being raided looked horribly familiar. He said: 'The Office in Rotherhithe got done on the telly. One minute I was sitting there, thinking this looks really exciting, then I realised it was my fucking bar. I never made any money in it, but from then on, that was it, I wanted out.'

David then found his good life in Spain rudely interrupted by the Spanish police. 'I was getting a lift with a friend to see a couple of French guys, who were in the same line of business as me, when the car I was in was pulled over by the police,' said David. The driver, Paul, had been arrested after going into a phone box that was under observation by the Spanish police. He fitted the description of the man the police were hunting – six feet two inches tall, stocky with fair hair. The .38 calibre gun he had stashed in the car didn't help matters and nor did the fact that when the police tried to arrest them, they drove off. David explained: 'The trouble was the Geordie bloke I was with was a dead ringer for another man, who was being hunted by Interpol on suspicion of murder. To make matters worse, there was a gun in the car – it was nothing to do with me, but I was there and that was that.'

It was the start of more than two years on remand in Spanish jails in Malaga and Madrid. Firstly he spent several months in Malaga and then Patrick stood bail for him. On the day that he was given bail, on the steps of the court, he was given extradition papers by Interpol, and was sent straight back to his cell. His drug dealing arrest with Kevin Cressey in Streatham had come back to haunt him, just as he feared it would. After a few months he was transferred to Madrid, where the conditions were harder because of the heat. 'In Malaga, you could buy fans to bring in but in Madrid there was none of that and it was so much hotter, it was unbearable.' It was a relief after several weeks to be flown back to Malaga to face the gun charge.

David said: 'The Spanish prosecutor showed the court a gun and I couldn't believe it because it wasn't even the weapon that was in the car. This was a tiny little gun, not a big .38 calibre one. I pointed this out to the judge and the prosecutor threw his cigarette on the floor, stamped it out and said: '¡Es un pistole!' (It is a gun!). He shrugged his shoulders, as if to say: "What are you complaining about?" It was unbelievable. I was sent back to Madrid to wait to find out whether I would get out of it or not. They don't give you a verdict straight away.'

In the end, he was found not guilty on the gun charge but languished in Madrid for a few more months. 'I learned Spanish properly – we had classes. We could have visits and get out on exercise. There was a gym and I worked out a lot. In fact, all the Spanish locals called me James Bond because I was working out all the time and the fat Welsh guy I was also in jail with was known as Benny Hill,' he said. 'I don't think he was too pleased about that but they were the only words of English they knew.' He was eventually extradited back to the UK to face trial with Kevin Cressey on the fifty-eight kilos of cannabis.

Just as things were getting tricky for David, his dad Frank was finding a new lease of life as a celebrity criminal. He had started working on his autobiography with the solicitor, James Morton, who had represented him during the Park-hurst Prison riot trials. Frank spent hours reminiscing, as he loved to do, into Morton's tape recorder. True to form, his stories were at times rambling and in places somewhat in-coherent, stuffed chock full with names and places and faces from a bygone time. The resulting memoir – in which Frank glossed over his relationship with Kate and all but airbrushed her from history – was a hit and a career as a celebrity crime pundit was launched. Although he was prepared to share his dark deeds and violence in prison with the world, he preferred to keep secret the fact that he cheated on Kate, got Doreen pregnant while they were still married and abandoned his three sons as small boys.

Book signings and television chat show appearances followed, bringing in much-needed cash, despite rumblings from some parts of the Establishment about him making money out of his career on the wrong side of the law. He even had a cameo role playing an enforcer in a low budget Brit film, *Hard Men*. Throughout it all, Frank lavished money on his girlfriend Marilyn, who was hoping to start a career as a singer. The couple rented a flat in River Street, Islington, for a while – close to the home of his old mate, Albert Dimes. They opened a cafe but they didn't stick at that for long. There were exotic holidays and Frank even paid for plastic surgery to boost Marilyn's self-esteem. There was nothing he wouldn't do to make her happy. Plus, his charity work continued and he would lend his name to a good cause when friends asked him to make an appearance. 'The public seemed to love him and the biggest queue at signings would always be for him,' said David. 'He could never say "no". He loved chatting to people and if it was for a good cause, then so much the better.'

Trading on his expertise as a criminal voice of a bygone era, he also launched tours of the Krays' old manor in the East End and his haunts around Soho, which were hugely popular and which he thoroughly enjoyed. Frank was at his best reliving the old days to an eager audience; he had great comic timing and knew how to please a crowd.

His services were then called on to try to help Ron and

Reg's brother Charlie Kray, who was facing charges of drug smuggling in a cocaine ring. He was taped talking to some undercover policemen who had offered him two kilos of cocaine and said he would like to buy it off them. Charlie always claimed he had been set up by the police. He needed a character witness. Frank played to the gallery at Woolwich Crown Court and his appearance was reported in the national newspapers. He did his best to try to persuade the judge, Michael Carroll: 'He is as innocent as you are, My Lord. He is a coward, but a lovely, lovely man. You couldn't trust him to steal a penny. He would run a mile.' As he was discharged as a witness, Frank quipped: 'It's the first time I have ever walked out of a court free.' But his attempt to help failed – Charlie was given a twelve-year sentence and died in 2000, after suffering a stroke in prison.

The court case against David became a hugely complicated affair, as it was embroiled in a landmark ruling on police corruption. His co-accused, Kevin Cressey, was involved in corruption with Metropolitan Police detective John Donald. Cressey had been recruited as an informer after he was arrested in 1992 with David. But by 1993 the relationship with his police handler Donald had soured. Cressey then went to the *Panorama* television programme and was secretly filmed discussing bribes with Donald. A court case heard that Donald and Cressey had worked out an agreement to destroy an incriminating surveillance log for £40,000 and remove a police file on Cressey for a further £1,000. Donald was jailed for eleven years for corruption and Cressey received seven years.

When David and his lawyer were preparing his case on the

drug charges, he was astonished to find enough evidence on police corruption to fill a room. 'There were two boxes of paperwork on my case; the rest was all Donald and police corruption. It made very interesting reading,' he said. David had access to all the files to do with the case, including those on police informers – but it transpired that people were listed as 'informers' simply because the police had managed to plant bugs in their houses and cars and were therefore able to eavesdrop on their conversations.

However, David managed to crack the codes that revealed exactly who had been informing on him. He also worked out everyone on the list of Met Police informers at that time. From the information he had been given as part of his court case, there were no fewer than 500 names on the sheets. Women were given men's names and vice versa, to disguise their true identities; for example, there were informants code-named 'Sharon Stone' and 'Billy Ocean'. But they all had serial numbers and these serial numbers corresponded to other police logs in which these people's real names were used. 'It answered a lot of questions for me about Kevin Cressey,' added David. 'I also had lists of informers which turned out to be fakes. There was a lot of intrigue going on. It could have been that someone was creating lists of fake informers to cover their own tracks.'

He had a lot of time to think it over – the judge jailed him for eight years.

Patrick sold up in Spain and returned to the UK. Lisa was missing her Nan and with David arrested, Patrick felt the shine had gone off their Spanish sojourn. They returned to the UK and Patrick made sure he kept up the family tradition of prison visits. On one such occasion he passed David a small package of cannabis to trade with the other prisoners. Although David wasn't a smoker, a lot of inmates used the drug – and harder stuff – to escape the grim reality of life on the inside. To prevent the package being discovered, David had to hide it about his person. 'As Patrick was leaving, the screw looked at me and made a comment about it being an emotional visit,' said David. 'Let's just say, it brought tears to my eyes.'

There were plenty of people David did not want to associate with in prison, such as the serial killer Dennis Nilsen, who he met while working in the prison gym in Whitemoor in Staffordshire in 1997. 'A screw pointed him out to me, in case it wound me up that he was in there, having killed all those poor gay guys,' said David. 'I just stayed well out of his way.'

Another highlight was when the Great Train Robber Tommy Wisbey took him on a day release from Spring Hill Prison in Buckinghamshire. 'Off we went in his car, with Tommy driving down all these little back roads,' said David. 'We were well off the beaten track and he was turning left and right all over the place. I hadn't a clue where we were. He parked the car and we both got out. We walked up to a little bridge overlooking some railway lines and he turned to me and said: 'And this, David, is where I did the train.' David went on: 'It was all those years ago but he still knew exactly how to get there. They had rehearsed it and learned all the routes off by heart.'

Shortly after his release in 2000, David and his dad Frank had a final phone call with Reg Kray before he died. David said: 'He spoke to me about the Lambrianou brothers, Tony and Chris. We all knew they were innocent. I had never heard him say it before, but he acknowledged that they had done a lot of bird for a crime they never committed.'

David's second marriage, to Jane, did not survive the jail term but the pair remain on friendly terms: 'She has raised my daughter Charlotte brilliantly and I am hugely grateful to her and to her mum and dad for that and all the support they have given.' But David wasn't on his own for long. On a night out in Bermondsey, when he popped into a pub to see his friend Dennis Arif, who had just been released from a sentence for armed robbery, he met girlfriend Charlie, who was twenty-six years his junior. The Arif brothers, Dennis and Mehmet, were long-term friends of the Frasers but had gained a reputation as tough crime lords and drug dealers. 'We've known and liked them for years,' said David. 'Dennis had invited me over to the pub for a family afternoon and I was taking my daughter Charlotte along and we met Charlie walking along. I knew she worked behind the bar so we stopped and gave her a lift. The relationship just took off from there but there was a big age difference – twenty-six years – so I was worried it wouldn't last.

'Charlie was really easy-going and got on great with Charlotte. That afternoon in the pub, all these kids came running in from the beer garden and said there was a right posh girl out there bossing everyone about. Then, my daughter, Charlotte, came in and said in the plummiest voice: "Gosh, Daddy, it is so exciting out there in the garden!" and I felt really proud because they were talking about my daughter. She'd been brought up so nicely by Jane and her family. That was the first inkling for me really that things could be different – better – for the next generation of Frasers. There was a way other than a life of crime.'

CHAPTER 24

BE LUCKY

The crowd at Wembley Stadium, where Frank had come to see Millwall FC play Swindon, were singing with one voice. But the chant was not for the players: 'One Frankie Fraser! There's only one Frankie Fraser!' Frank waved and a roar of approval rose up around the stadium. He took the applause like a pro but it never ceased to amaze him that the nation had taken him to heart, lifting him up to the status of a folk hero. He remained very humble about fame and would sign autographs endlessly, without complaint.

As time went on, Frank was more than happy to play up to his image as a hardman for laughs. One incident involved a leaving party for a reporter at the *Sunday People*, who had incurred Frank's wrath over a story about a fight he had with former Kray gang member, Freddie Foreman.

The article in 2002 by reporter Neil McLeod claimed Foreman and Frank – who by then had a combined age of 145 – slugged it out in a cafe in Maida Vale and Foreman dragged Frank out by the ankles after trading insults. Frank was privately deeply unimpressed by Foreman's confession in his 1996 autobiography, *Respect,* to the murder of Frank Mitchell on behalf of the Krays. David said: 'He didn't think it was wise to make a confession of murder like that, especially when you had been acquitted, but he also didn't want to criticise Freddie publicly for it because he was very diplomatic about people's reputations and it wasn't his way.' The row is believed to have started after Marilyn had told Foreman what she thought of him for the confession. When Foreman had a few words back, Frank stepped in and a tussle ensued. Frank issued his own version of the fight on his website and insisted that Foreman had started it – grabbing him around the throat – but he had fought back and was never 'floored' or dragged outside. He even rang up the newsdesk to let them know he was very unhappy – which was not a call many would want to take.

When the time came for the reporter to leave the *Sunday People* to start a job on another national newspaper, the then News Editor, James Mellor, came up with a ruse to scare the life out of him. At his leaving party, just as the reporter was warmly thanking his colleagues for the happy times they had shared, in walked Frank. Mellor recalled: 'He came in and asked: "Where's McLeod?" and then proceeded to pull a pair of pliers out of his jacket pocket. A hush fell over the pub as he walked up to Neil and said: "I hear you need the services of a very good dentist."'

Fortunately, Frank wasn't bitter about any rift he might have had with the newspaper or with Neil McLeod. Mellor said: 'He was a good sport, although I will never forget the look on everyone's face when he walked in. He was every bit as menacing as I had hoped he would be. It made me realise what it must have been like to be on the receiving end when Frankie Fraser wanted to put the frighteners on.'

Frank and Marilyn, meanwhile, had split up. The couple had set up home in Walworth, back on Frank's old stomping ground. He showered her with gifts, gave her everything he had, but it wasn't enough and the relationship failed. It broke his heart. When Patrick went round to the house afterwards, he found his dad sleeping on the floor, with no furniture. Patrick said: 'He had done that so often in jail that he thought nothing of it. Possessions weren't really important to him but he was getting on a bit and we couldn't have him living like that, so we took him to Ikea and got him sorted out. It was very sad because he was lost without her at first but he picked himself up and got on with it.'

To his many grandchildren, Frank was a doting and proud grandfather – albeit with an unconventional past. Lisa Fraser, Patrick's wife, said: 'He was so sweet with Amy. She was very lucky to have Frank and Kate. Kate was like a best friend to me, she was ageless. Kate wasn't like a normal grandmother either. She didn't dress her age, in fact, she liked nothing better than to swap handbags and shoes with Amy when she was a teenager and she always wore high heels and Jaeger coats. She loved to look smart and was so stylish. Amy used to say that her gran looked nothing like the others at the school gates. I remember once she came to watch Amy sing at the Rotary Club for the old-age pensioners and I teased her that they'd think she was one of the old girls from the home. Kate grabbed my arm and said: "Don't you leave me here!" She wasn't joking.'

When Salvador Manzi died in 2003, the family treated Kate to a bigger caravan and a trip on the Orient Express. But old resentments between Kate and Frank still simmered.

When Eva died, passing away at home, Frank was still so bitter about his ex-wife that he refused to let her attend the funeral. David said: 'We all felt that my dad was cruel about the funeral, because Kate was Eva's lifelong friend but he said if she was going, he wasn't, so, of course, she couldn't go. I pulled him up on it and so did Patrick. My dad didn't like it and he got really sheepish but it had to be said.'

Eva had been ill for months but had kept it a secret from her family because she was so mistrustful of doctors. Without realising it, she had suffered a perforated ulcer, which led to peritonitis. She had been devastated only two years earlier by the death of her youngest daughter, Shirley, of a sudden brain haemorrhage. Eva's daughter Beverley was by her side when she passed away, along with her daughter, Evelyn Wolff, Eva's granddaughter. 'She refused point blank to see a doctor, no matter how we tried. She lay down on the sofa, and told us she loved us,' said Evelyn. 'Then she just slipped away in her sleep.'

Eva's death came as a terrible shock to Frank, who was never the same again, according to his family. Patrick said: 'He was lost without her. She was his closest friend, his ally, his sister, who had stood beside him through it all.'

Frank said of his beloved sister: 'She was my best friend, my pal, my everything. I thought of her as one of those amazing women, like Joan of Arc, a complete one-off. I could rely on her one hundred per cent. In my world, you couldn't easily say that about anyone. I would pop over and see her often and we would talk every week on the phone. Then, one day, she was gone.'

His family began to fear for his health, as he pined for Eva, going off his food for several days after her death. On the day of the funeral, Eva's daughter, Beverley, moved him to tears by offering him her mother's favourite gold chain and sovereign pendant. Beverley said: 'I handed it to Frank and as I did so, he turned away and put his hands up to his eyes. He told me not to look at him because he didn't want me to see him crying. Frank was a strong man, not someone I had ever seen in tears before. It was all too overwhelming for him to be parted from her.'

Without Eva in his life, Frank relied more on his family to look after him, as he made friends easily in the pub and was known for his generosity, to the extent that people would knock on the door and ask for cash and he would give his money and even his food away. When Patrick and Lisa popped round one afternoon, they were horrified to find his face had swollen up and he appeared to be suffering a serious allergic reaction. They rushed him to hospital. It emerged he had kept the hair-dye he used to give him his trademark black locks on far too long. It was the first sign of forgetfulness, which was an early warning of Alzheimer's Disease.

David missed some of those final years of his father's life because, despite efforts to stay out of trouble, he found himself on the receiving end of another ten-year sentence. This time, he was charged with demanding money with menaces – the same charge Frank had faced during the Torture Trial – after getting caught up in a sting operation involving a police informer.

A friend of his, Terry, was owed £60,000 by a man called Blake and Terry, in turn, owed David £7,000. Blake arranged to meet Terry in Blackheath with the cash. Terry travelled to the 'meet' in a car that was being driven by a mate of his, with David following in his own car – because he wanted to get his money back. But David became suspicious after seeing a white van and a motorbike and several other cars following Terry. Meanwhile, Blake had told Terry in a phone call that morning that the cash was in the boot of a parked car, waiting for him to collect it because he was too scared to see him in person.

David made ten calls to Terry, warning him it was a ready eye – the police were on to them – and telling him to leave the cash, but despite David's warnings, Terry picked up the bag from the boot and set off in his friend's car, with a cavalcade of undercover vehicles in tow. David said: 'I overtook them, because they were travelling so slowly, and put my car in between them and Terry. He then saw my car and his friend pulled over. He got out of his car and into mine with a bag and showed it to me, saying: "Look, it's all paper, I want my money."

'Blake had double-crossed him and left a bag full of newspaper and about £20 in notes on the top of it. I told Terry it was a set-up but still he wouldn't have it. I knew we had to get away quickly, so I put my foot down and suddenly we were being chased. Terry asked why I was driving so fast. I said: "Because those cars behind us have just stuck blue flashing lights on the top of them and the Old Bill are chasing us, Terry."'

David thought he had managed to shake them off but a police car then came head-on from the other direction and rammed him. 'We were basically stuck in the car then, the front had come right in and my knees were hurting me because they had got jammed up against the dashboard when they rammed us,' said David.

Armed police jumped out of their vehicles, pulling David and Terry out, throwing them to the ground. Having handcuffed David, face down on the ground, they then proceeded to break three of his ribs and kick his teeth in. 'One of them was armed with a single barrel pump-action shotgun. The wheels had come off the car, it wasn't going anywhere, but he blasted a shot into the tyres and then put the barrel of the gun to my head. It was so hot it burned me and left an imprint on my scalp.

'Round the other side of the car, where Terry was, another cozzer did the same. Everything went quiet after the bang. I thought they had killed him. When we were pulled to our feet, I was covered in blood where they had kicked two of my teeth out and he had what looked like blood all over his shirt. It turned out he'd been lying in radiator fluid from the car and wasn't bleeding to death as I had feared.'

David was taken to hospital to have his broken ribs checked but was returned to the police station, where he refused to speak. He pleaded not guilty at Maidstone Crown Court but said: 'I could have called Jesus Christ as a witness and I still would have been found guilty.' He was treated as a double Category A prisoner. He said: 'There was so much noise every time I came to court, sirens, police outriders, there is no way I could get a fair trial. The police had spent a lot of money on the investigation, which meant you knew you were going to get a lot of bird to justify it. I knew that from the start.'

Terry took a guilty plea straight away and got eight years

for demanding money with menaces. 'He told me at the start, he was one of those people who would just hold his hands up, he couldn't give evidence, he wasn't any good in court, so that was the way he wanted to do it,' said David.

David's girlfriend, Charlie, had told him she was pregnant not long before his arrest. 'I wasn't planning more kids but, of course, I was pleased and then suddenly I was in the nick and in agony with my knees busted, my ribs broken and my teeth done in by the cozzers,' said David. 'It was a really hard time. I started off in Belmarsh and Charlie came to see me, to say she would stand by me. I was handcuffed to two screws, my legs were in shackles and I was looking at her and she was so young and pretty and I just knew that it wouldn't last.'

During David's trial, things took an almost farcical turn when one of the witnesses, who was giving evidence behind a screen so that he couldn't be identified by the accused, told the court how he, a young man standing six-foot-four-inches, had felt intimidated by David, who was five-foot-eight and then in his late fifties. The only time they had met was when David came between the young man and Terry, who was irate about not getting his money, the day before the arrest. In court, it emerged that the father of this witness was a police informer. 'It was beyond belief,' said David. 'I got ten years and I knew I would end up doing half of it at least.'

He had only just been sentenced when Charlie gave birth to a boy, James. 'A screw knocked on the cell door and told me I was a father again. I was over the moon, of course, he was beautiful.' James is named after David and Patrick's cousin, Jimmy Fraser, owner of the Tin Pan Alley club, who was knocked over and killed crossing the road in Florida in 2002, in a freak accident.

David spent the first two years of his sentence back in his old cell at Whitemoor Prison, with the other double Category A men – murderers and terrorists. He was even offered his old job back in the gym. He refused: 'I got a ten for doing nothing other than trying to get my own money back, so I wasn't going to play the game.' Charlie was a regular visitor with the baby but David was increasingly troubled and feared the relationship would end. 'When the baby was eighteen months old she brought him to see me and he was playing on a toy and, as he fell off it and picked himself back up, she told me it was over, just like that. It came as a relief really because I knew it wasn't going to work. It was a burden off me because I could just focus on getting on with my bird without having to worry about her any more. I had been having trouble sleeping, and that night I slept like a log. She is a great mother to our son, James.'

When he came out in 2009, having served the recommended half of his sentence, David had clocked up more than thirty years in jail and determined to try to keep out of trouble. He found his dad Frank much changed when he came home. Frank knew he was becoming forgetful and, trying to impose order on his mental chaos, became obsessed with knowing the time. Patrick put clocks all over the house to help him keep track of things. Eventually, it became clear he couldn't manage on his own and so he was found a place in sheltered accommodation in Peckham. Patrick said: 'His first reaction was that he didn't want to go to Peckham – because that's where the Carters came from, his rivals from all those years ago. Old memories die hard and he decided he didn't trust people from Peckham. But once he got there, he loved it.'

He still enjoyed public appearances and evening talks, as his memory for the old days held firm. There was also a sense of his boys not wanting him to go into a mental decline. They saw that he had good days and bad days but by keeping him active and engaged with people, he seemed to do better. After one public appearance in the North of England, they were all travelling back down to London on the train and David went to get some teas, while Patrick popped out of the carriage to have a cigarette. When they returned, Frank wasn't there. David said: 'We knew he couldn't have got off the train because it hadn't stopped so we went along through the carriages and there he was, with a huge crowd around him, telling stories, with everyone listening and laughing.' Patrick added: 'It was a relief to find he was OK. We needn't have worried – he really was quite an entertainer.'

It was on one of these evening talks shortly after his release that David was to meet the woman who he has shared his life with ever since; Hayley, a carer thirty years his junior. 'There was something about her voice the first time I spoke to her, we just clicked. We became friends first and then lovers and we have been together ever since.'

As Kate's health started to fail, David took her for a trip down memory lane, driving her to the hop fields in Kent, where she had spent so many happy times with the family. It was to be their last such visit, as several months later, in 2010, she had a suspected stroke and was put on warfarin to thin her blood. She died of complications not long afterwards. The night before she died, Lisa stayed by Kate's bedside in hospital. Kate's eyesight was nearly gone but she told Lisa she could see a little girl, running away down the hospital corridor.

At her funeral, the priest paid tribute to her, saying Kate was legendary in the community, for all the right reasons. She took more dinners up to Brixton Prison for family, friends and friends of friends than anyone else. She once even gave her own dinner to a homeless man sitting outside her maisonette. At the height of the Brixton riots, while shops burned and Molotov cocktails were hurled at the police, the rioters made sure one little old lady – 'It's David and Patrick's mum. Evening, Mrs Fraser!' – got safely home through the chaos with her shopping.

She had married one of the most violent criminals of the twentieth century and given him three sons, who all went on to carve their own careers as villains, but Kate was, undoubtedly, a kind-hearted soul who only looked for the good in people. If someone needed help, they could always turn to Kate. She spent decades embroiled in a criminal world – they were her best friends and family – but the kindness she showed when she first met Frank as a little boy remained unchanged. It was with her until the day she died.

One by one, the old faces from Frank's world predeceased him.

Billy Hill was long gone and Albert Dimes before him. Billy Blythe, Jimmy Brindle and Dido Frett had all passed away. Ronnie Kray died in 1995 and Reg followed in 2000. The residents from his sheltered accommodation also became his friends and they left him too. His was a world of ever diminishing numbers. Every time one died, he would sigh and say to David and Patrick: 'Another one off to Boot Hill' – that was his name for the cemetery up the road.

The boys tried to keep his spirits up, bringing him money, which he liked to count out – and then give away to everybody else in the home. David said: 'We'd have a running joke with him that we were coming in to rob him and he would laugh his head off and say: "I've got loads of cash under my mattress, please don't steal it!"'

He also kept up with his television appearances, doing a final documentary on his life. He was frequently asked for his opinions on society and often provided some surprising answers. For all that he fought the system relentlessly, Frank was no anarchist. 'We need rules, the police, the courts and government,' he said. 'I am not interested in anarchy. Society needs rules – but that doesn't necessarily mean I am going to stick to them.' To any female interviewer, his opening shot was always: 'Wasn't I in Parkhurst with your grandad?' Asked if he had any regrets, he would reply: 'None. No, that is not true, only one – getting caught.'

And talking about his epitaph always raised a smile: 'I would like to be remembered as a very good dentist.' The big question, which always met with a twinkly eyed response from Frank, was whether he was really mad. He would say: 'Well, I had a bang on the head when I was little, you know.' Privately, to those who knew him best, the answer was a resounding: 'No, of course I'm not!' But 'Mad' Frank was far more complex than that.

During the Second World War, the army didn't want him

because of his mental and physical condition and he then went on to feign mental illness to escape from a brutal prison regime in the late 1940s. He played the system to suit his own ends but he found, to his cost, this ruse cut both ways. In the 1950s, the Prison Service had endured enough of his extreme violence towards the staff and had him certified and sent to Broadmoor to get him out of their jails and give everyone some respite.

His hair-trigger violence and lack of empathy to people he perceived as being his enemies – on many occasions, his jailers – led the Prison Service doctors to diagnose him as a dangerous psychopath throughout his sentences in the 1950s through to the 1980s. By the end of his time in jail, medics found that his psychopathic tendencies were largely 'burnt out'. Being branded a psychopath is not classified as insanity but a personality disorder. However, secure hospitals such as Rampton and Broadmoor are home to many violent psychopaths. In Frank's early sentences there was little attempt at therapy, but the chemical cosh was used instead to calm them and render them harmless. By the same token, jails are also full of people with psychopathic tendencies who have committed crimes but who are not insane; they are deemed fit to serve out their punishment on the wings. They are not mad, just criminals. One might also say that the business world is full of psychopaths who use their lack of empathy to succeed.

For Patrick and David Fraser, knowing their father intimately, they feel certain the 'Mad' Frank tag was not deserved but that his extreme violence and refusal to play the game and settle into prison life was the result of some stubbornness of character, which had its roots in his childhood on the streets of Waterloo. 'I only ever saw it once, when I was brought up from Lewes prison to visit him in Birmingham in 1983 and I had two screws from Lewes who were hanging around us and they were winding him up,' said Patrick. 'He leaned over and said to me: "I can see myself losing twelve months' remission here." I had to tell him not to do it and that seemed to calm him down. They would wind him up and he would just go for it.

'The thing about my dad was he knew people and he knew how to manipulate them. If he got it into his head that he was going to do something, he would not let it drop but he was very clever. He wasn't mad at all, far from it. He just made them believe he was crazy when it suited him.'

David Fraser added: 'He used to tell us a brilliant story about when he was on the hospital wing with a broken leg after the Parkhurst riot and he worked out that the two medical screws looking after him didn't like each other. He started setting them against each other by moving things around and blaming it on whoever was not on duty. In the end, over a number of weeks, he wound them up so much that they had a fight in the ward and were slugging it out while he sat in bed, looking all innocent.'

In terms of their father's violence, David and Patrick have seen first-hand that he was not always the thug people made him out to be. 'He was violent to the screws in prison,' said David, 'because he hated them and they hated him, but on the outside I have seen him walk away from drunks and people behaving like idiots, giving them the benefit of the doubt. It was only if it was to do with money, people owing him money in business, he would get heavy and that is the same for me and Patrick. That is business. Everything else, well, you would have to think: "Is it worth it?" Usually it isn't.'

David takes after his dad in that he has a long memory when it comes to being owed money or insulted. 'I waited ten years to catch up with someone once, who owed me several thousand pounds and was mouthing off about what he was going to do to me. Well, I caught up with him, quite by chance, about a decade later. I waited for him to come out of a restaurant and jumped into his car next to him, as he got into the driver's seat. It was dark and raining and he didn't realise what was going on until it was too late, I was sitting beside him. He just about shit himself. I told him to take me to get the money he owed me, and he did. Then I gave him a clump on the way out of the house, just for good measure. That is the thing about me, I have a long fuse these days but it is not a good idea to cross me because I do bear grudges and I will get even in the end.'

'In some ways, I think I take after my father in that respect. He was very diplomatic, he wouldn't call anyone a rat or a grass without firm evidence, he didn't like rumours but when you crossed him or owed him money, you would live to regret it because he would get his revenge, even if it took years.'

His memory was fading but Frank proved, one last time, that he still had the energy to get into trouble with the law, even when living in sheltered accommodation. He hit the headlines by being handed an ASBO at the age of eighty-seven for assaulting another pensioner who had sat in his favourite chair. Frank liked that particular chair because not only was it comfy, it also had a good view of the street, which meant he could see people passing by. Another resident, who suffered dementia, refused to budge when Frank asked him politely if he could sit in his usual place. Frank tried to move him and a slanging match ensued. The staff, fearing matters could escalate, called the police. By the next day, the other resident had forgotten all about it – his dementia was a lot more advanced than Frank's. But Frank was handed an ASBO. When the police came to explain this to him, he flicked a V-sign at them. Patrick said: 'It was all a bit ridiculous because no one got hurt and Frank loved being there, so he really didn't want any trouble. We had to laugh. It did show he still had a bit of the rebel in him.' His extraordinarily stubborn streak never left him, as even towards the end of his life, if he was having a bad day, he would refuse to get out of bed – his family joking that he was 'on a protest'.

A final sadness was the loss of his mate Charlie Richardson, who he had grown closer to over the years than his old business partner, Eddie. Matters were made worse after a comment by Eddie Richardson at his brother Charlie's funeral, which meant that Eddie was lost to Frank as well. Relations between Eddie and Charlie had grown very strained in the years before Charlie's death. The brothers had long had their differences but Eddie had felt that Charlie had asked too much of him financially and was taking advantage.

Frank had arrived at the funeral with David and their friend, Richard Hunt, in his Rolls-Royce, to pay their respects. As it was a cold day, they all gathered in a small side room next to the chapel, and Eddie came in. David said: 'As we were all chatting, Eddie made a comment, saying: "I've only come here to see him burn."

'Frank turned his back on him and just blanked him. He said to me, under his breath, it was a total liberty to say that about Charlie. When we went in to the funeral, Frank got up, walked over and kissed the coffin. It was a dramatic thing to do but he made his point.'

David and Patrick had thought that with their father's short-term memory becoming so unreliable, the incident would be forgotten. But the next day, when they went to see him, the first thing he said was: 'I didn't like what he said about Charlie. It was a total liberty. A brother should not say that.' His sense of honour and respect in the criminal world was undimmed and Eddie Richardson had crossed a line.

Frank's favourite trip was on a boat up the River Thames, past the places he used to play in as a grubby-kneed little boy, with holes in his boots. Some cousins from Bermondsey would take him out for the day but after one trip, they came back saying they thought his Alzheimer's might be getting worse. David said: 'The girls who took him out came back and said he had a great time but he'd been a bit confused because he kept mentioning someone called Kate and they only knew about Doreen and Marilyn. As they were sailing along past Waterloo Bridge he'd been saying he used to go down by the river with Kate. They didn't know who she was and thought his mind was wandering off somewhere but he was with her, reliving his past and remembering my mum. Maybe it was the passage of time or because he knew Kate had gone now, he was able to allow his true feelings for her to come out. But it was very sweet that he was enjoying happy memories of their time together at last.'

He was a regular at his local in Peckham, the Hollydale Tavern, and David recalled how some rowdy teenagers became suddenly very subdued when someone at the bar pointed out that the little old bloke in the corner, quietly supping a pint, had probably killed and sliced more men than they had eaten hot dinners. 'These kids couldn't have been nicer. They helped him with his coat and helped him into the taxi, calling him Mr Fraser the whole time. It was nice to see that level of respect for him.'

As Frank approached his ninety-first birthday, Patrick and Lisa started planning for him to spend Christmas with them, as usual. But as he was trying to sit down on the bed in his sheltered accommodation one morning, he slipped and had a bad fall. His cries for help were heard by the staff and he was sent to hospital, where he complained bitterly that he was in agony. 'The doctors told me they had X-rayed him and there was nothing wrong and so we basically told him he had to get out of that bed,' said Patrick. 'After a few days, he came home, and he was screaming in pain. This went on for over a week and then we got a phone call from the hospital.

They had made a mistake. Whether they had X-rayed the wrong hip or looked at the wrong medical records, God knows, but they admitted then he did have a fracture and in fact he had had it all along.'

David said: 'We were furious that he had been left in such pain. We thought it was like the old days in prison, when he would refuse to get out of his cell because he was on a protest and we were encouraging him to get up. Dad was saying he was in agony and no one believed him.'

The fracture was on the left thigh and hip. An untreated fracture can lead to serious complications, such as infection, and in the elderly who are already in a weakened state, such a delay can be life-threatening. Frank was quickly booked in for an operation to try to repair the fracture. Doctors explained that, due to his age, any surgery would carry a risk but there was no choice but to go through with it, as to leave him would prove fatal.

On the day of the operation, he was visited by David and Patrick. He told the boys: 'I have had a good innings, I'm ready to go now.' David said: 'We were being really positive about it, trying to gee him up and we fully expected to see him after the op. He squeezed my hand and told me to "be lucky".' Turning to Patrick he said: 'I do love you, you know.' Patrick added: 'He was never one given to great shows of emotion. For him to say it, he must have felt it was goodbye.'

David said: 'After we left, the Bermondsey girls, who took him on days out, came to visit and he was laughing and joking with them. He remembered all their names and was chatting happily. When it was time for them to go, because they had to get him ready for the surgery, he winked at them all, just as he always did. 'One of them had her little toddler with her. As they were leaving the little boy turned round and smiled and Frank said to him: "You're terrific, Arthur."' That was the last time anyone spoke to him. I thought it was lovely that he was fussing over the little boy like that.'

During the operation, his blood pressure dropped dramatically and he died on the table. He was resuscitated but was now only kept alive by life support. Twenty-four hours later, the decision was taken to turn off the machine.

Frankie Fraser had survived more than forty years in prison, countless punishment beatings in the cells, razor fights and bank raids. In the end, there was just old age, a fall and the complications of a missed fracture in an NHS hospital. His death, ironically, had many of the hallmarks of those of other pensioners whose families feel the health service has let them down at the crucial moment. But scratch below the surface and Frank, the gangland legend, was still lurking, rebellious to the last; the leg that caused his demise had already been fractured in three places during the Parkhurst riot. This is not a medical history that many silver-haired nonagenarians could lay claim to. The reason the surgery was so complicated, was because there were already a number of metal plates and pins holding it all together after the bone was smashed to pieces by prison warders wielding batons in the aftermath of one of the worst riots in prison history. Perhaps Parkhurst got him in the end.

Frank's passing brought headlines in the national newspapers and gangland turned out en masse on a cold, bright December day to honour one of the major criminal players of the twentieth century. He didn't want a hearse pulled by horses adorned with black plumes, as the Krays had done. Frank wanted less fuss. His family had requested donations to the Alzheimer's Association in lieu of flowers but still the floral tributes came. Gangland was going to give Frank a fitting send-off, whether he liked it or not; huge wreaths adorned the hearse as it was led into Camberwell New Cemetery by the funeral conductor in his black silk top hat, carrying a silver-topped cane.

Mourners, many resplendent in gold jewellery – including at least one necklace made of bullets – and a few well-placed tattoos, were faced with a wall of press cameramen from around the world and did their bit, turning out suited and booted, giving each other firm handshakes and hugs on the steps of the crematorium.

If the police had swooped, they probably would have had enough felons to keep them busy for years to come. Tommy Wisbey came to pay his respects and Chris Lambrianou was there, along with Eddie Richardson – the last of the so-called Richardson Gang – stooping slightly to talk to his old associates and friends. So many people crowded into the chapel that every pew was packed and there was standing room only; they gathered in front of the altar, in broad-shouldered clumps, hands clasped in front of their double-breasted suits. For many, the last time they had seen the inside of a house of worship was during a stay at Her Majesty's Pleasure. One friend of the family raised a smile when he said: 'Wherever Frank has gone, either upstairs or down, you can be sure he will be protesting about the conditions.'

There were no hymns but, instead, Sinatra songs, during which the mourners were asked to reflect on the Frank they knew. His coffin was brought in to the strains of 'I Get a Kick Out of You', which lightened the mood further. Doubtless, many will have thought about the things they got away with together, which is exactly what he would have wanted. The final word was left to the priest, Father Michael Branch, who addressed a congregation of highly suspicious looking characters: 'Brothers and sisters, go in peace – and don't get caught.'

Frank would have approved of that sentiment whole-heartedly.

EPILOGUE

For David and Patrick, after clocking up more than fifty years in prison between them, the most important thing in the world is their family and being able to spend time together. 'When I look back at Frank's life after he left prison, I think he was really lost for the last twenty years or so,' said David. 'The world he inhabited had gone, the Chaps were not there anymore, times had changed and I think that is the challenge for so many criminals when they get out. Looking at our kids, I think education is the key. It gives you the world without having to steal it.

'The problem with doing big jobs like Hatton Garden for people like us, is that we are old school – just as they were old school – but they didn't take note of the fact that the world had moved on. You might get a bit of work, you might get a way in, you might get away with the tom, but what are you going to do with it then, in the age of mobile phones and video surveillance and cameras everywhere and everything being monitored?

'No one has a God-given right to steal anything and think they are going to get away with it, but the old way might be to sit on it for a bit, wait and wait and then sell it – and you'd get away with it. There were times things got nicked and they would be back in Hatton Garden a few months later, being re-sold to the punters. These days it is just too difficult. Our view is that we are too old to run away any more and the whole robbery business has got to be that much more sophisticated if you are going to pull off a massive job – you have to ask yourself, is it even possible? For us, the answer is "No".'

Patrick shares his sentiments: 'Crime used to pay but it doesn't pay now. I'm not complaining – I've had a great life, with lovely holidays, living abroad, owning a bar. I had the luxury apartment, the carpet with the pile so thick you sank into it, it was wonderful but like all these things, it couldn't last. The money runs out eventually.'

Two of Patrick's three boys experienced life on the wrong side of the law. Jamie, who died suddenly in 2013 at the age of forty, had turned his life around in prison. He had been jailed for ten years for robbing betting shops with a replica handgun in 2001. 'He had been having a bit of a breakdown at the time but prison worked for him. He took exams, got qualifications and I was proud as punch. When he came out of the nick he got a job running the cleaners on the London Underground and was a manager of the company when he died.' Paul, forty-two, got two years in prison when Patrick and Lisa were living in Spain, for possession of cannabis after a chase across Blackheath. Three years ago he was caught with three kilos of cocaine and got seven and a half years in prison. 'He really got into books in jail,' said Patrick. 'It was self-education. It changed him. He has gone straight since.'

His youngest son, Sam, thirty-seven, is 'as straight as they come'. 'I asked him once if he would come in with me and the other lads, doing a bit of work, and he refused. He has always had his career and I think that is brilliant. He installs air conditioning in offices.' Patrick and Lisa's daughter, Amy, twenty-one, is doing a degree at Sussex University.

'I don't think I have been a particularly great father – I wanted my kids to go straight and when they turned to crime, I was choked,' said Patrick. 'My kids tell me I have been a good dad but I wasn't around much when they were younger and missed out on a lot. I felt the only reason I was breaking the law in the end was so that they didn't have to. I know so many people who have made heaps of cash from crime and educated their kids in posh schools and then those same kids also turn out to be criminals. So, maybe we are fooling ourselves that we can change the way we are by just having money. What matters in the end is your family. It is no good if you are going to be spending all your time doing bird.'

David's children, too, are an immense source of pride for him. His eldest daughter, Rachel, thirty-six, now a happily married mother-of-two, used to work for Merrill Lynch. 'Working in the bank, rather than robbing it, how about that?' said David. Charlotte, twenty-one, recently graduated from Bath University with a degree in English and Drama. James, ten, is a 'lovely little boy who enjoys doing what ten-year-old boys do'.

David said: 'I think I have done a bit more for my kids than my dad done for me. In fact, I know I was a good son to him. I do feel guilty because I haven't been there for my kids, being in prison for such a long time, but I have always tried to show them I love them and I am really proud of how they have all turned out.

'I was with my son, James, recently in the corner shop and I found a fiver on the floor near the cash machine. He immediately asked me: "Are you going to hand that in, Dad?" Well, I did my best to try to persuade him that it was finders-keepers, or that the bloke in the shop would just pocket it and it was OK to keep it, but he wasn't having any of that.

'I got him in the car but the only way to shut him up was to tell him I was going to hand it in. He is so honest, it is lovely. I kept it, of course, but I gave him an extra fiver in his pocket money that week. You can't say fairer than that.'

'Mad' Frank Fraser was a man of extremes – violence and kindness; wealth and poverty – but he never managed to achieve the one thing he wanted most: a happy and stable family home. David said: 'The thing about our dad Frank is, he was so loyal to the underworld that he forgot how hard it is to live in the real world. I would like to think we have learned from his mistake.'

ACKNOWLEDGEMENTS

I would like to thank my brilliant agent, Tim Bates, for his support and enthusiasm for this project and to Kimberley Chambers for introducing me to Frank Fraser and his sons, David and Patrick. The patience and charm of Gemma at PFD was also very much appreciated during our many 'meets' at the office. Thanks are also due to Ingrid Connell at Pan Macmillan for her encouragement and expertise at every stage and to editor, Fraser Crichton, for his eagle eye.

The Fraser, Brindle and Wall families helped us to piece together the family history and the bygone world of Waterloo and Lambeth in the first half of the twentieth century, with their wonderful stories about the characters who lived there. Maggie Wall, her daughter Diane Cain and the lovely Lisa Fraser provided invaluable help by recalling Kate Wall and her side of the family. Particular thanks are due to Beverley for memories of her mother, Eva, Lady Margaret and the old days. Thanks also to Beverley's daughter, Evelyn (Bub) Wolff, for her enthusiasm and sheer determination in tracking down the Native American past of her elusive great-grandfather, James Fraser, in Canada.

ACKNOWLEDGEMENTS

To that end, thanks to Fred 'Jumbo' Fraser and all at Fort Chipewyan in Canada for insight into the Métis way of life, and also to the archives of the Hudson Bay Company. The National Archives at Kew were an invaluable resource in our research, as was the British Newspaper Archive and Southampton Naval Archives, with particular thanks to Joe Baldwin. Consultant forensic psychiatrist, Dr Sian McIver, provided advice on offenders with mental health issues.

And the biggest debt of gratitude must go to Frank Fraser, the last true Boss of Soho, for his patience in his final year, recalling his life in such vivid detail.

The following resources also proved invaluable when writing this book:

Hart, E. T., *Britain's Godfather*, London, True Crime Books (1993).

Hill, B., *Boss of Britain's Underworld*, London, The Naldrett Press (1955).

Hill, J., and Hunt, J., *Billy Hill, Gyp and Me*, London, Billy Hill Family Ltd (2012).

Pember Reeves, M., *Round About a Pound a Week*, London, Persephone Books (2008).

Richardson, C., and Meikle, D., *The Last Gangster*, London, Random House (2014).

Richardson, E., *The Last Word: My Life as a Gangland Boss*, London, Headline (2005).

GLOSSARY

bird – jail sentence
block, on the – held in isolation, in the punishment block
book, on the – a prisoner who is a security risk (describes the process of warders signing a Category A prisoner in and out as they move around the prison)
brasses – prostitutes
chiv – a razor blade or knife
clipping, getting a – being given a beating
clouting – hiding stolen items about one's person during shoplifting
clumps – blows
cozzers – policemen
creeping – sneaking into offices or hotels to steal
faces – criminals, well known in gangland
fence – someone who receives stolen goods in order to sell them on for a profit
ghosting, ghosted – moved from one prison to another, without prior warning
grass – a police informer
hoister – a shoplifter

GLOSSARY

hoisting – shoplifting

hopping the wag – playing truant from school

in the death – in the end

jump up, the – stealing from the back of lorries

lay-down – a stay of a month or two in a prison

nick – prison

nonce – paedophile

on his toes – on the run from the police

on the pavement – a career criminal who robs banks

on tick – on credit

on top, come on – to go wrong, go pear-shaped

ponce – someone who lives off the earnings of another, by taking a percentage cut

ready eye – a criminal enterprise watched by the police after a tip-off

screwer – burglary, break-in

screws – prison warders

spielers – illegal gambling dens

star prisoner – a criminal spending his first sentence in an adult prison

straightened – paid off, bribed

taking a bit of crooked – buying or receiving goods, in the knowledge that they are stolen

tom – jewellery, from the rhyming slang 'tom foolery'

tool – gun, pistol

to tumble – to work something out, realise what is going on.

verballing – an illegal police practice, in which a statement is falsified, to the effect that words have been put into a criminal's mouth

INDEX

INDEX

INDEX

INDEX

INDEX

INDEX

INDEX

INDEX

PICTURE CREDITS

Fai - Wood

extracts reading groups
competitions books new
discounts extracts
competitions extracts
books new
new events books
events
extracts reading groups
new titles reading groups
interviews events new
events extracts extracts
discounts new books
new books events interviews
events new interviews books
discounts extracts discounts
www.panmacmillan.com
extracts events reading groups
competitions books extracts new